The Country of the Risen King

The Country of the Risen King

An Anthology of Christian Poetry

Merle Meeter, Compiler

BAKER BOOK HOUSE
Grand Rapids, Michigan

This collection of Christian poetry
is dedicated to our Triune God
and Eternal King,
and also to all the poets
whose poems could not be included here
because of editorial limitations.
All of the poets have given me
encouragement, loving counsel
and sustaining prayer.
The Lord of the Church
will surely reward them all
with his earthly
and everlasting blessings.

Contents

Preface......ix

Introduction......xi

Part One

Contemporary Poets......1

Part Two

Historic American and English Poets......293

Medieval Poems, Renaissance Madrigals, Spirituals......415

Biographies, Acknowledgments, Indexes......421
    Biographies of Contemporary Poets......423
    Biographies of Historic Poets......431
    Acknowledgments......433
    Index of Poets......439
    Index of Titles......441

Preface

This book is an anthology of Christian poetry. And, although most of the modern poets included here are from the United States, the rest of the world is indeed represented: England (W. H. Auden, Jack Clemo, Edith Sitwell, et al.), Ireland (Colin Duriez, Joseph Campbell), Canada (Margaret Avison, E. Margaret Clarkson, Ralph Huizenga, etc.), Mexico (Hester Hogan), South America (Norberto Wolf, Nancy Thomas), and Africa (Ronald Klug). The translation of the wealth of foreign Christian poetry is, however, beyond the range of this volume.

The scope of the anthology also affected my selection of the historic Christian poets. Other poems could certainly have been chosen from Donne, Milton, Herbert, and Hopkins, to mention a few. I have included several minor poets because of the unique worthiness of form and content in a small number of their poems. Some poets have been omitted that the reader may consider Christian writers, and I may, indeed, have overlooked one or two. However, I have tried to use the normative teachings of Scripture to evaluate the Christian content of each writer's work. Artistic sensitivity and craftsmanship were also important factors in my choices.

Included among the contemporary poets are several young writers who illustrate the vitality, breadth, and beauty of Christian poetry as it is developing today. There are, no doubt, a number of other fine Christian poets I have missed; they will enhance the volumes of other anthologists should our Lord stay His return.

Merle Meeter

Introduction

There is a country unknown to many who live upon this earth, a kingdom known only to its citizens, a commonwealth delineated in the Scriptures and celebrated also in the literature of those who serve the eternal and unseen King. Bunyan led us into this perilous and wondrous country through his *Pilgrim's Progress*; Milton took us back to its glorious and terrible beginnings in *Paradise Lost*; and C. S. Lewis opened up its fabulous vistas of magic and miracle to an indifferent age in his *Narnia Chronicles, Perelandra,* and *The Great Divorce.*

But these are only a few notables among the commissioned explorers who have ventured to visit and describe the landscapes and inhabitants of the invisible, yet clearly seen, country, its affairs and monarchs, its conflicts and festivities. Our guides, however, are also the biographers, dramatists, lyricists, and fictionists of the Sovereign of that land. Among them are wise and intrepid adventurers with a vision to objectify and present: Donne of the holy songs and sonnets, Herbert with *The Temple,* Crashaw and Vaughan, Bradstreet and Taylor, Thompson with his *Hound of Heaven,* Gerard Manley Hopkins, and T. S. Eliot. And there are the hymnists of the realm, such as Newton and Cowper, Watts and Wesley, as well as storytellers like Lawrence Dorr, Flannery O'Connor, Elisabeth Elliot, and James Johnson.

Yet even this listing represents only a few of His verbalizing servants, a small contingent of that chorus who praise and adore the Almighty One, in English for the time being. However, through the Living Word, the crucified and risen Lord Jesus Christ, whose Holy Spirit reverses Babel, all tongues will unitedly and perfectly bless the Triune God, without linguistic barriers, in His completed Kingdom, the New Heavens and Earth.

Today also has its adventurers, those hearers of the call who go out in faith obeying, blessed in that they believe the Gospel of liberation, proclaimers of Truth. These warriors, witnesses, sinners released by the gracious power of the Deliverer, are the rejoicing subjects of their King's domain. And as the Fellowship of the Resurrection, they are fearless of defeat, death, and the devil. So our day too has its lyric spokesmen, godly prophets through the genres of literature, poets of the everyday and the eternal. This is their book—and ours—for the glory of God, and for the encouragement and joy of all those who walk or desire to walk the True Way of Life through the wonderful Country of the Victorious King.

PART ONE
Contemporary Poets

Carol Addink

The Way of All Flesh

You were, till now
When I stepped in, unexpected,
To ask you to do mending,
Never old, just—Grandma.
But today, your hair down,
Flying about your face in aged frizzes,
As you sat facing an evening alone   ·
And talked of the pain returning
(For the first time with a shade of "Why?"),
You suddenly seemed all your eighty years.

I came home to tell you, "Mother,
Grandma is suddenly old."
You were on the couch,
Collapsed after another day's work
Slightly harder than yesterday's,
Your second chin appearing
And more new crow's-feet,
Facing an evening of ironing.
I choked the words back,
Not sure why.

And you, self in my mirror,
First crow's-feet just appearing
(But only when I'm tired),
Frizzes not from age but choice,
Your freshness slightly faded,
Why so wooden?
Had you forgotten
The way of all fall flesh?

Charlene M. Anderson

I
Waste
Dead

I
waste
    dead
bones warped
crooked
    dry and raw.
Brittle wind
hissing through
a crackling
    hunk of spoil.
Come
Holy Spirit
    revive this stubborn
parched creation of flesh
blow and fill
the vacuum of my soul
    so I may live again.

W. H. Auden

from
For the Time Being: A Christmas Oratorio

"What shall we say then? Shall we continue in sin, that grace may abound? God forbid" (Rom. 6:1–2).

Well, so that is that. Now we must dismantle the tree,
Putting the decorations back into their cardboard boxes—
Some have got broken—and carrying them to the attic.
The holly and the mistletoe must be taken down and burnt,
And the children got ready for school. There are enough
Left-overs to do, warmed-up, for the rest of the week—
Not that we have much appetite, having drunk such a lot,
Stayed up so late, attempted—quite unsuccessfully—
To love all of our relatives, and in general
Grossly overestimated our powers. Once again
As in previous years we have seen the actual Vision and failed
To do more than entertain it as an agreeable
Possibility; once again we have sent Him away,
Begging though to remain His disobedient servant,
The promising child who cannot keep His word for long.
The Christmas Feast is already a fading memory,
And already the mind begins to be vaguely aware
Of an unpleasant whiff of apprehension at the thought
Of Lent and Good Friday which cannot, after all, now
Be very far off. But, for the time being, here we all are,
Back in the moderate Aristotelian city
Of darning and the Eight-Fifteen, where Euclid's geometry
And Newton's mechanics would account for our experience,
And the kitchen table exists because I scrub it.
It seems to have shrunk during the holidays. The streets
Are much narrower than we remembered; we had forgotten
The office was as depressing as this. To those who have seen
The Child, however dimly, however incredulously,
The Time Being is, in a sense, the most trying time of all.
For the innocent children who whispered so excitedly
Outside the locked door where they knew the presents to be
Grew up when it opened. Now, recollecting that moment
We can repress the joy, but the guilt remains conscious;
Remembering the stable where for once in our lives
Everything became a You and nothing was an It.

➤➤➤

And craving the sensation but ignoring the cause,
We look round for something, no matter what, to inhibit
Our self-reflection, and the obvious thing for that purpose
Would be some great suffering. So, once we have met the Son,
We are tempted ever after to pray to the Father:
"Lead us into temptation and evil for our sake."
They will come, all right, don't worry; probably in a form
That we do not expect, and certainly with a force
More dreadful than we can imagine. In the meantime
There are bills to be paid, machines to keep in repair,
Irregular verbs to learn, the Time Being to redeem
From insignificance. The happy morning is over,
The night of agony still to come; the time is noon:
When the Spirit must practise his scales of rejoicing
Without even a hostile audience, and the Soul endure
A silence that is neither for nor against her faith
That God's Will will be done, that, in spite of her prayers,
God will cheat no one, not even the world of its triumph.

He is the Way.
Follow Him through the Land of Unlikeness;
You will see rare beasts, and have unique adventures.

He is the Truth.
Seek Him in the Kingdom of Anxiety;
You will come to a great city that expected your return
for years.

He is the Life.
Love Him in the World of the Flesh;
And at your marriage all its occasions shall dance for joy.

All Out or Oblation

Where sandstorms blow
and sun rots and blackens and wrinkles and
the ocean of bright glare licks up into
emptiness all the small
stragglers
        exposed
              alive . . .

There.
Clean   cold   water
  throat-laving
    for living.
Water.

        They cluster there.
        Sun flashes
        on sword-bright water-disc in
        earthenware bowl
        uplifted.

God.
  God.
    Saltwater runs in the engraven lines of their
    cheeks in mouth corners bitter.

WHAT ARE THEY DOING?

        They are crazy. They are
           pouring it
                out.

Sand coats the precious droplets and darkens
                with the life stain.
Earth's slow and unspasmodic swallowing is slowly,
           slowly accomplished.

    No. I do not understand.

But I do want to care so totally that I can
pour it out
into deserts . . . to find out what it is.

For Tinkers Who Travel on Foot

What if it *was* a
verse in the
Epistle to the Hebrews that
kept Bunyan
at concert pitch through
deaf and dumb months?
He found
resonance.
He stuck it out till then, too:
not for one instant sure it
would come to anything, in all his
mute madness, nor ever
diverted for one instant.

"On the one hand"—N.B.
    "he was difficult"—
his wife, loyal, was, and no wonder,
hysterical.

On the other hand though—N.B.—
when the sky was finally sundered with glory
and the cornet
rang out, created stillness,

    he knew it, instantly.
He consented, himself, to
the finality of
an event.

The Word

"Forsaking all"—You mean
head over heels, for good,
for ever, call of the depths
of the All—the heart of one
who creates all, at every
moment, newly—for
you do so—and
to me, far fallen in the
ashheaps of my
false-making, burnt-out self and in the
hosed-down rubble of what my furors
gutted, or sooted all
around me—you implore
me to so fall
in Love, and fall anew in
ever-new depths of skywashed Love till every
capillary of your universe
throbs with your rivering fire?

"Forsaking all"—Your voice
never falters, and yet,
unsealing day out of a
darkness none ever knew
in full but you,
you spoke that word, closing on it forever:
"Why hast Thou forsaken . . . ?"

This measure of your being all-out, and
meaning it, made you
put it all on the line
we, humanly, wanted to draw—at
having you teacher only, or
popular spokesman only, or
doctor or simply a source of sanity
for us, distracted, or only
the one who could wholeheartedly
rejoice with us, and know
our tears, our flickering time, and
stand with us.
But to make it head over heels
yielding, all the way,
you had to die for us.
The line we drew, you crossed,
and cross out, wholly forget,
at the faintest stirring of what
you know is love, is One
whose name has been, and is
and will be, the
I AM.

A Hearing

In remote Ur of the Chaldees
a primitive man utterly alone
is struck, a coal shedding stars
deep as space has grown.

In elegant brightness, linen and stone
finality, Egypt rose
mirage-clear under the blue when
the famine was stalked by the Jew's

deep prisonrock-born eyes.
His people—near that throne
and articulated slaves—by force
were (skeleton or steel) withdrawn.

Crumbling waves behind, a dune-
carved sill on nothingness
except sandstorms and silences to hone
down an arrowing purpose

fire-cruel on cluttering cities,
other cities, petal-queer on the clean
stem of the water-freshened place:
the ununderstood life flowed on.

Judgment and corruption
coming up, tumbling aside, release
the kingly gold and ivory, the stone
raising its awful grease-smudge and incense.

From the shepherd-king's loins
through refugee years, mean
resignation, compromise,
essential fires burned down

to an outcast's child born
in the cot of the beasts
(shepherds heard silver horns
from remotely royal stars).

That life against our own
makes much make no sense.
Who doesn't hear wild John?
Yet even his repentance

won't let even him in
to kneel to the sandals of the source man.
"Unworthy" he can
only wait till that one

himself comes, puts on
the towel, looses the sandal thongs,
washes his guests,
and stoops to give them freshness.

He began,
being alone, the singing
that (listen!) from the farthest down
murmurs, and will resound.
          ("Make room . . . ").

Circuit

The circuit of the Son
in glory falling
not short, reaching
not for that being-in-light
but stripping, putting on
the sacrificial animal
form (lambent silly/*selig*)
and the livery of "man"
servant of men, obedient
even to death
till glory touched again
(reaching down to the flesh
marred, and the tossed
cup of our darkness, and the spilt
blood, and the silence—
stone and rotting place out of the light . . .)
till prising, he touches even
us to celebrate
the Father of Lights, open to
this Son   to His giving. . . .

Hymn on and to
the Holy Ghost

How should I find speech
to you, the self-effacing
whose other self was seen
alone by the only one,

to you whose self-knowing
is perfect, known to him,
seeing him only, loving
with him, yourself unseen?

Let the one you show me
ask you, for me,
you, all but lost in
the one in three,

to lead *my* self, effaced
in the known Light,
to be in him released
from facelessness,

so that where you
(unseen, unguessed, liable
to grievous hurt) would go
I may show him visible.

The Dumbfounding

When you walked here,
took skin, muscle, hair,
eyes, larynx, we
withheld all honor: "His house is clay,
how can he tell us of his far country?"

Your not familiar pace
in flesh, across the waves,
woke only our distrust.
Twice-torn we cried "A ghost"
and only on our planks counted you fast.

Dust wet with your spittle
cleared mortal trouble.
We called you a blasphemer,
a devil-tamer.

The evening you spoke of going away
we could not stay.
All legions massed. You had to wash, and rise,
alone, and face
out of the light, for us.

You died.
We said,
"The worst is true, our bliss
has come to this."

When you were seen by men
in holy flesh again
we hoped so despairingly for such report
we closed their windpipes for it.

Now you have sought
and seek, in all our ways, all thoughts,
streets, musics—and we make of these a din
trying to lock you out, or in,
to be intent. And dying.

Yet you are
constant and sure,
the all-lovely, all-men's-way
to that far country.

Winning one, you again
all ways would begin
life: to make new
flesh, to empower
the weak in nature
to restore
or stay the sufferer;

lead through the garden to
trash, rubble, hill,
where, the outcast's outcast, you
sound dark's uttermost, strangely light-brimming, until
time be full.

Sestina for Professor William Blisset

Eyes keen, because you licked sticky wood-honey,
Jonathan? You snort at news of a fast
for scared, unequipped men. They quake to see
the fierce Philistines milling around in their blood,
earth heaving underfoot, friends' faces hostile
enough to kill first, under the dire bright arc.

From the felt virtue of the holy ark
how should this king-of-the-tribes extract the honey?
Your father is tall, Jonathan, hasty not hostile.
The skyhigh household that truly holds you fast
can shine through shielding royalty, through blood,
& this wild breakfast that gives you eyes to see.

In the printed word, astigmatic, I see
your name, in the sacred calorescence an arc-
lamp bright through my carbon generation's blood.
The enemy braces our leaf-stuck stoney honey-
combing metropolis. Our young heroes are fast
with a buck. And the holy licks at us all, as if hostile.

Is it the host on earth now that makes us all hostile?
Our day too soars, a cliff where the Prince could see
The other unafraid climbing, following fast.
Tales rot to easy magic, a moviehouse arc
lantern and cellophane: "Jonathan has a honey
hid at the cliff-top, his as he risks his blood." . . .

Samuel's grief was harsh, foreboding the blood.
The priest is no popular leader. Don't tell us the hostile
megatons hide under the affluent honey
of words. We will hide our eyes. We do not see
mercy in this queer story of an ark
for paired progenitors, nor in high promise, held fast.

The young, sensing aliens everywhere these days, fast,
too angry to earn or eat, afraid of blood.
A million candles per square inch burn the arc
light on them. Time and Fortune are hostile.
Most are forlorn. Only a handful see
their place still out with the locusts and wild honey.

Who dares any longer break fast—dares be not hostile?
The Son's Blood clears a dayspring's arc—o see
One risen, with his friends sharing the fish, the honey.

No Matter What

I KINGS 17

Elijah's raven was a bird
of prey, a scavenger.
And yet he was—Elijah heard
it right—God's messenger.

His wafer from no holy fire.
"This grisly flesh, or die."
Cherith Brook alone was pure
and Cherith too went dry.

Elijah swallowed what the bird
of doom there dangled down
until the desert. Then the Word
came and he could go on.

The widow had not needed ravens.
Now her one son lay starving.
Elijah begged. "Well, all I have is
gone, if I risk serving."

She did. The boy lived on.
The Prophet still endures.
The unfailing meal and oil a stone
of Bethel for our ears.

It consecrates a time
of bony men and doom.
That bread, the flesh of Him
who makes our brooks His home.

Josiah Bancroft

On That Eighth Day

On that Eighth Day
    of Creation
He stepped forth,
    an everlasting Lazarus,
Who, brilliant in renewal,
Came to walk among our death
    once again,
Just as unrecognizable in resurrection
    as before
When He deigned to become
   enfolded in our shroud of dust.

Walking with the blind,
He bade the very rocks
    to silence
their joy,
    and whispered stillness
to His cavorting creation—
       Then,
proffering pierced palms,
He plucked darkness from a soul
    and stood,
    revealed
as He shall appear.

That day His coming shall
    quick-catch-snatch away
our blind and dark-glass gropings
   as He did before.
   But never before
has He been seen as He is:
    King of Kings
      and
    Lord of Lords.

My Desire Is

My desire is
        that
The Fire
   which rushing fell cloven upon my first brothers
Should today descend
   that bright patriarchal stair to touch
     my wrestling soul
        to lap
   the very dregs of my ezekiel existence into
   a sacrificial pure fury (once called Charity)
Igniting
   even the altar with the very flaming zeal
   of Those Burning Ones
Who
   quick to do His Word
Flash the sky to light
   with everlasting cries of
Holy   Holy   Holy.

Cor W. Barendrecht

Word to World

on the beach the sandy soil was soft with thirst
a digger wasp with all its energy
worked its way into a dune

in the field the red clay skin of earth
cracked like a long-deserted honeycomb
a desolate earthworm failed to break the crust

in the town a young woman in a cave
near a sandstone inn
dilated on dead crackling straw

nature is alive in the pulsating universe
expansion and contraction is present everywhere
even in human life
sometimes in clouds we cannot push aside
it seems that even God recedes
in preparation for exertion

one child God put his arm around 280 times
in cloudformations in the crystal skies
compassionately rocking it
through macrowaves and microwaves
polarized on planet earth

at zero hour God came
a baby on the bloody thirsty earth
with vernix on its skin
little sheep in a sundown pasture
and wrinkles on its face
little year rings of untimeliness
like summer wood in a balsam fir
and twenty billion invisible nerve cells
with a live reminiscence of heaven
and more knowledge than
100 volumes of encyclopaedia Brittanica
in the dna molecules of one cell string

when shepherds knocked noisily at the door
of the sepulchral-sounding cave
his arms and legs swung out with a jerk
and he cried an earthly roar of flesh and blood
a simple startle reaction

God spoke one small creative word
a benediction for creation

at 33 expansive wide his hands spread all around
arms thrown out wide to embrace the universe
purple of passion in a sunset sky
day without end

the Word has reached the beach, the field, the town,
bloodthirsty earth of men to retrieve
chief sinners and braves
break out of your crust
it is time to be born.

Swaddling the Word

Joseph wrapped
the mother of the Word
in woven clothes and
sent her on a donkey
into the dark night
We stopped to look
but feared it was a hoax
—so many tried
to break into our homes
dressed even as priests
or nuns, but underneath
their habit was a threat
to our possessions
and our lives—

And who can tell
what damage He will do
inside, once born into our homes,
what silent corners
cover by His acts,
or what dark deeds
uncover by His light?
Maybe today we wrap
the Word in swaddling cloths
for our own comfort or
to ease our consciences;
does the infant cry
ever disturb the silence
of our muffled nights?

Name

A name written in sand
by a child's hand;
on a San Quentin wall
by an inmate's fingernail;
in blood stains
on doorposts;
in small-print footnotes
of dissertations

A name sprinkled
on little heads;
sung over bodies
in immersion tanks

A name breathed
in wind-touched silence
of lost paradise;
carried on wings
of one-day butterflies

A name on quivering lips
of a combat soldier
alone in a foxhole;
clattering between teeth
of an aging woman;
tremored by a
protestant voice

A name remains
when writing is no more
and voices die

A name given to
what has no name

Between desire
and silence
falls a name:

Jesus, the Christ.
Paradise regained.

Swimmers
at Leelanau Schools

FOR JOHN E. MEETER

We come from the open seas
If we ever knew
we don't remember
how far we've been
or where.

We gather
at a fisherman's wharf
like dark olive Pacific salmon
winging soft fins
in still waters.

Near the Homestead
we lay in waiting.
We want to go
but are afraid
to leap upstream.

We linger, drift,
then fight to perform
a last creative act,
turn to face the
fisherman.

Joseph Bayly

A Psalm at Children's Hospital

I find it hard Lord
agonizing hard
to stand here
looking through the glass
at this my infant son.
What suffering
is in this world
to go through pain of birth
and then through
pain of knife
within the day.
What suffering
is in the world
this never ending
pain parade
from birth
to death.
He moves
a bit
not much
how could an infant
stuffed with tubes
cut sewed and bandaged
move more than that?
Some day he'll shout
and run a race
roll down a grassy hill
ice skate
on frosty nights like this.
He'll sing
and laugh
I know he will Lord.
But if not
if You should take him home
to Your home
help me then remember
how Your Son suffered
and You stood by
watching
agonizing watching
waiting
to bring all suffering to an end
forever
on a day
yet to be.
Look Lord
he sleeps.
I must go now.
Thank You for staying
nearer than oxygen
than dripping plasma
to my son.
Please be that near
to mother
sister brothers
and to me.

A Psalm
for Maundy Thursday

Tonight
Lord Jesus Christ
You sat at supper
with Your friends.
It was a simple meal
that final one
of lamb
unleavened bread
and wine.
Afterward
You went out to die.
How many other meals You shared
beside the lake
fried fish and toasted bread
at Simon's banquet hall a feast
at Lazarus' home in Bethany
the meal that Martha cooked
on mountain slope
where You fed hungry crowd
at close of tiring day.
Please sit with us tonight
at our small meal
of soup and rolls and tea.
Then go with us
to feast of bread and wine
that You provide
because afterward
You went out to die.

Daniel Berrigan

Thirst

In him no beauty was
but body racked and robbed
and blood predicting darkly
no comeliness   no wonder

against his pinioned arms
legion seas came marching
winds ran through his caved
breast   and the sun was armored

in seamless womb on womb
unborn interminably
I started in his longing
and puffed his tongue to drought

in him no beauty was
no comeliness   no wonder
who yet when he was lifted
had drawn all things to him

a fist to his face came sorrow
a thirst   the thought of me

Lazarus

Sister, you placed my heart in its stone room
where no flowers curiously come, and sun's voice
rebuffed, hangs on the stones dumb. What I could not bear
I still must hear. Why do your tears fall?

why does their falling move Him, the friend, the
unsuspected lightning: that He walk our garden
with no flowers upon His friend, but a voice splitting
my stone to a dream gone, my sleep

to day? what, what do tears say to Him?

what did He say in tears, that His grief fall
scalding my hands, that cold hands sprung
sleep like a manacle, and drew my eyes a space
that had seen God, back to His human face?

Paul Borgman

Joseph

He wrestles straining flesh
To free the stubborn child
From clutching womb
While whispered grumblings slip
With sweat from trembling lips,
An awful fit
Compared to angled boards
With just right joints
On firm wood bench.
How far from steady here,
Away from home and youth's
Clear questions, answers cleaned
And ready.

These knots once came with looks
Of age, their smiles and frowns
Among wood grains—
Like hill-side grass in fact
Where wheat and barley browns
Joined pasture greens,
Where rough met smooth
And flat reached round
And sun out far kissed stone in close
Quite warmly. There he soared
In pictured thoughts and deeds,
Or slipped between the blades
Quite nimbly.

To frame those thoughts and deeds
He worked with wood from day
To ordered day.
But here the blood-strewn straw
Brought all the gnarls of Mary back
Again. Her screams
Were caught in slimy folds
On babe's dark head from womb
Now pushing through
But how? And how or what
Began these months of mess
And sexless tomb?
Just how then?

But most of all he wished
A simple peace
With her whose life seemed strange
And far from his own skill
To please. Her fears and joys
She had apart.
Elizabeth alone
Might know those dream desires
Of womb—apart from him,
A man of faith but not
Much hope, belief without
Clear vision, ready though
For waiting.

He shared some good times too,
And once her angel came.
But all in all didn't fit
At all since Mary—
There! And Mary smiled.
Joseph looked around
At dumbly staring cows
Then back again
To see the baby out
Against the breast that he
Loved too, a picture good
Enough to frame,

He dried his hands and heard
New sounds. The baby cooed,
Or was it cried?
Joseph smiled, then Mary smiled
Again. "And didn't I do
Quite well? And didn't I tell
You God was here?
What was it like for *you?*—
It didn't *feel* like God!"
Joseph kissed the child
With Mary's hope and smoothed
Her knotted string-wet hair
Just now then.

Flesh, World, Devil

We wrestle nays of our own devising
In windowless castles with darkened rooms
From long ago.

And far away
The old familiar voices whisper
Tangled pleas wishing against
The rain-dripping, dreary walls.

Winds moan within the echoing
Damming chambers of our mind,
And the mind itself spins spidery trickeries,
Dizzying halls.

Spun despair,
We only rest with intricacies
Fine but not fragile, superior knots
Harnessing life
In bitterness built on air.

We wrestle yeas of other's devising
On living room windows that deaden the gaze
From each other to it.

Tell us a vision,
Swoop in, coax out, slide us to here and now,
Glide us to where it's at, channel our woes,
Alter our sighs.

Difficult height and depth blur into mellow marsh,
Landscapes with no scope, windless and dry,
Adjustment and focus
But minus the sky.

Cure for despair:
We rest with these lunacies,
Mad but unshakable, yeas molding life
And its leftovers—
Of loneliness unaware.

We wrestle grays of great deceivings
Through windows obscured by angels of light—
Bright darkness.

Rattling gets smothered with roarings that purr;
Prowls of contentment finger the soul,
Smudging its mirror
To dim-witted ease.

We toss between yeas and nays, tempted by does he say,
Ravaged down days where we hear
Without hearing, see without seeing
The final disease.

Quiet despair:
We rest at our peril when comfortably safe
On a shore not our own,
With sand that shifts quickly—
Destruction without the scare.

Brother Antoninus

Passion Week

Christ-cut: the cedar
Bleeds where I gashed it.

Lance wound under the narrow rib.

Eve's orifice: the agony of Abel
Enacted out on the Tree.

Blood gushed
From the gash.

The Holy Ghost
Gusted out of the sky
Aghast.

Our Guest.

Bleed cedar.
Little cedar,
Lanced,
Axe-opened,
The ache of sacrifice.

Pour out,
As Christ,
Those pearls of pain,
Bequeathed.

O bleed
Little cedar,
Bleed for the blooded Heart,
For the pang of man . . .

The earth's
Old ache.

Zone of Death

Wind is not nigh.

No Holy Ghost,
Spirit outspilt,
Burnt this charred day.

What sin did this?
Could I?

Hot light blares.
Stars, outblistered now,
Mark time, extinct.

Night might bring
The seasonal constellations
In its sphere,
But night is nowhere.
Sun. Sand.
The noon-crazy jays
Cackle and gibber,
Jar on the gritted ear.

Dawn sneaked in unsmelt.
No wine, no water here.

Now the lance-riddled man
On yon pronged tree,
Stretched in the death-tread there,
Opens his executing eye
And gibbets me.

John 3

Dusk's
rooftop;
night and house
cast in questioning blue.
Cricket's abrasive song
rebirthrebirth rebirth.
I ascended the gravelly stair.
Strange truth
shone in his eyes
when I first saw him—
authority,
different from my bickering order.
Without greeting
he set before me
the strangest thing...
he spoke of spiritual
labor pains—
the meaning plagues me.
Marvel not,
he said,
the body of wind can be had
but must be born.

On the Day of His Deliverance

Between the alder trees
Whose fingers stroke
The close dark ceiling
I have sailed.

And shall sunlight glint
In the hair of the waves
Before my prow?

I glimmer; the
Olive whispers rumour
Jesu, Jesu.

The Fields Are Already White for Harvest

JOHN 4:35

The fields plead over endless hills;
The eclipse of a cloud
Falls over the heads of grain.
A breeze bothers the sycamore leaves'
    silver.

The harvest heeds no storm.

Can grace hold those
Acres against autumn?

Pick up the sickle of intent—
Bent,
And too heavy....

The fields pleading over endless hills
join my pleading
for an arm of strength to lift
    my arm.

29

Shake My Eye

*"One thing I know, that whereas I
was blind, now I see!" (John 9:25).*

Shake my eye
Until it see
The order
In Your hand.
Let it stand.

Let it stand:
With its roots
Move the con-
crete of my heart.
Let me start.

Let me start,
Dear Jesus, now
To praise You
With a fitting ring.
Let me sing.

Let me sing
You, Daystar,
To the eyes
That will not read.
Plant Your seed.

Plant Your seed—
It will grow;
Deeper trust,
A deeper root.
Spread its fruit.

Spread its fruit
In our lives
Till we all
With one desire
Seek Your fire.

Seek Your fire
In my life:
With Your light
Until I die,
Shake my eye.

Perfect Wresting

GENESIS 32:24–31
MATTHEW 26:36–39

Every knarry thing speaks
Of struggle,
Tension, growth;
God's wrestle with Jacob,
Battle of dreams:

Willow,
Wisteria;
Burl, boxelder;
Figure in cabinet wood;
Stalactites, helictites
In niches' night;
Icicle's knob till
Melting mines it;

Mud dripped from fingers
Or crawdad-heaped;
Moss hummocks in shade;

All flow, ooze and freeze,
And railroads mapped on a man's face
All mirror Gethsemane growing.

Truly This
Was the Son of God

MATTHEW 27:45-54

Though it was early
The clouds closed like curtains
After the first act;
The ground opened like a sore
And showed the blood it had eaten.
I remember the sound of curtains
Ripping inside us,
Doors creaking open on their
    hinges.
Three days He sat in the earth like
    a root.
Rising, he tore and sifted the earth
    of its dead.

Two Inscapes

1

When I lay down
& died to my manheight,
Weeds became
New trees,
Sweeping with blooms
The sky
When I lay down.

2

With sense
I turn
To my Lord;
That without
Sense these lichens
May not be forced
To stand & sing alone.

The Branch

Spreading out,
my tendrils
seize barbed wire,
roses,
briar.
I tangle,
search,
in blind handhold quests,
spiraling
ropelike toward light,
circling posts and rocks,
bearing flower,
fruit
in season,
holding the Vine.

Sietze Buning

Obedience

Were my parents right or wrong
not to mow the ripe oats that Sunday morning
with the rainstorm threatening?

I reminded them that the Sabbath was made for man
and of the ox fallen into the pit.
Without an oats crop, I argued,
the cattle would need to survive on town-bought oats
and then it wouldn't pay to keep them.
Isn't selling cattle at a loss like an ox in a pit?

My parents did not argue.
We went to church.
We sang the psalms louder than usual—
we, and the others whose harvests were at stake:

> *Jerusalem, where blessing waits,*
> *Our feet are standing in thy gates.*

> *God, be merciful to me;*
> *On Thy grace I rest my plea.*

Dominie's spur-of-the-moment concession:
"He rides on the clouds, the wings of the storm;
The lightning and wind His missions perform."

Dominie made no concessions on sermon length:
"Five Good Reasons for Infant Baptism,"
though we heard little of it,

for more floods came and more winds blew and beat upon that
House than we had figured on, even,
more lightning and thunder
and hail the size of pullet eggs.
Falling branches snapped the electric wires.
We sang the closing psalm without the organ and in the dark:

> *Ye seed from Abraham descended,*
> *God's covenant love is never ended.*

Afterward we rode by our oats field,
flattened.

"We still will mow it," Dad said.
"Ten bushels to the acre, maybe, what would have been fifty
if I had mowed right after milking
and if the whole family had shocked.
We could have had it weatherproof before the storm."

Later at dinner Dad said,
"God was testing us. I'm glad we went."
"Those psalms never gave me such a lift as this morning."
Mother said, "I wouldn't have missed it." And even I thought but did not say,
How guilty we would feel if we had saved the harvest!

My father once asked why I live in a black neighborhood,
and I reminded him of that Sunday morning thirty years ago.
If my sons ever ask why we live in a black neighborhood,
I shall sing my favorite psalm in answer:

> The Moor, with the Philistine and the Tyrian,
> Shall soon, O Zion, throng thy holy gates.

And I hope my sons forgive me
(who knows exactly what for?)
as they will hope their sons will forgive them
(who knows exactly what for?)
as I have long ago forgiven my father
(who knows exactly what for?)

Fathers inevitably fail to pass on to sons
their harvest customs
for harvesting grain or real estate or any crop.
But Christian fathers pass on to sons
another more important pattern
defined as absolutely as muddlers like us can manage:
obedience.

Carol for Christmas Morning

At break of day we get the tiding:
"The long-expected baby came.
The naming took but brief deciding:
'God-will-deliver' is the name!"
We go to check the evidences
and there we find this fact sublime:
The Verb of God beyond all tenses
is happening to us in time.

No other sign to us is given,
no other sun with such red glow—
like God's bright company to live in!
The Noun of God: we look and know!
Sing to the baby who has shown it,
that God is loving, just, and wise.
When human flesh has seen and known it,
our earth will turn to Paradise.

The rising sun contains the power
to end his race with bridegroom joy.
God's Word is here: it is his hour!
"This bridegroom is a baby boy!"
He'll bind each person to all others,
from mouth to mouth his cup he'll give,
entrust his flesh to sisters/brothers.
In new community we'll live.

Huub Oosterhuis (1929–   )
trans. Sietze Buning

Annunciation

"Be it done to me according to your word,"
she tells the angel with a curtsy.
Well brought up, she knows her place,
knows what to say to her betters.

Well brought up, she does not wonder aloud
but wonders silently about the Refiner's Fire
and how will she abide the day of his coming
and how will she stand when he appears?

Well brought up,
she bothers nobody. Alone
she waits for the apocalypse
of birth.

Jesus Our Hope

Faith cannot do too much expecting.
The words of Jesus all come true.
Friends offer only weak protecting;
Jesus our Friend will see us through.
What limit to the power He gave us?
All power exists for Him to use.
Since Love desires and plans to save us,
how can Omnipotence refuse?

This hope must soften every sorrow.
March onward, comrades, heads up high!
All those who march toward God's tomorrow
Find mountains flat and oceans dry.
What limit to our jubilation,
each trace of pain forever banned?
Forgotten is our alienation.
And we? We're in our fatherland!

Hieronymus van Alphen (1746–1803)
trans. Sietze Buning

35

Barnyard Miracle

Paulina the heifer would not stand still
while I milked her.
Five times she had kicked
so viciously
that the steel hobbles had sprung
from her legs.
Despite the tender welts where the hobble clamps
had been attached,
she was angry enough to do it again.
The fifth kick had lost me the milk
so I was angry too.
In adolescent temper I took the gutter shovel
and beat the heifer five, eight, eleven strokes
until I heard your voice, Mother.
You were in the barn for some heifer milk
for oyster stew.
Milk from other cows would do,
but heifer milk is better.
"Sietze, Sietze,
God's blessing can never rest on such temper."
You went to the heifer's head,
served her an extra portion of cornmeal,
and talked to her woman-to-woman:
"You've got to be quiet inside, Paulina,
in order to be quiet outside."

Paulina stood perfectly still
while I finished milking her.
I wondered guiltily
what manner of woman you were
that even the raging Paulina
obeyed you.
And what's more,
in addition to the pailful spilled,
she still gave enough milk
for oyster stew.

I Am the Mountainy Singer

I am the mountainy singer,
And I would sing of the Christ
Who followed the paths through the mountains
To eat at the people's tryst.

He loved the sun-dark people
As the young man loves his bride,
And He moved among their thatches,
And for them was crucified.

And the people loved Him, also,
More than their houses or lands,
For they had known His pity
And felt the touch of His hands.

And they dreamed with Him in the mountains,
And they walked with Him on the sea,
And they prayed with Him in the garden,
And bled with Him on the tree.

Not ever by longing and dreaming
May they come to Him now,
But by the thorns of sorrow
That bruised His Kingly brow.

Thomas John Carlisle

Coming and Going

   The word came
and he went
in the other
direction.
   God said: Cry
tears of compassion
tears of repentance;
cry against
the reek
of unrighteousness;
cry for
the right turn
the contrite spirit.
   And Jonah rose
and fled
in tearless
silence.

that gust

constantly I live
expecting daily
minute-ly
his Spirit blowing
me over
and over
and over me
to the next
target of love
i try to stand
on my own
whatevers
but they shiver
in that wind
and disinte-
grate before
that gust of grace

Counselor to the Almighty

Think twice before You pardon.
Men repent
even in ashes
but repent again
of their repentance.
Take the wiser bias
of my advice.
Confine Your charity
to such good neighbors
as Your humble servant.

Supper with Jesus Christ

At first they didn't know him
didn't even see him
till he said
something
something which said
something to them
as always.

Always to them he spoke
always to him
or her
whoever
looked to his lips
fastened upon
his face
he spoke directly
and in person
person-to-person
until distance shattered
and vanished altogether.

Immersed in all that ailed
them and the world
they thought no hope
could interrupt
their dialogue
with doom and death.
But he was Life.

They let him slip
into that conversation
and insert a new
prevenient dimension.
They began
again with him
and saw all time
spread out before them
until it all
led to the hill
that crucified their dreams.

Him whom they had not welcomed
at first at last they would not
let go. They haled him into
their home for bread
he held within his hands
until the breaking
burst their blindfold.

Five Days Before Friday

Why should I join
an indecent demonstration
chanting loud folk songs
defoliating trees
messing up the highway
inspiring officialdom
with hysterics at the rampage?

I no more than they
desire to welcome
some fool who will
upset my money changing
and preoccupation.

I shall carry no signs
of his seditious coming
nor shout *hosanna* even once.

Under the Sun

Under the sun
there was no one
to comfort them
sons of oppression
daughters of fears
no one to comfort them
none to explain to them
none to sedate
sores and torments
and tears.

Under the sun
there was no one
to speak for them
no one to cry for them
under the sun
save for a brother
they treated as traitor
the tender
compassionate
grief-bearing one.

Some set their faces
in anger
against him.
Some double-crossed him
and some let him down.
Under the sun
there is none
who can help us
save for the healer
with hands like our own.

Hands like our own
but all ruddy
and bloody
bent by the burdens
he wittingly chose.
Committing himself
to a hill
of crude hardwood.
Under the sun
we have one friend
God knows.

The Great Intruder

It is exasperating
to be called
so persistently
when the last thing
we want to do
is get up
and go
but God
elects
to keep on
haunting
like some
holy ghost.

Negotiation with a Higher Power

I will demonstrate
my immediate
obedience
providing You comply
with my demand
for a more satisfying
assignment.

Albert Howard Carter, III

Annunciation

Lo! Like flares the angels came,
Brilliant zones of white-cold flame;
Point-blank the dazzled shepherds heard
Of man's warm flesh, incarnate Word.

E. Margaret Clarkson

Prayer from a Stryker Frame

Lord, I lie here,
  Strapped down, motionless, almost insensible,
Skewered to this strange board
By the cruel, incredible pain;
Unable to move hand, foot, or head
  Because of pain's intensity
    And the exigencies of the Stryker.
Pain wracks my body through and through;
  I lie on a bed of pointed, red-hot nails,
Invisible forces pressing, pressing me down
  Harder, harder into them. . . .
I scarcely knew such pain could be.

Once You lay on a bed of coals,
  Spiked to a stake by pain
Far beyond anything I experience now
  Or can possibly imagine.
They lifted You up
Till the nails must have seared Your very soul,
Tearing Your body with the awful thud
  Of a cross dumped roughly deep in a pit,
    And You impaled upon it.

I lie here of my own necessity,
   Hoping to be made well in time
By mystery of surgery;
   Willing to be purified by pain
      For my own advantage.
You hung there
   Out of pure love,
Willing to be crucified, to die
   For my sake;
Hoping to gain nothing for Yourself
   But Heaven for me.

Your anguished cry, "Forsaken!"
   Wrung from parched, sinless lips,
Goes echoing down the ages; finds me here
   And meets my need.
No "Why?" torments my fevered brain today
   For I am not alone:
You answered all the questions
   Of tortured human hearts
      Once and for all.

Your risen life
   Within, around, above, beneath,
   Supports me
      In my pain,
And in Your peace I rest.

They turn me over now. Circulation
   And other physical requirements dictate
      This painful thrust
   Three times each day.

Here I lie, prostrate,
   Throbbing, rigid,
      Face to the dust,
   Humble before Your feet.

Face to the dust, I worship You, my Lord,
   In this strange, love-lit sanctuary,
Bowed by compulsion, true,
   But also by new love
      Freshly born of pain,
Adoring You in wonder and in awe
   Who for my sake
      Hung on Your cross.

Jack Clemo

The Winds

There is a tree grows upside down,
  Its roots are in the sky;
Its lower branches reach the earth
  When amorous winds are nigh.

On one lone bough there strakly hangs
  A Man just crucified,
And all the other branches bear
  The choice fruits of the Bride.

When Pleasure's wind goes frisking past,
  Unhallowed by a prayer.
It swirls dead leaves from earth-born trees,
  Old growths of pride and care.

The gracious fruits are hidden by
  These leaves of human stain;
The Crucified beneath His load
  Shudders, as if in pain.

But swift springs down a credal wind,
  It thrills through all the boughs;
The dead leaves scatter and are lost;
  The Christ renews His vows.

His hands direct the Spirit's wind
  Branch after branch to shake;
The Bride's fruit drops, and at the touch
  Elected hearts awake.

Broad Autumn

True faith matures without discarding:
All I unearthed, each sky-sign crudely mapped
On the white rasped hills of youth,
Warms me still by rowan-tipped crags
Far up the autumnal mountain,
Incredibly remote in climate, texture, weathering
Of bare stones, from my first insights:
I left no wreckage on those low rasped cones.

There is no snarl of tools
Where broad wisdom calls across the cordial heather,
But the hacked glints my young heart stored
Still tone the subtle comforts and the sharp
Fearful shifts of shade as the blood cools
To admit, and clarify, the expanding mental range.

No pestilence of proud ripeness,
Urbane, agnostic, cankers the wide braes
Which my spirit, eagle-keen now, calls native
In the pale sun's gloss. The spikes of raw praise,
Sparse once on the white hills,
Glow ruddier here against the thinned
Thieving of the schooled foreign crows.

I have not changed my country;
I have grown and explored
In my faith's undivided world.
I discard no primal certainty, no rasped
Sky-sign of the Cross;
But now in broad autumn, feeling a new peace
And the old poise of defence,
I accept the pure trysting lochs,
The full antlers in the glens.

Josephine Butler

These brothel steps lead back to Mersey grime,
Gas-jets and a foul wind fretting the street,
Spidery shadows everywhere.
It's past midnight, the waiting rooms are packed:
Troops, boys of eighteen. . . . I have been inside,
Spoken to some of them, made contact
With girls tripping out to solicit.
My tears and prayers go burning into the slime,
The web that trails from the blood's tricked heat.
God, why do I dare—
I, married and fifty—defy the established crime?

While a million wives lie free, soothed with their husbands,
Unhaunted by harlots' laughter, in a sweet swell
Like that which cured my unstrung girlhood's
Acid of questions, I am driven to docks and stews,
To the soul's vicarious, bitterest black sands,
Where the urge of rescue receives the bruise
From the stony chattel, the cynical male stride,
The trafficker's manipulation
Of a State licence to buy and sell.
I lead my period's
Christ-war on vice, on a vast betrayal—England's.

I've fought the C.D. Acts and Bruce's Bill,
Morals police, the regulated sewer,
And apathy in decorous pews.
My life was sometimes threatened: brothel keepers
Worked up the mob, set buildings blazing. Still
I thrust at public conscience, gave lepers
The tender truth, slipping through the official
Cordon of steel-toned disgust
To bid Christ's martyred love conquer.
Fire in me cannot choose:
Pure flame would gut cruel threads,
    snap the last thrill.

Priest Out of Bondage

Dark, mutinous land: I shared
Its moods through my dead youth, but I am spared
To wake and live and know it a husk and tetter
Which faith and sunrise peel from my soul.
I slip with every other fetter
The Cornish bond, for I must be whole
Within the eternal Moment, and have no root
In soil or race, in the annals
Of the Celt, or in the dubious channels
Where idiosyncrasies and tensions shoot.

I rise, no longer dark,
No longer mutinous, and embark
On the journey outward, the escape
To air that is rid of superstition, to a pulse
That draws no heavy blood from the obscure
Cycles of savagery, the historic shape
Of atavism. I shed the lure
Of a dim mother-breast I have outgrown,
And while the Moment's hot fierce joys convulse
My heart I take the irrevocable step beyond
Loyalty to this dead land: no longer bone
Of my bone is its granite, nor flesh
Of my flesh its clay:
The bright blade of the Word severs the barbarous bond.

Christ calls from the tarred road and I must go,
Not as an exile, no,
Nor as one deprived, but as one
Moving to fulfilment, moving home
Out of the ancestral mesh,
Out of the bitter moorlands where my tears
Fell on the sullen bramble and the dun
Rock of the derelict years.
Heir of the Moment and the electing Way
Whence all my treasures come,
I tread in the newness of truth
Where dawn-flushed pylons trample the uncouth
Spells of the tribal night. And this dead land
Which bore and molded me for a fate
Sour as its soil and hard with its hate
Smoulders and glowers behind the plucked brand
It will never regain or understand.

Harpoon

TO JOHN KNOX

Knox, it was from your seal-sleek,
Eagle-clawed coast that the harpoon winged,
Stilling my fabulous white whale,
Sperm-taut with its spout and plume
Of hot texts, your texts, that scalded
Cool modern currents and shook the minstrel winds
Over untrafficked straits of my clay.

I've been called kin to you who knew
Only the treachery of Mass-drugged queens—
Gay smiles above the saddle, the dirk concealed
That leapt soon at your Kirk's gullet.
For the rest, Berwick moonlight and apple blossom
Flicking Marjorie's face, pledged faithfully,
As Genevan exile proved. You the much-loved,
Never-betrayed husband—how far removed,
As man, from my white whale, speared near harbour,
Harpooned from the pale sands of Skye.

I reach farther back
Into your gaunt story: a black winter at Nantes,
The galley humped like a dark whale
At the Loire's mouth, anchored midstream;
Gale and thong on the stripped Scottish captives,
Clawed from their birthright to the low craft
Laden with loot, moored abroad for their brute death.

A winged mockery struck in dry dusk or at noon;
You threw the Virgin's portrait overboard,
Even with manacled hands, there on that hell-ship.
Your drunken guards had passed it round,
Bidding you kiss their goddess
Who blessed the galley, the floggings, starvation and stench.

You cast away the only grace of colour,
Beauty, charm, for your dour creed's sake.
Nothing remained but the grimy bench,
Bloody chains clanking on hollow skin,
And the untrafficked prayer as you swooned.

Is this a truth for me, for my harpooned
White whale of vision, speared beyond youth?
I cast off the idol beauty

When the ancestral stench seemed all my world;
But only beauty as mute pagan earth
And as man's art, the soft smear you barred,
With your strong thunders, from Scotland's soul.
I never cast to seal or eagle
One image of living face or limb
That spurred my white whale to warmer waters
And its oiled gloss of human sun.

Harpoon means swoon, then richer loveliness
For the miscarried grace, now waking
In prepared currents dear to your Kirk.
The undying texts again plume and spiral,
And my fantastic inner fable
Reshapes in wholeness at a new mouth.

Tested

No, I am not afraid
To trust, even now, that sign
Of covenant corn and wine.
Let the sullen grit descend
Around the miraculous blade,
It will not bend;
Let the rubble fumble and fume
Where the fiery seed lies hid—
God promised, prepared room
And will halt the grating acid.

Let the field be fenced from me,
The wintry wash of gravel foul the road,
Where His golden gesture showed
The gate to fertility—
I trust and affirm:
When the destined flash recurs
I shall be there, beyond grit and worm,
Where the full harvest stirs.

Edmund P. Clowney

The Singing Christ

Their mighty song burns heavenward
   And glory shines in sound;
The herald angels praise the Lord
   In shouts that shake the ground.
Sing, O sons of heaven's joy,
   The wonder of his ways;
The birth-cry of an infant boy
   Perfects his Father's praise.

Sing, O Jesus, Mary's son,
   The pilgrim psalms appointed:
How great the works the Lord has done!
   How blessed his Anointed!
Sing in Nazareth, young man,
   The songs of jubilee;
Today fulfill redemption's plan,
   Proclaim the captive free!
Sing, O Saviour, lift the cup,
   "Jehovah is my song!"
The sacrifice is offered up
   Before the shouting throng.
"I come to do thy will, my God,
   My body is prepared
To drink the cup and bear the rod
   That sinners should be spared."

Sing, O Christ, up Zion's brow
   From Kidron's rocky bed;
The pilgrim songs are silent now
   And all thy friends have fled.
Sing in agony, my King,
   The God-forsaken Lord:
Count thy bones in suffering
   While malice mocks thy word.

Sing, ascending King of kings;
   Lift up your heads, ye gates;
The King of Glory triumph sings,
   The Lord that heaven awaits.
Sing, O Son of God's right hand,
   Our Prophet, Priest, and King;
The saints that on Mount Zion stand
   With tongues once dumb now sing.

Sing, Lord Christ, among the choir
   In robes with blood made white,
And satisfy thy heart's desire
   To lead the sons of light.
O Chief Musician, Lord of praise,
   From thee our song is found;
Ancient of everlasting days
   To thee the trumpets sound.

Rejoicing Saviour, sing today
   Within our upper room;
Among thy brethern lift the lay
   Of triumph from the tomb.
Sing now, O lamb, that we may sing
   The glory of thy shame,
The paean of thy suffering,
   To sanctify thy Name!

David Cochrane

Tables and Stars

It was that time of day
When the sun and the moon and the stars
Were playing hide and seek in the sky.
Every few minutes another star
Would come out of hiding and try to catch the sun,
But the sun quit and went home.
Then I thought about what I had heard today
And I was no longer sad for the sun.
He would chase away the stars tomorrow.

I opened the coarse wooden door
Which always creaked when I stepped inside.
I peered into the dimly lit room
Where I had spent my nights for the past twelve years.
I saw my mother pull out a slab of freshly baked matzo,
Golden warm and crisp.
I was hungry
And my eyes were wide.
I asked her if I could have some.

"When it cools," she said softly.
"And where have you been this afternoon?
I wanted you to help me
Clean the soot
Off the brick
Above the oven.
I wish you would ask
Before you go running off
To play."

I explained that I had gone down the street
To watch the carpenter make tables and stuff.
"I made friends with a kid there," I said.
"I think he's the carpenter's son.
He doesn't seem like a carpenter's son.
He told me some really neat things
About the stars and—"

"You can wait until your father comes home
From the synagogue and tell him about your day.
Right now,
I want you to set the table and light the candles."

When father came through the door that creaked,
I could see a smile through his big bushy beard
And a little fire in his eyes.
"Sarah, my wife, I am ready to eat!
And what did my first-born do this day?"

"I went to watch the carpenter make tables
And made friends with his son
And he told me all sorts of neat things about stars
And about birds
And then he spoke about the Holy One
And quoted things from the Torah
And the prophets
And he said everything the way you do,
Father.

"He told me that every star has a name
And there are some red
And some large
And some white
And some small
And the sun is a part of a family
And there are many families in the sky
And that birds can fly because they have hollow bones
And—"

"My son, tell your friend not to dream so much
And to learn his father's trade;
And as for you, you are a Levite,
And you will learn the covenants
And the Law from myself
And other rabbis,
And you will be properly trained in the synagogue
And you will obey the commandments
And you will learn to love God!"

I turned to my mother,
But she turned away.
I could not understand
Why they could not understand.
I ran outside and gazed at the stars and
Wondered if all he said was really true.
I knew he could build tables like his father.
Yet, somehow, I do not know why,
I believed he could build more than just tables.

Hugh Cook

Crucifixion

racked by a driving wind
the snow is plastered
on the oak tree
manacled to every niche
black oaken arms sag

under white heat
from the winter sun
the snow
    slowly
    soddens
drops
    seep from the tree
rivulets slither snakelike
down the stem
new seed to barren soil

Christ
your water spring
my germination
let me grow
as a new
white oak
rock-rooted
in your garden

Sand Castles

this man

a small stone
at the bottom
of a murky sea

but

God collects beach stones
his hand reaches down
and he plucks them
from their slime
and he polishes them

and when he shapes
his indissoluble
sand castles

he lines the walls
with stones

Higher Vision

in a moment of startling recognition
  we see likenesses in the world
an insensate stone has a man's face
  dull eye hollows, the nose's bridge
a writhing cherry tree in winter
  has Grünewald fingers for branches
a time and water-worn driftwood piece
  is a miniature emu, down to the clefts
    between the finely sculptured toes

better yet to see God in a sunflower
  his infinity in the iris of a cat

E. Neil Culbertson

Death Drowned

Death drowned dead
in His Blood.
Death pounded in its head
by the nails in His Cross.

Fountains of the deep
break.
Earth
shakes,
and Hell backs up
in the sewers.
Two hundred Saints
go marching home.

Mad clouds and darkness,
like a funeral shroud,
got ripped.

Chaff

Chaff.
Sorted and sifted,
good from bad when God brings Judgment.
Sordid and twisted, victims from villains,
when we try to do it for Him.

Driving the supposed chaff from us
with our own hot air,
instead of the appointed four winds
of the Revelation,
we often trample the elect-yet-unconfessed
as pearls before swine,
forgetting what pearls look like
from the outside of the oyster.

The silo barn is
filled with fat-bellied wheat,
layer upon layer,
prouder upon proud stacked in pews.
We reach the vantage of the silo top,
yet from greatest to least
we are carpeted wall to wall,
suspended by the chaff that is
pressed into the damp dirt reality . . .
in every crack chaff fills.

Settled wheat
ground down under so much pressure
looks (to us) like any chaff hogs walk on.

A Crazy Man
Myself Sometimes

Could you help me?
You're a Christian;
let me capture your attention.
The symbolism's obvious—
a net cast in the sight of any bird
able to be caught.
I never liked hiding.
If you'll encourage me to speak,
I'll pray with you all that I've done.

I've thought poetry before
that I can't write down.
It rakes my throat with digestive acid;
hope put off makes the heart sick.
Some poems I just throw up.
Still dizzy, undiscerning, caught off balance,
vomiting angry words,
I mistake my capacity for pride
to be inspiration.
Afterward, wishing to cry,
to sprinkle the earth to a complete
remission of sin,
able to pray.
I know I've got it backward.
Repentance is grace,
not a snake-oil cure to be used only
when it hurts.

Let me capture your attention.
My capacity for introspection
can resurrect Babylon.
I'm not the Triune.
I have Legion, for we are many.
Don't withhold that Word!
... clothe my naked shamefulness
   with sanity and praise.

Everyone Begins

bound in the pregnant womb,
born by gut reaction
with slippery skin,
pretty eyes, Adam's sin,
and a mouth waiting for the first smile.

Words,
like army ants
paragraphed in rows,
are pressed to attention
on newspapers
a child does not read.
Riots and bombs
explode beyond his range.

Not abreast of all situations,
just happy being fed—
the first Kingdom task.

His Workmanship

He strikes me with
His good sense,
pounding dents.
Welding my frame
with a Holy fire,
He joins the impossible
alloy.

Set in a jig
and cut down to size,
I am snapped into place.
It clicks.
I have no clearance
for the grabbing and growl
of most machines.
Structured with high-stress capabilities,
wonderfully and fearfully
am I engineered.

Three-in-One Oil—
like for a child's skates—
smooths any abrasiveness
I might have
about doing my part.

Grandfather

Canals travel without moisture,
except when you cry.
Grandma's gone now, to God.
They journey upward,
time-worn across your face
to rest at twin oases,
refreshing that desert place.
Their blue water breaks over me
with kindness when you look at me
with approval for the path I am set to take.

You are an old dusty book.
A confession!
The years just make you shine
with another, greater Light,
to comfort me for the years ahead...
for the years I'll leave behind.

Eternity is fixed and mitred neatly
to the joy in your relaxing smile.
Excited words crowd memories
that refuse to age with you
through teeth set eagerly with your smile.
Rousing words, swift with soldierly precision
lay siege to my heart,
demanding a treaty with my imagination:
"'Och! Papa!' Mama would say to me..."
You speak her part as if Grandma
were somewhere in the next room.
"'Your feet! Like ice, Papa!' and Mama
would rub them with her feet until
I was warm again. Oh..."
Your words seem to leap the distance between us
with the proud desire to stretch each muscle,
aware of their special power
to mark my life with their impression.

Sin will never shake you,
though a sharp wind assaults your lungs
and sets your heart racing.
You make me glad you're the adopted grandfather
of this orphan in the family of God.

Heritage

FOR HAROLD JACKMAN

What is Africa to me:
Copper sun or scarlet sea,
Jungle star or jungle track,
Strong bronzed men, or regal black
Women from whose loins I sprang
When the birds of Eden sang?
One three centuries removed
From the scenes his fathers loved,
Spicy grove, cinnamon tree,
What is Africa to me?

So I lie, who all day long
Want no sound except the song
Sung by wild barbaric birds
Goading massive jungle herds,
Juggernauts of flesh that pass
Trampling tall defiant grass
Where young forest lovers lie,
Plighting troth beneath the sky.
So I lie, who always hear,
Though I cram against my ear
Both my thumbs, and keep them there,
Great drums throbbing through the air.
So I lie, whose fount of pride,
Dear distress, and joy allied,
Is my somber flesh and skin,
With the dark blood dammed within
Like great pulsing tides of wine
That, I fear, must burst the fine
Channels of the chafing net
Where they surge and foam and fret.
Africa? A book one thumbs
Listlessly, till slumber comes.
Unremembered are her bats
Circling through the night, her cats
Crouching in the river reeds,
Stalking gentle flesh that feeds
By the river brink; no more
Does the bugle-throated roar
Cry that monarch claws have leapt

From the scabbards where they slept.
Silver snakes that once a year
Doff the lovely coats you wear,
Seek no covert in your fear
Lest a mortal eye should see;
What's your nakedness to me?
Here no leprous flowers rear
Fierce corollas in the air;
Here no bodies sleek and wet,
Dripping mingled rain and sweat,
Tread the savage measures of
Jungle boys and girls in love.
What is last year's snow to me,
Last year's anything? The tree
Budding yearly must forget
How its past arose or set—
Bough and blossom, flower, fruit,
Even what shy bird with mute
Wonder at her travail there,
Meekly labored in its hair.
One three centuries removed
From the scenes his father loved,
Spicy grove, cinnamon tree,
What is Africa to me?

So I lie, who find no peace
Night or day, no slight release
From the unremittant beat
Made by cruel padded feet
Walking through my body's street.
Up and down they go, and back,
Treading out a jungle track.
So I lie, who never quite
Safely sleep from rain at night—
I can never rest at all
When the rain begins to fall;
Like a soul gone mad with pain
I must match its weird refrain;
Ever must I twist and squirm,
Writhing like a baited worm,

►►►

While its primal measures drip
Through my body, crying, "Strip!
Doff this new exuberance.
Come and dance the Lover's Dance!"
In an old remembered way
Rain works on me night and day.
Quaint, outlandish heathen gods
Black men fashion out of rods,
Clay, and brittle bits of stone,
In a likeness like their own,
My conversion came high-priced;
I belong to Jesus Christ,
Preacher of humility;
Heathen gods are naught to me.

Father, Son, and Holy Ghost,
So I make an idle boast;
Jesus of the twice-turned cheek,
Lamb of God, although I speak
With my mouth thus, in my heart,
Do I play a double part.
Ever at Thy glowing altar
Must my heart grow sick and falter,
Wishing He I served were black,
Thinking then it would not lack
Precedent of pain to guide it,

Let who would or might deride it;
Surely then this flesh would know
Yours had borne a kindred woe.
Lord, I fashion dark gods, too,
Daring even to give You
Dark despairing features where,
Crowned with dark rebellious hair,
Patience wavers just so much as
Mortal grief compels, while touches
Quick and hot, of anger, rise
To smitten cheek and weary eyes.
Lord, forgive me if my need
Sometimes shapes a human creed.

All day long and all night through,
One thing only must I do:
Quench my pride and cool my blood,
Lest I perish in the flood.
Lest a hidden ember set
Timber that I thought was wet
Burning like the dryest flax,
Melting like the merest wax,
Lest the grave restore its dead.
Not yet has my heart or head
In the least way realized
They and I are civilized.

Joann Deems

Perspective on
St. Joseph's Day

the swallows are returned
to Capistrano!
flown north from the pampas
to the mission at San Juan

above the clouds their wings and tail
outline bells, catch sound
suggest the ring of hatchet blades
how Nazareth's trees were hewn

down, the swallows tend their business
restore the chipped mud nests
just south of Los Angeles
and mate near them

yesterday in New York State
bearing north on seventeen
we're brought up through the southern tier
near Fish's Eddy

and watch above the black-edged snow
beige deer fill in bare hillsides
the winter of their searching gone
bend to taste new grass

this Monday morning, spring
I think of tractors plowing in the middle states;
one from Iowa, south; another, Missouri's
west; the last in Kansas

south, sewing the winter's wheat
planning row on row
Christ's trademaster evenings
planing cabinets for his home

Just a Housecat

PSALM 113:9

Like a lioness I leap to their defense—
Be it physical or emotional—
And like that same cat I pace
the bedroom dens when they are ill.
I carry them with me as closely and
securely as if held by my jaws
And provide the same nudges of direction
with head moves and naked paws,
claws carefully withdrawn.
I search the supermarket jungles to feed them
And lie in peace when they sleep
and feel the awe of holy gifts and yet
when the wild one raises her head
in powerful pride and dignity
I am—ashamed?

They Were Going Somewhere

Eunice finished talking and looked up
    at the Lord,
Waiting for Him to speak.
"So the women newly arrived have been
    telling you
That Timothy—is—not enough?"

And the Lord tilted back His glorious
    head, and He laughed.
And His laughter rumbled and the
    clouds collided,
And the rain fell upon the earth.

And the women below covered their heads,
And put up their umbrellas, or turned
    on the windshield wipers
Because they were all going somewhere—
    anywhere—
To get away from home.

It Still Sings

I wrestled with it and threw it to the ground,
I denied it, I cursed it, I trampled it, and scourged it.
And then I buried it in the deepest hole I could dig.

But it came oozing to the surface as quietly as
the unfolding of the tight buds on the trees.

I tried to ignore it until it got too big—
as big as the moving branches and green-covered hills,
and shouts of color from petals.
I hid it in the mountains and rolled a stone across it.
And for two seasons I thought it slept.

I tried, I tried, to rid myself of it.

Then one day I heard its singing behind me,
but I could not turn to face it again.

I cried, I cried, and shouted over my shoulder:

> There is no judgment!
> No right!   No wrong!
> No justice!   No mercy!
> No Love!   No Plan!

It still sings softly and offers much.
But I am no fool! I shall not turn and embrace it.
I hate and dread that promising song.

David DeGroot

Though Still
in Filth I Run

No beaming sun am I,
Cloud-caressed and aloof to life,
Ever above the turbulent world,
Apollo in the sky.

In squalor was I reared
As bastard to an ugly trull,
With a cesspool for a soul.
Dark death I daily feared.

The Son a wonder wrought!
Glory-girding my twisted hips,
He set on me a cloak and crown,
Bright garments all blood-bought.

Though still in filth I run,
I challenge everyone I meet
With the glory of His birth,
With the garments of the Son.

Sandra Duguid

If Christ Had Lept

If Christ
    Had lept from the cross
    Had
Recalled the blood
          that
            striped
              His
                face
    the blood
    that colored
  the head
Of each
    Prove-Thyself
      driven
        nail

      If
      He
Had   uprooted that tree

From Golgotha then

    Had   hurled it at men

They might have believed
He was   as He said
God's Son

And He would not have been.

Crucifixion: Communion Service

Be bone of my bone,
be flesh;
I hang from something,
let it be Thy cross;
let that be a straightening
I might lean against,
Power I'd not offend,
then, set me free,
the implementation of Thy perfect
form in me.

Spring Stanzas

The melting snow recombines
Giant awkward flakes
Hurl themselves against the
    budding lilac;
Cherry blossoms batter
Frail petals against marble

Suitcases of crocus bulbs
Rot beneath bare sunporches
Of our ancient homes;
Seeds germinate in the wet
Newspapers saved
In downtown cornerstones

Christ, when this is
Some metaphor of spring,
Show us the real and bruised
Body darkening at Jerusalem.

The Tearing Veil

From within the sanctuary
of the whitewashed church
I looked out the closed window
saw a starling, flying east
flown into summer's screen

Dead for days
dark breast, sides, back
circled with the soft
splintered wire

It had never imagined such panic
and aiming toward no particular inside
did not find itself, even then
half in, half out

Dying at noon
he would have swooped from blue
to no blue, the sun emblazoning rainbows
on his back

Dying toward dusk
the sun would have cast his shadow
on the inside glass
to show another starling

Wings pinned back
trying to fly forward through the screen
the bird would not have pitied, failed to pity
been saved by the other starling

The moon became memorial for that scene
I leave it for worse

Men
crucified
have closed their eyes
back some moments
as from magnifying glass
to see The Christ
bolt upright
pinned to rotting wood

They have appealed to Him
whose wreath was the black sun
who told that moons, the need for them
shall fall
have heard the tearing veil
done with dark glass
and live that inner place
where nothing bears reflection

Save The Light.

Complaint: God's Patience

If I were the Truth, wouldn't I
gather the errant quickly
by hook or by crook?
Use a snapping bait,
a staff with a switch-blade,
a little threat?
Enough of everyone's hedging, holding
back, trifling with his Maker.
I would not hear of Will;
Fierce Talon God, I'd
drop them roughly into Life
on their sweet
soul's pomposity;
kidnap them into The Kingdom, War
whoop!

O but who
in the hot sun quietly
as though still on vacation
is rippling a pool with his rod,
relentlessly climbing through tangled briers
for one caught, bleating sheep? What
kind
of shepherd or fisherman? What
sort of
suitor or dove.

Miss Weld

Emma S. Weld, you always signed your name
in books you loaned,
on jar labels of peaches
for deliverance after Sunday School.
Your voice shook in a violent alto,
too loudly, above the bright blue hymnal;
your prayers, too long, took us all in.

Lunch at your house
was a special occasion;
a former home economics teacher,
you didn't invite just anyone.
Outside, you would point out the big brass bell
that used to call the help, several kittens,
the stained-glass window.
We ate by the pot-bellied stove in the dining room,
but later you opened the parlor doors
and showed me the stained-glass window,
bright purple and red over the stairs.
After lunch, we had our ice cream in cut-glass bowls.
Dust in every cut outlined the rim too perfectly . . .
Tonight, clumps of dirt, newly agitated,
settle around your coffin
like small bunches of grapes,
alveoli.

My sister told me that the Sunday School
collected over thirty dollars in your memory;
we'll purchase our first Communion set,
the silver tray, the little glasses.
Come to the first service . . .
Tonight, with a newer friend,
I ate orange-rice casserole,
cider and red tea
before we went to church.

At the service, each one sang God's praise,
a separate song, separate key,
the Bread,
moist between my teeth,
and clear
the Wine,
spreading in my lungs, Miss Weld
like lavender

the last Word

Be still and know . . .

But they walked and they ran,
And they marched and they rode,
And they flew and they drove,
And they bused and they commuted.

Be still and know that . . .

But they gathered and they met,
And they communed and they congregated,
And they assembled in circles,
And lined up in rows and they organized.

Be still and know that I . . .

But they conversed and they spoke,
And they shouted and they shook,
And they cried and they laughed,
And they murmured and complained.

Be still and know that I am . . .

But the marchers went forward,
The buses rolled on,
The circles went round,
The lines kept moving,
And the shouts and the cries,
And the laughter and the sighs,
And the murmurings and the complaints,
Grew louder and stronger
Whirling and swirling
Faster and faster
Until suddenly—it stopped.

And everybody fell off.

Be still and know that I am God.

Colin Duriez

Words Are a Dying Sun

Words are a sun
              finally
              sinking
                        behind the rim of silence;
    words
          are
              a dying sun.
Our cold twilight words
                        before darkness and silence
are slow words
              that sing in the evening of man.

Who can give words of love
                        to the aged
                        and tired
                        and hoar-headed;
who will love man,
    man empty and decaying and near blind
    man who hides the ugly death signs
    with senile dreams
                        of long-ago youth
                        and beauty
                        and innocence.

The Sun of Righteousness,
    the Word of Truth,
      will give words of love to man,
    will rise in the vision of those
whose eyes He has opened in fear,
                opened to the coming silent death
                              that
                        is
              dark
dark,
      death darker than a cold
                        sunless solar system

The Sun of Righteousness,
    the Sun of Righteousness,
      the Sun of Righteousness
shall arise with healing in His wings.
Then only will the earth have its rest,

its peace,
   its fulfilment,
      its meaning;
then only will it break into cries of joy.

But those that see Him will be few:
they will first tread
the sinking and setting of the sun
before its time of death;
   they alone will therefore dance the new arising,
for they alone will see
     their sickness and their
       age and their decay
and they alone will first have early been caught
    in their lonely vision
by
  the dying
      of the old tired sun.

Words
    are
      a dying sun,
and words of love give long shadows.

For Everything There Is a Season

ECCLESIASTES 3

The time to weep is in the heart's winter.
   Grief is the grip of ice and silence,
snow and vast grey skies. Bending under
   tree-caught snow, nerves hold the sad immense.

The time to laugh is when new is sprung
   suddenly. Renewal—new love, new
light, new green, new morning, blossom-hung
   delight—makes the Spring of the heart due.

There is a time for living. Into
   a wide green under a thoughtful sun
we move and struggle. Who is the True
   must reach here, must judge what we have done.

There is also a time for dying.
   The green leaves become brown, the grass fades,
the unplucked fruit drops and rots. Sighing
   tree-sung rain makes cold decaying shades.

On Prayer

Lord, I am slow
to speak
with You.
Not that You are
coins
to be cashed
in time
of need; not that
You are
words
to cry or to sing.
It is just that it is a slow thing to speak
with anybody.

"Whence? What? Whither?"

Where, from where do I come? What am I?
    where do I go to? Whence? What? Whither?
ask all sorrow-weighed men: men who were,
    who are, who will be. All who will die
ask, and their anguished, fluent eyes speak.
    Laughing, bare rocks clang back in echo,
jeering echo of pain-edged cry; woe
    ignored by grit and rock. Man is weak.

A young man melts into his girl's arms,
    hoping she is soft, soft like her breasts,
sensitive as the pool's face that rests
    on green depth yet a wind's breath alarms.

But a girl's love cannot break ages,
    aeons of finite uncertainty:
one girl, one boy. Are they cursed to be?
    and trapped between shrieking nothingness?

What is truth? asked Pilate; stalked away
    not waiting an answer. The marble
felt cold underfoot, Christ's stern eyes full
    of warm tears. It was rejection day.

The painting titled "Whence? What? Whither?" was done by
Paul Gaugin, the French artist, in Tahiti in 1897, just before
he attempted suicide. It is now in the Museum of Fine Arts,
Boston, Massachusetts.

Journey of the Magi

"A cold coming we had of it,
Just the worst time of the year
For a journey, and such a long journey:
The ways deep and the weather sharp,
The very dead of winter."
And the camels galled, sore-footed, refractory,
Lying down in the melting snow.
There were times we regretted
The summer palaces on slopes, the terraces,
And the silken girls bringing sherbet.
Then the camel men cursing and grumbling
And running away, and wanting their liquor and women,
And the night-fires going out, and the lack of shelters,
And the cities hostile and the towns unfriendly
And the villages dirty and charging high prices:
A hard time we had of it.
At the end we preferred to travel all night,
Sleeping in snatches,
With the voices singing in our ears, saying
That this was all folly.

Then at dawn we came down to a temperate valley,
Wet, below the snow line, smelling of vegetation;
With a running stream and a water-mill beating the darkness,
And three trees on the low sky,
And an old white horse galloped away in the meadow.
Then we came to a tavern with vine-leaves over the lintel,
Six hands at an open door dicing for pieces of silver,
And feet kicking the empty wine-skins.
But there was no information, and so we continued
And arrived at evening, not a moment too soon
Finding the place; it was (you may say) satisfactory.

All this was a long time ago, I remember,
And I would do it again, but set down
This set down
This: were we led all that way for
Birth or Death? There was a Birth, certainly,
We had evidence and no doubt. I had seen birth and death,
But had thought they were different; this Birth was
Hard and bitter agony for us, like Death, our death.
We returned to our places, these Kingdoms,
But no longer at ease here, in the old dispensation,
With an alien people clutching their gods.
I should be glad of another death.

Gracia Fay Ellwood

November 22, 1963

Your eye was keen enough, that far away,
To find your brother's head between the cross-
hairs: and a single bullet hurtled straight.
But not quite keen to see the scope
Had found your own head, nor ear to hear
What your brother's blood cried from the ground.
Wound for wound, life for life, unmurdered cry.

Not so!

The trumpet-tongue evoked an apt reply,
A carmine rushing stream from higher ground
That swept up Abel's blood in swift career
And cried for gracious things: mercy, Hope,
Slain, take vengeance in the death of hate;
The triple grave marked with a single cross
Quiet awaits the third and final day.

Red Jordan

His blood is on us, warm and dark. We seem
Helpless to climb out of the rising stream—
The knee that pressed His arm against the beam,
The fist that drove a spike into a dream,
The mailed shoulders that shrugged to hear no scream
Are spattered, soaked, corroded to the seam;
No polish can restore our armor's gleam,
No perfume make our reeking bodies clean.

His blood is on us: in a cataract
We kneel, with open hands and shoulders bent,
And we are washed and clean at last. See, see
Christ's blood streames in the firmament, and we
Are wholly deluged in its warm descent.
His blood has met His blood, and made a pact.

Et Incarnatus Est

FOR JAMES VANDER LAAN

                                        Outof
                                        Light
                                       sheer
                                      down
                                     heavn
                                    thru
                                   f a r
                                  high
                                 reach
                                es of
                               blue
                              great
                             wind
                            deeps
                           Light. A
                            very
                          cut-flawless
                        uncloudy cleardark
                      still   moved   moving
                          Diamond   sorts,
                       sifts   shiftsshapes
                     vital blinding   white
                       into an irised promise
                     A sinistra the unawaited
                    unwelcome infralight leav-
                   es dark-night-charred galled
                  embers underneath the tenuous
                 flame-of-living-love red-orange,
                Sun gold, crown gold, vision gold,
                Rainwind fresh gardenfragrant green,
                Maryblue—waiting, startled, assenting
                Courtly violet velvets breathing myrrh,
                All-eye-unseen heart-unentered plus ultra.

The Fool

*"Some people will probably say I was a fool. . . . But you
have to live an open life; you have to be available. I drove
away with him. He pulled a gun and said, 'Mr. M_____, you
have been kidnapped'. . . . He shoved me into the trunk of
the car."*

The wise man keeps behind his castle wall
While eyes above the ramparts sweep the hill.
A stranger with a plot to his downfall
Will find the bridge is drawn, the moat is full.
The walls are stout and windowslits are small;
The air is dim and stifling in his hall,
But he is his own man, no thrall.

I am the Fool who leads an open life
And looks to see a stranger as an I.
A man can smile (and smile) and lay a snare
And jerk it tight. I fell. Hands sealed my eyes,
Hands bound my limbs, hands locked me in, and I,
Submitting, was infected by their guilt.
With terror wound like weeds around my head,
Gasping I journeyed aeons in dense night,
Close as my coffin, laden and dark as earth.
I was unmade as I . . . a stolen thing
To be concealed in wrappings, shifted, stored
Until the bargain over it is struck.

From past the End and from before the Naught
A lavish flow of Light, by holy luck:
The wrappings fallen, the stolen thing rebought,
The fish's jaws forced open and its prey
Cast up, breathing, on marble shores; undone
The covering stone the third and final day,
And I am born, and free, and dancing in the sun.

Coronation

FOR MY MOTHER

You had an eye that saw, on hill and tree,
A Light not of the sun; you had a hand
Gifted to wield a subtle brush, to catch
The glory on a canvas for us blind.
But not a master's hand, a servant's; its tools
Ladle and pan, scrub-brush, a needle and thread
By toil to prepare for us a place.
More: to clasp a stranger's cold-stung hand
And take her in; by Light in-fleshed to warm
A child through the Shadowed Valley's arctic night.

Your light to us is dark now: glints remain
Only, caught on these canvasses, our selves;
May you approach the place that light had birth.
May the Creator who took a servant's form
Enfold your hand within His pierced ones,
Escort you to the heights: His throne, His crown:
Alice, artist, Bearer of God, and Queen.

Robert Emshoff

Elohimmyyahweh

There is no private world,
nor language,
but His voice is heard.
His line spins out
to all earth's ends,
slingshot swung round thundering suns,
spanning expanding galaxies,
through empty flat space plains
that never have been known
by tug of mass,
then spirals back
over arcing tangents of disaster,
stitching gracious tapestries in time
and casting out an ordinal net
that squeezes the spacious womb of stars
and regulates their fire.
   This net is whole,
enabling both
the tunneling of neutrons
and the birth of blues,
    straight
as the locus of a light-mote
bending past the sun,
    true
as no man
but One is true
   and clean—
His perfect act
confounding time,
   and good
to taste and see
and seek.
This net was thrown
wisely by Your love, Lord,
taking in its folds my soul.

Node

I remember Him: His coming in,
with palm fronds waving in the wind
that swept out straight, smelling of street,
out to the desert heavy with wild ashes.
But the wind died,
and the last hosannahs die
(a bird swooped sudden
to its hole,
and the people huddled
in their homes)
and the weighted wind
is waiting rain.
The palms on the ground were green;
saccharine bitter wintergreen—ozone bourne,
the strong green before the storm.

Seascape: Recalling the Wind

Above the by-pass
the sound of many motorcars and square-backed trucks
outrushing on expresslane random purposes
recalls to me the oceans of my birth,
the cataracted roar behind the waterfalls
where I, secure, played Captain Nemo: pirate king—
and later of the sea-bird circus throng where first
she kissed me when I won a dimestore loving cup.

But now this streaming nightsong sounds so like a lynch mob
or like stormblast breakers hurling tender polyps back
against the anviliron sharp black rocks of shore,
that I with eyes of underwater creatures cry
to have my roots wrenched off the reef
by the Krakatoan roar within the membranes of my brain
when my most screaming cries of prayer are met at best
by chasmed silence, or by further buffeting beneath the surf.

My wings are broken, Lord:
wind-wings on which I rose,
kiting on the thermals of Your love,
higher than the heavy clouds where Odin rode,
and I am falling fast and falling faster
falling fastest toward the smashing shore below—
Snatch me from my self-destruction, Christ!

Walk in Fog

Fog produces transmutations of perception,
limitations on the walking eye
whose yellowing lights' contentions
shudder and succumb
to the inverse square of radiation—
Einstein whistling in the dark,
confronting Heisenberg
with a Heraclitean dream of fog.

There is no moon in fog
or stars to specify location
on a labeled cork topography.
Here there is only here
and not-here flowing
timewise one
into another as you walk.
Black trees come lumbering
out of fog;
lost ships' masts sleeping
in a Sargasso of mist
are discovered, one by one,
as if I were not walking,
but as if by my efforts fragments
of dehiscent discontinua
are lifted for a moment up
from the dark well shining
in unmitigated singularity
and dropped again unknown
and unbegotten as I walk
from here to not-
here, not here and now.
I am afraid
of dawn.

The Eastern Sun outspilling blood
upon the punctured waters
of the dying eye of night
threatens yet another labor,
but now the fog has fallen on the ground
and I have come
from the freshened womb of morning
young with dew.
There are etched against the lightened distance hills
and I will walk with God today.

Mia Fagerstrom

The Cleansing

For fourteen days our world's been torn and wrung
By cold uncheerful winds and damp and fog
And brooding clouds that cover up the sun
With every gray and black. A chilling bog
Has mired the sun's bright endless sapphire fields.
Or if the sky was clear, then it was night,
And every star poured down a cold so steel
We trembled, as if frightened by the sight.
But now it's warm: the air's so bright and sweet
Each mark on the gray stone chapel tower
That rises from across two sunlit streets
Is hard, scrubbed of haze that misted summer.
   The Lord lashed this fair world with wind and storm—
   May He lash me; may I be so reborn.

Dan Hawkins

Lazarus

was wrapped in broadcloth.
His stinking flesh stayed near the bone
And kept a mocking semblance of the man;
But for his eyes, which
Left two hollow holes that could not see
The dusty cave, no place for any former man
To rest.

Others used their eyes for him.
Even Jesus wept.

Dear God

I see You
Draping Your infinite arm
Across the back of the universe,
Feet propped on the planet
Of Your dreams, which have died,
As men have died since Eden.

Still, You take Your
Sabbath rest
And fail to speak a second week
Of words.
It is as though You expect Paradise
to rise again.

Hester Hogan

Blood Thaw

The world is pressed to freezing
When winter's deathly blanket falls.
Earth's blood is bitter, chilled;
A pulse is barely heard
  As winter shrills its own keen lust
  Of death and bloodlessness
  In groaning winds and piercing breath
  Through trees that wave their bony arms
  To grayly laden skies.

In this,
Winter's most ruthless hour,
One tree stands proud.
  From that tree
  Blood flows free—
    Blood that winter's foulest breeze
    Cannot freeze.
And winter dies.

Ralph Huizenga

The Furrow

PHILIPPIANS 3:13–14

The pasture should be plowed, I thought,
for years of grazing had done the sod no good.
The dip left from plowing the furrows apart,
years ago, could hardly be found.
Searching, I found a slight hollow, and at the end
a cottonwood with rusty barbwire grown into its bark.
I tied a red kerchief on a branch close to the trunk,
high enough to be seen above the horse's head.
Dad had shown me this, years ago.
Two branches, one to the left and one to the right,
a little below the kerchief, would help to guide me
when I looked alongside the horse.
Dad would not have approved.
"Make sure you see the beacon between the ears,"
he would say, and as soon as coulter had cut sod,
Dad's eyes would be frozen to the spot
between the horse's ears
where the beacon could be seen.
I still hear him say:
"Without the beacon you can't do it, son."
His furrows were always straight.

I gave Nellie a lump of sugar and adjusted her collar.
"Makes the horse feel more at ease," Dad would say.
He never seemed to depend on the horse, though.
I felt it was different with me.
"The first furrow should not be too deep,"
I told myself, and adjusted the gaugewheel.
To hold the reins and balance the plow
at the same time was not easy.
I gripped the handles firmly, held the reins tight.
Nellie did not like the feel of things;
I could hear her grinding on the bit.
We'd better try, though, I thought.
"The first furrow sets the pattern for the others."
"Let's go, Nellie!"

The horse's head was pulled down to her chest;
she dribbled, but she did not pull.

I gave her enough rein so she could pull freely:
It seemed that I gave the leadership out of hand;
this made me feel ill at ease.
Without my urging her again, Nellie started to pull—
I could see the red beacon when she lowered her head.
It was more to the right than in the middle, though.
A forceful pull turned her to the right—too much!
"Whoa, Nellie, whoa. Let's try to do better."
Nervously, I jerked Nellie back into line with the beacon
and held the reins a little tighter.
Nellie pulled slow with short, quick-tempered steps;
White foam spluttered around her mouth—
she stopped.
The beacon was centered between her ears.
I urged her to go, but again she dribbled . . .
Pulling her head hard forward, she snorted;
I felt the reins slip from my sore hands—
Nellie started to pull.
She caught me off guard; I tried to get control.
Panicking, I grappled for the reins.
The plow tilted to the right,
skidded without cutting the sod.
It took all my effort to balance the plow.
The whole cottonwood tree could now be seen
on the left side of Nellie,
red beacon and all.
We kept going.
I stumbled over a sod half turned over.
"Keep going, Nellie, just keep going."
She seemed to understand and plodded laboriously
in the general direction of the beacon.

When we came to the poplar,
I looked back on the finished furrow—
and wept quietly.

Roderick Jellema

Four-Square Gospel

Old Uncle Fred could squint along forty-foot beams
And catch the gentlest wayward drift toward a curve
That no one else saw. His calloused, pitch-stained hands
Would tenderly stroke the flush seams of a perfect joint.
We used to see him astride his unwavering rafters,
Tall as the echoing blows of his worshipping arms,
Looking with pride on the loving work of his mitred,
Four-square world. He always looked sharply to see
If some sinning board in somebody's house were off square,
And longed to redeem it with the righteous tongue of his plane.

And then he slumped into arches and curves of age,
Propped up in a bed, looking out at the slanted east
While unseen termites encircled his squared-off house.
Puzzled, he eyed the long, sad arc of the geese,
The easy bend of a tree-limb heavy with fruit,
And then—we knew by the softening line of his mouth—
Saw the curve of a neck swinging free from the beams of a cross.

James Weldon Johnson

O Black and Unknown Bards

O black and unknown bards of long ago,
How came your lips to touch the sacred fire?
How, in your darkness, did you come to know
The power and beauty of the minstrel's lyre?
Who first from midst his bonds lifted his eyes?
Who first from out the still watch, lone and long,
Feeling the ancient faith of prophets rise
Within his dark-kept soul, burst into song?

Heart of what slave poured out such melody
As "Steal away to Jesus"? On its strains
His spirit must have nightly floated free,
Though still about his hands he felt his chains.
Who heard great "Jordan roll"? Whose starward eye
Saw chariot "swing low"? And who was he
That breathed that comforting, melodic sigh,
"Nobody knows de trouble I see"?

What merely living clod, what captive thing,
Could up toward God through all its darkness grope,
And find within its deadened heart to sing
These songs of sorrow, love and faith, and hope?
How did it catch that subtle undertone,
That note in music heard not with the ears?
How sound the elusive reed so seldom blown,
Which stirs the soul or melts the heart to tears.

Not that great German master in his dream
Of harmonies that thundered amongst the stars
At the creation, ever heard a theme
Nobler than "Go down, Moses." Mark its bars
How like a mighty trumpet-call they stir
The blood. Such are the notes that men have sung
Going to valorous deeds; such tones there were
That helped make history when Time was young.

There is a wide, wide wonder in it all,
That from degraded rest and servile toil
The fiery spirit of the seer should call
These simple children of the sun and soil.
O black slave singers, gone, forgot, unfamed,
You—you alone, of all the long, long line
Of those who've sung untaught, unknown, unnamed,
Have stretched out upward, seeking the divine.

You sang not deeds of heroes or of kings;
No chant of bloody war, no exulting paean
Of arms-won triumphs; but your humble strings
You touched in chord with music empyrean.
You sang far better than you knew; the songs
That for your listeners' hungry hearts sufficed
Still live—but more than this to you belongs:
You sang a race from wood and stone to Christ.

Carolyn Keefe

Prophet

His voice is heat-wave thunder
unannounced, a long way off,
a break in the skyscape,
a dreary day respite,
a hint that things may change.

He scares me at times,
the deepness, low, growlly,
fanged prelude to rainstorm
and uncertain crops.

I wish he'd not come.
We have priest and king;
they don't rumble so
and wake me at night.
God knows I need my rest.

The Trading Post

What is my search for God's will
but the haggling of a fool?
"O Lord, when, where,
and how You will," I sing
in a falsetto key.
The chorus is a swap—
His peace for my blatant pledge:
I shall endure the disdain,
those echo chamber laughs
which keep reverberating.
Just for a word,
a sign from a star,
a line of bread crumbs to follow,
I proffer my love boxed in gold,
as though I can give something
I do not possess.

You fool! Seal up your lips.
Deviousness mounted upon your
tongue trades favors with God. Not
to be bought, the Immutable
in command of His own will
sets the price.

Easter

A woman with shoulders bowed only since Friday
steps deep into death's lair.
Stupified by guilt or sorrow or not caring,
the town had been silent as she passed.
Behind the hedges insensible cyclamen
and violets drink life from the dawn,
giving their moisture back to the sky.
They too should have perished with Him,
blasted to their very root hairs
tenacious in the ground. Gather
some for Him and with the aloes
make an ointment for His bloodied brow.

    O joy! Her bitter myrrh
    had become obsolete at daybreak.
    Through ground and rock,
    sky, sea, and stars,
    He bursts His putrid casing
    and confronts the universe!

She folds the linen, taking it home
to wash from it the stench of death,
joyfully laying it out in the forever sunshine.

Love Seeking

I could understand if You had found me
a porcelain among the rubble of earthen cups
stained dark with tea from many lands,
but I have nothing except brokenness to offer,
an encrusted shard lost deep thousands
of years in Babylon's tell, a relic marked
for oblivion, dead to use and the hands of men,
having no power within myself to restore
the beauty my Maker fired in.
Look at me, a dirt heap resident,
the neighbor of earthworms and slugs,
scorned by wild asses and the boars
which tramp nightly on my roof. Yet
You chose to uncover my ancient hill
and cut away the resistant layers one by one
till You could lift me from my filthy bed.
You are Love seeking, and I can feel
my degradation drop off behind the years.

Incarnation

How can I talk with you
now that the garden is gone
and my mountain voice has grown hoarse?
My prophets lie in uneasy graves
straining to give a single word
through the battle tramp
that stuns the stars.

But my handmaid has silence in her soul,
the quiet spot where lilies grow
in untrammeled love, dew-fed
by some invisible stream.
She will listen to my heartbeat,
the slow, steady pulse of my long sleep,
the dark womb bed, the wet wall
that veils my eyes from the sky.
I shall lie still and learn the feel of man
   firm pounding down at the river's edge
   The gentle swish of her garment
   cool repose under the willow
   the hot bleaching sun
   a soft hand against my face
   the man's resolute grasp
   jostling along the roadway
   the door's sudden slam
   the long tunnel into starlight
   my first man-child wail
I shall use your nouns and verbs,
the sentence half-said,
the halting phrase swallowed
by fear, the sighs and giggles,
the worn-out slang,
the quiet acquiescence.
And when I speak my words,
you shall hear in your hearts
the sound of God talking with men.

Dream Combat
at Claibourne Church

The mailbox spilled its contents so inadvertently
that I might have thought this happened often
and without consequence.
I had not courted the honor
given only the brilliant and adventurous;
some other hand must have singled me out
as worthy and wise enough
to match opportunity with desire,
money with study, freedom with performance.
I showed you the letter which I hoped
would repay the teacher more than the taught
and evoke a stunned silence greater than my own.
But your reply was as rehearsed as a long-running play
whose vigor, mounted by habit, convinces all
except those trained to see.
You sighed that you were full,
not of pride, but of fear,
the sinister kind unable to spot any one enemy
but many working centerward.
I must beware lest I be snatched away
from your jot-by-jot tutelage sustaining us both
and making me the marvel others now sought.
With you I had caring akin to God's
and wisdom sufficient to make the world take notice;
leave, and my mind would be plucked like Eden's fruit,
devoured, rather than given back to my Maker.

I wish you could view the portraits
engulfing my room in multiple stance,
your form drawn more cunningly
than I had ever imagined and without your leave.
Earlier I should have studied them
for light change and texture,
noting the period shifts
and how your eyes nuance the unspoken,
your hands tap out both rhythm and rhyme.

But then the letter had not arrived,
a day went forward more than back,
the now was yours, the future too,
and what was passed was praised but not reviewed.
"One who puts his hand to the plow
should never look back," and

►►►►

"Remember Lot's wife!"
your adage whips against my protruding will,
the ever-so-slight shaping, the shaper God-high,
more handsome than a crown prince and quite as dashing.

I must have been six or seven
when you sprang out of Cinderella
and filled the empty church and manse,
you with your white suit and shoes,
ebony hair caressed by jewels,
the whitest hands that ever held
the fitting glass slipper.
What impelled you carriage-bound
to my threshold, not for a queen
but a daughter?
It was the ebony hair encircling my face
like a dark halo, you said,
and the body of an angel disguised as a fairy,
and a fairy as a girl,
and a girl who could become Athena,
the Wise, the Reasonable, the Pure.

Then before I could unprince you,
my regimen began:
parent-approved theology at seven,
foundation course in creation,
original sin, and redemption;
by eight, one-hundred texts from card to brain,
my payment, a Bible you signed in red
and presented to your half-grown Athena,
her dusky halo still in place;
pulpit reading before twelve,
the church-bred wonder atop a covered milk crate
for audience view and focalized worship;
a complete sermon two springs later,
the wooden box gone,
the preacher's hair vibrant, long,
her dress wispy and white.
Your plan may have begun that day
with your eyes upon my back,
the faces of your holy kin
framed against the giant Word and standing palms.
The staging was your design—
a dome-strung purple banner hid
the three trumpeters whose piercing blasts
became rarified like music from a deep valley;
three dozen candles were properly mounted,
each growing higher until a flaming path
reached the cross and ended there.

"The child is ours," I heard you say,
"brought to this house by good Claibourne stock,
and, like Samuel, reared from the womb
to know God's Word and night decrees.
Now Claibourne's pride, the Church's favor,
stands before you awaiting your seal."
The twelve elders (never off cue)
walked full-aisle length to cage me
within their sacred circle of laid-on hands,
their burning hopes the watchers' sweet sign,
my accursed brand.
Still, no one asked your black-haired goddess
if she wanted her way initial-struck
with your name, her bounds fixed,
her days, her years ordered for God-gifting.

Of course, I believed your early pansied words
sown when eager gardeners spy the first spring stirrings
and plan for long blossoms,
the nurtured care a joy equal to the plucking
and thrice as hard.
I did not fathom that the urging was yours,
not this way, but that,
growth clear of the driveway, the path,
the bramble bush.
I submitted to your coaxing,
the hand with God-feel,
generous, ungloved, mother-earth-warm,
a warning to slugs and cutworms,
sacral to me.
You thought you knew the culture for tender plants,
the filtered shade till roots dig deep
and high-sky sun is past the wounding,
but you would not await the turning
like a man who senses the seasons
and does not press for what has not first slept
the quiet, dark, embryonic night.

You never guessed that some day
the tutor would turn on the prince
and mock his feeble vanity and whitened hair,
or that the brander would trample the pansies
before they had dropped seed.
Each pose has startled the other,
one man costumed is seen as four,
and four unsettled increase their terror.
If only remembrance would put bite on my sword,
engage my courage to do you mortal harm,
avenge your gate-keeping done in God's name,

but you turn my private, unschooled thrusts circus-silly.
I am more buffoon than Athena,
less warrior than coward,
the simpering heir to a great name.
In training me for wisdom, you have reaped a reward
which reeks of your favor,
the I-shall-be-happy-to-please, my dear sir.
It fascinates, it delights,
but it diminishes me
precept by precept,
intent by intent
till only your mazed words are audible.
The battleground disappears
like a violet cloud riddled by thunder.
I stand alone,
unarmed,
my secret wisdom displaced,
your steady voice the sound that enables.

Yet an honor bestowed is a cruel goad
that makes past efforts seem preliminary,
one hank spun gold must multiply
until a whole bin is full;
first a single tree stripped clean,
then an orchard awaits.
The lesser task commands the greater.
One instant the conscience is mollified,
the next it pleads for more.
There is no end to the demands made by honor.

The past has come to me
like a long-forgotten dream
which hangs between one year and another,
a hair's breadth to walk on and less to grasp,
more spider web than bridge,
formless except for trapping.
But a dream can reveal as well as hide—
my mind is a sun-gullied creek bed,
the blurred edges roll back,
slowly the land's awash.
The ruffled days cry out from infant's sleep
when untaught brain had no term for the act;
once disclosed, your hollow virtue must assume
its new, murky name, its refuge forever gone.
No ground is safe for standing
when rankled memory sunders the devil
from the god and shuns mercy,
lest the one spared turn back consumptively.
Now I am ready to gut the ugly form behind the fair.

Ron Klug

Joseph's Lullaby

Sleep now, little one.
I will watch while you and your mother sleep.
I wish I could do more.
This straw is not good enough for you.
Back in Nazareth I'll make a proper bed for you
of seasoned wood, smooth, strong, well-pegged.
A bed fit for a carpenter's son.

Just wait till we get back to Nazareth.
I'll teach you everything I know.
You'll learn to choose the cedarwood, eucalyptus, and fir.
You'll learn to use the drawshave, ax, and saw.
Your arms will grow strong, your hands rough—like these.
You will bear the pungent smell of new wood
and wear shavings and sawdust in your hair.

You'll be a man whose life centers
on hammer and nails and wood.
But for now,
sleep, little Jesus, sleep.

Bonnie Kuipers

Babel: A Warning

Mad stackpiled anthill
erected in a busy mound
rises up
in glory from the earth.
Thick black masses
move steadily
with single-minded intent,
full of this day's
errands and gains.

Don't you realize
one foot coming down
from above
your small world
could churn or crush
this all to dust?

The Last Birth

Dried daisies in her lap,
covered by hands
brown as the sweet earth,
wrinkled as the furrows
plowed open to the sun...

I sometimes dream wistfully
that I am you,
feeling the morning sun
kiss my hollow cheek,
tasting bitter water
as if it were new wine.

Through the thin cotton of your dress
your dried frame shakes
like wheat in the wind
begging to be harvested,
crying out sharply
that the season of ripeness
has passed.

And when the flowers close
deep in their shell of night,
your smile will crease wide;
you have known for years
that you would be
a daisy in His lap,
the healing element
for His bleeding hands.

The Few

ON THE LAST DAYS
AND THE CHOSEN

I feel the circle tightening,
    the quarter moon
has passed into the full
and it is frightening
    to know we are the few
who
    grasp the silver lining
    in the stormy clouds—
        the few
who
    alone will be there
to see the sunlight.

Creature Praise

The snow lies deep
    on darkened hollows
and in its gentle coming
    it has not missed
a single tree
    or blade of beaten grass.
It is the sole traveller
    on the backwoods paths
    and waits silently
        for evening to come
    and with evening—
        animals,
    that stop a breathless moment
to watch and worship
    beneath a
    lonely, dying sun.

Creation

Born on the Potter's wheel,
it dances to His tune—
summer skies and sun
were on His mind
and He could find
no other way to express it.
It should bring you joy
to know you were created
from the swiftness of His hands,
and you are the smile
on a child's face,
having the strength
of a mountain stream
falling over itself
in an imaginary race—
you are a separate sun.

Howard Laing

from *The Equation of Mystery*

PROLOGUE

"Step back, old man. Stand here.
The portrait is called 'The Mystery Man.'"
"What is mysterious about him?
I imagine Apollos looked like that—
Your lighting is too bright.
The whole canvas looks like a shimmering pool.
I apologize, it's my eyes;
All I see now is a solitary spire
Shepherding a flock of grazing fog."
"Young man, would you help this good brother?
Tell him what you see."
"A man in coat of camel's hair,
Wind-blown by desert air,
With bowed gaze into Jordan's mirror
As open heaven and descending dove appear."

I. LIFE

Our vision, winged by wind,
As Paul was upward borne,
Outsoars the hordes
Of cosmic clouds.
We all break through into bliss,
Co-pilots into scurrying skies.

In vine and branch
Entwined—the mystery:
Two equaling many.
Men put out the flaming bush,
Marvel at its burning and shining,
Back away from the unconsumed.

But the One who may live in us
Can home heaven,
Mold mansions in the mind,
Home earth,
Stir the hearth in the heart—
Put a welcome mat at the door of the universe.

II. LIGHT

No one dreamed it,
Sunrise over the rim of his heart—
Like Zebulun and Naphtali
Startled out of darkness.
Dawn dazzled the temple
Before one knew there was a temple.
So mid-dayed in the morning,
He groped for a hand
And heard footsteps
Spraying waves of light.

Arrayed in panoply of day,
The Saul-man surpassing men,
Standing a head taller—
The man of promise,
Stretching his arms
Around the shoulders
Of the seer and the singer—
The slayer of thousands,
Striving with Philistines
Upon the heights of Mount Gilboa—
The Glory of Israel.

Two, the new I,
And many, the co-inherent we,
Rejoice in the splendid city
As grain the ground:
Swing on the tree of life,
Picnic in the park
Bathed in rainbow splendor,
Walk down the strangerless street,
Linger by the river.
City on the summit,
Hidden until seen.

III. LOVE

Knights are known by the Round Table,
The gift that Arthur prized the most.
As the sun's slanting rays
Converge above the clouds,
The courteous lift their eyes
To their invisible King—
One with hair of white and eyes of fire—
Enjoying milk and meat from His hands
And spending gifts—a tear, a smile—
To ready themselves for the good fight.

He knows their knightly combats,
Self-inflicting thrusts
While holding Table Round.
"Lord, is he the one?
Not a crumb for him!"
Table manners disgraceful,
Clumsy fingers for Pauline silver,
Causing outraged faces and empty places.
The sun stares at the cup,
Tipped over in remembrance of Him.

➤➤➤➤

New man, the Poet's masterpiece,
Of great price: song after separation,
Catharsis of Cross and Pentecost,

Man with the Book, in love,
On the field of battle,
Exulting in desire to do His will.

As a bud unfolds in sunshine,
He matures on the bosom of Love,
Far from the foot of thunder and lightning.

With the signature's flourish,
Words rise to welcome the Author,
White pages waving in the air,

Forerunner of the greater gathering,
Encircling dance round the bride-city.
Some see but a quaking reed,

Friend of Sorrows, acquaintance of Grief,
Muddled as a flower with center of green,
Archaic as an orchid beside a rose.

"Who are you?" they query.
Man knows man. New man knows new man.
Even angels look into the poem from the outside.
When a word assumes position
As it is written,
Every jot relates, every tittle means,

Astounding the critic, crowning the Laureate,
The One making a home out of heaven
And a new earth for heaven someday,

Building a city in the mind
And bringing it to earth
On the morning of all new things—

The summer breeze, laden
With the fragrance of Lebanon, quivering
The inscape of mystery, I equaling we.

Poem for a Girl Who Limps

Your built up shoe
helps but does not
hide the strain
of your turtle steps
heaving your heavy shell
of a body
rhythmically forward.

Embarrassed to pass you
on the narrow walk,
I lag behind.
The hair on your spine
must know the stare
that can't quite force itself
to see you broken
but has no way
to see you whole.

If only I could take you,
as I take my child,
play Christ to your need,
touch each wounded foot
and tell you, *Run.*

But I have only grace
enough to play words
alive in poems.
They've yet to raise
a body from the dead.

Still, one never knows,
the word has powers
we can't predict.
Listen, I'm writing for you
and playing my words
into prayer.

The Dove

GENESIS 8:11
JOHN 1:32

Twice sent to signal
God's relenting,
my flights were short
but to the mark.

I lighted first on land
and then on light:
the flood of grace
the grace of blood.

I saw both times,
His mercy spent,
Christ buy what God
could not redeem.

The Worm

ACTS 12:21-23

Consider my host,
Herod. Does not
the Holy Ghost
work also in him?

The Snake

ACTS 28:3-6

Nature conflicted. The weather was cold
But heat drew me out. I struck flesh
And fastened on fire. For yielding to
Nature I burn unnaturally.

Bass

the way you brag about it afterwards.

took the canoe
below the ripples
and back up the eddy
quietly   quietly
dropped a whole crawler
on a lily pad
and twitched it off
right into his mouth

played him   letting him run
stopping him short of the weeds
brought him   sun on his side
to the net
slipped the coin out
and let him
                    go

Compound Metaphors
for Sunday Morning

No war of earth and heaven darkens
the stillness of this timely church.

Earth is ours:
It blusters against the windows
and shakes the panes
we eye the sky through.

And heaven too:
Falling, it intersects the wind,
cuts through all panes
and fills with light the eyes
we close to see.

The long division of the saints
is set aside.
In the mathematics of the cross
all products, sums, and quotients
equal one.

Grandmother:
Dying

Aged in one stroke
the old woman lies
in silence,
her lips caved in
in unaccustomed severity
around her toothless gums.

Yet she is not without
dignity. The lines
of her life betray
no hidden gall,
no secret sin for years
eating at her conscience.

Others shout and scream,
abuse their nurses, and
their long-dead husbands.
The grace she learned
in childhood
still wears new.

And when she speaks to us
and says, "I've been
talking with an angel,"
we know that if our eyes
were opened we would see
a company of angels
standing at her wounded side.

The Brass Salvation

Evening. A barred owl barks
doglike in the woods.

Only the frogs and crayfish
fear him;
his talons are small and weak.

Our fears come not by air;
they creep about the earth,
seeking to enter our soles
and crawling veins rise
to stop our hearts.

We laugh at their pits.
Our salvation is forged in brass;
it coils on a pole near the fire.

My Father's Acres

Like an army preparing a siege
the woods mass
around my father's acres.

They've taken the cornfields,
the neighbor's orchard and swept
across the field of winter wheat
that bowed in the wind
like a kneeling congregation.

No farmer seeking profit
from the land, my father
had no quarrel with woods.
His code read, *Love your enemies.*
He cast his lot against the grain;
he planted trees.
The dogwood, maple, hemlock
and tulips rooted
with my youth have prospered
in his soil and rise
twenty feet above his roof.

Outflanked, the woods have lost.
Ordered and in place,
they shade his evening's rest.

Finding the Word
LUKE 12:12

The Spirit must scream
plummet down
like a bird of prey
and sit   fierce
talons clenched
in your bleeding lips

and your words become
His Word
and His Word become
your words

that your speech
dead in the agony of self
might be resurrected
in self-extinction.

After the Stroke

The embolism loose
from the heart
lodged in the brain
a sudden confusion of language
paralysis
and the end of speech

> *As for man, his days are as*
> *grass.*
> *Psalm 103:15a*

Beside your bed,
I cannot speak the prayer
that begs for your recovery.
The Groaning Spirit
who gives us leave to pray
withholds that comfort.
He has given me, instead,
sleeplessness,
open eyes to watch
the sweet liquid, fortified,
drip three days
into your needled arm.
My mouth stays shut.

> *Bless the Lord, O my soul.*
> *Psalm 103:1a*

It is no easy thing
to bless the Lord in Buffalo
where you lie
stroke still and dumb.

My watch is pointless,
kept only for myself.
The nurses, crisp professionals,
need neither me
nor my questions.

The heat of your room drives
me out into the street.
The 5 A.M. winter wind
is cold. Its voice
a quick thin blade, slips
through the layered wool I wear

and speaks deep into my side
the word that alters all.

> *He hath not dealt with us after*
> *our sins, nor rewarded us*
> *according to our iniquities.*
> *Psalm 103:10*

In the therapy room
they held you by a belt
stood you up
and told you,
Walk.

You thought hard,
clutched the rails
and throwing your foot
like a loose shoe
stepped into the pain
and did not stop
until you'd walked it through.

But there were others there,
almost as young as you,
whose only grace
was the white webbed belt
around their waists.

> *Who satisfieth thy mouth with*
> *good things.*
> *Psalm 103:5a*

When your words returned,
they came at random
jumped from your lips
out of context
and refused to lie down
in sentences;

but they did return.
And slowly felt your lips
and tongue divide the syllables
until, one day, dominated,
they spoke as ordered
and blessed the name of God.

Poem for Melissa

AGE THREE

The squirrels you never see
except, perhaps, to catch a glimpse of
scratching around
to the back side of a tree
squeak like your rubber
nursery toys.

Across the valley hunters' rifles crack.
I think, how hard
in the autumn foliage
it is to shoot a squirrel.

Adam's daughter,
I've taught you well.
The weight of death
you handle falls
easily to the ground.
You gather leaves
and name them
accurately,
maple, oak, and elm.

At our approach
a gray squirrel
flattens, St. Andrew's crossed
against an oak trunk.
I watch him with a hunter's eye,
but I have only clumsy weapons,
hands incapable of striking distances
greater than my reach.

And I have willed
to discipline their eagerness
to reach for blood
they have not shed by birthright.
We should not beg another death,
when all the deaths we need
are done.
Take one; hold it in yours.

Poem Written on Request

Asking for a poem
about God
        come down
to be cramped in flesh
strung out
and nailed
on a cross

is

asking a poet to believe
the Word
is bound in words.
You won't find many
willing to deal in that
brand of magic. But here I am.

And here's your poem:

Break forth into joy
Sing together
The Lord hath made bare
His holy arm.

Sunday Morning

INVOCATION

Every Sunday, listening to the CBC,
we climb the steep slope of the Genesee Valley
then descend gradually into the interval
of Short Tract Church.

AT PRAYER

How easily I have said these words,
addressing the Mystery as Father
and calling myself by implication child.

My daughter tugs my sleeve.
God waits.

It is not in vain.

A JOYFUL NOISE

Hymnbook in hand
the only thing that saves me
is the volume of my voice.

If I were to end my praise,
the foolishness of this noise
would batter my ears
like angry fists.

There is no hope
apart from bellowing,

"Jesus Saves! Jesus Saves!"

RECEIVING THE SACRAMENT

Kneeling to receive the Lord,
I feel my eyes crawling on my back.

Do I really want to be here?

Suddenly the stained-glass dove
breaks from the window.
Light trails His swift descent.

I rise up shining.

BENEDICTION

Returning, after the hour
of commonplace observance,
our car pauses at the ridge,
gathers itself and leaps
over the brink into our valley
opening like another world before us.

The Current

THE GENESEE VALLEY

This is the landscape of order:
acres of corn and potatoes
split and measured
by roads disobedient
to the river's slow meanders.

Once, in a borrowed boat
I obeyed them
and under me felt
the current stronger and
further reaching
than the grip of concrete.

Mornings now, after rain,
I go out
to the edge of the field
and bending, place a finger
in the current's narrow spoor
and touch in the soil
the confirmation of my fear.

And yet, these Appalachian hills
receding an eighth of an inch a season
are not the measure of our lives.

It is the darker current,
not water,
that roars as silently as the stars
and rips the trees
from Calvary's banks
and tumbles stones before it
that replenishes the soil
and marks a man.

In it I find my proper fear
and in that fear, my life.

The Sureness of This Hour

The blandness of His body
still in my mouth,
the commemoration of His blood
cupped in my hands,
I pause in prayer.

Beside me my daughter,
too young to know
the verses that she knows,
draws a man
with a heart-shaped head.

She tells me it is me.
The sureness of this hour
is reconciliation.
The bread, the blood, her love
confound my double nature.

The Geography of Love

1

The sun is the fire
we dwell in.

It does not burn,
but we live in danger.

Its light is darkness
to our eyes.

2

The gaggle crumbles;
the sky is cluttered with geese.
Then one fronts the wind,
breasts it,
and breaks its battering
for the flock.

The air supports their flight
and bears the word
to us.

3

We have come into time by an act not ours.
The will that bears us
can be run like the flood current
of the Genesee
but not denied.

We run it by willing
its direction for our own
by digging deep into its power
by adding speed to speed.

There is no turn
we can't by grace negotiate.

4

We have come to this place by choice.

We have crawled like cicadas
from the years of darkness,
split our backs by will,
and left the old nature
fastened to the tree.

Yet, we will fall into the ground.
The grave, too, is Christ's;
it is His place.

5

Eternity is now.
What we are is what
we will become,
and what we are is here.

In the geography of love
the only place is Christ.
We dwell in Him,
the present of the Father.

Madeleine L'Engle

O Simplicitas

An angel came to me
And I was unprepared
To be what God was using.
Mother I was to be.
A moment I despaired,
Thought briefly of refusing.
The angel knew I heard.
According to God's Word
I bowed to this strange choosing.

A palace should have been
The birthplace of a king
(I had no way of knowing).
We went to Bethlehem;
It was so strange a thing.
The wind was cold, and blowing,
My cloak was old, and thin.
They turned us from the inn;
The town was overflowing.

God's Word, a child so small,
Who still must learn to speak,
Lay in humiliation.
Joseph stood, strong and tall.
The beasts were warm and meek
And moved with hesitation.
The Child born in a stall?
I understood it: all.
Kings came in adoration.

Perhaps it was absurd:
The stable set apart,
The sleepy cattle lowing;
And the incarnate Word
Resting against my heart.
My joy was overflowing.
The shepherds came, adored
The folly of the Lord,
Wiser than all men's knowing.

O Sapientia

It was from Joseph first I learned
Of love. Like me he was dismayed.
How easily he could have turned
Me from his house; but, unafraid,
He put me not away from him
(O God-sent angel, pray for him).
Thus through his love was Love obeyed.

The Child's first cry came like a bell:
God's Word aloud, God's Word in deed.
The angel spoke: so it befell,
And Joseph with me in my need.
O Child whose father came from heaven,
To you another gift was given,
Your earthly father chosen well.

With Joseph I was always warmed
And cherished. Even in the stable
I knew that I would not be harmed.
And, though above the angels swarmed,
Man's love it was that made me able
To bear God's Love, wild, formidable,
To bear God's Will, through me performed.

At Communion

Whether I kneel or stand or sit in prayer,
I am not caught in time nor held in space,
but thrust beyond this posture I am where
time and eternity come face to face;
infinity and space meet in this place
where crossbar and high upright hold the One
in agony and in all Love's embrace.
The power in helplessness that was begun
when all the brilliance of the flaming sun
contained itself in the small confines of a child
now comes to me in this strange action done
in mystery. Break me, break space, O wild
and lovely power. Break me: thus am I dead,
am resurrected now in wine and bread.

The Risk of Birth

This is no time for a child to be born,
With the earth betrayed by war & hate
And a comet slashing the sky to warn
That time runs out & the sun burns late.

That was no time for a child to be born,
In a land in the crushing grip of Rome;
Honor & truth were trampled to scorn—
Yet here did the Savior make His home.

When is the time for love to be born?
The inn is full on the planet earth,
And by a comet the sky is torn—
Yet Love still takes the risk of birth.

Second Lazarus

O come, dear Lord, unbind: like Lazarus, I
lie wrapped in stifling grave clothes of self-will.
Come give me life that I to death may die.
I stink: the grave of sin is worm-filled still
despite our turning from its rottenness,
unwilling to accept that we are bound,
too proud to mention our begottenness.
Come, open sin's sarcophagus. I'm wound
in selfishness, self-satisfaction, pride,
fear of change, demands of love, greed,
self-hate, sweet sins that come in fair disguise.
Help me accept this death and open wide
the tight-closed tomb. If pain comes as we're freed,
Your daylight must have hurt first Lazarus's eyes.

The Nativity

Among the oxen (like an ox I'm slow)
I see a glory in the stable grow
Which, with the ox's dullness might at length
    Give me an ox's strength.

Among the asses (stubborn I as they)
I see my Savior where I looked for hay;
So may my beastlike folly learn at least
    The patience of a beast.

Among the sheep (I like a sheep have strayed)
I watch the manger where my Lord is laid;
Oh that my baa-ing nature would win thence
    Some woolly innocence!

The Apologist's Evening Prayer

From all my lame defeats and oh! much more
From all the victories that I seemed to score;
From cleverness shot forth on Thy behalf
At which, while angels weep, the audience laugh;
From all my proofs of Thy divinity,
Thou, who wouldst give no sign, deliver me.

Thoughts are but coins. Let me not trust, instead
Of Thee, their thin-worn image of Thy head.
From all my thoughts, even from my thoughts of Thee,
O thou fair Silence, fall, and set me free.
Lord of the narrow gate and the needle's eye,
Take from me all my trumpery lest I die.

Heather Marsman

In the Hospital

My heart is sound,
so don't be fooled by the chart.
I am younger than that
(or maybe I am older)
because I started to die years ago,
and every so often
another part of me falls away,
some useless, gangrenous toe or
hand or foot.
I guess it started
when I saw the devil
and whether it was he or me
doesn't really matter.
You can call him cancer
or poverty or mental illness—
even just plain death
and he'll be happy.
In the hospital you can take your pick.
For me, he was hands—
puffy, putrescent,
caging me just by being there
overunderbesideandbeside.
It was a game to play
. . . sitting still . . .
the terrified still of a child alone
in a midway at night,
the still of a deserted house,
of heat without wind,
or a broken watch.
But I wanted out. I broke   the rules and jumped—
overthrough—
I was off and running!
Out the door down the stairs through
the door I shut the door and   jumped
for the chair   there.
i was safe   crouched in a ball,
       the pounding inside
          shaking me like a jack hammer

     but i knew   how?

i looked down   once
and i saw them, mine   the same
and there was nothing and no sound

The nurse was frightened
and the doctor couldn't laugh
Maybe that doctor had a pet name for the devil,
but he couldn't laugh.
He could listen.
He could poke and prod.
But only Jesus stretching out   His hands
for mine   could control that jackhammer heart,
widen the arteries for surgery
so the whole team could step back, strip their gloves
—and masks, smiling. "See! New hands!"

And here I am again,
friend, praise God and laugh—
let the whole blessed hospital laugh—
"Look! My toes!"

Brothers and Sisters

Before...
Before I knew Holland is not
        the Netherlands and no boy could ever stop a flood
        with his finger,
Before I ever heard of anyone eating tulip bulbs
        or hiding from the razzia,
Before I was told of families crossing the Atlantic
        and the Prairies like sick sheep only to be corralled
        in some Canadian's garage with a space heater,
Before I ever tasted Oliebollen or considered putting brussel
        sprouts on my list of regular vegetables,
Before a minister without a collar (a dominee who liked cigars
        and a little gin) shepherded me without an argument
        into the smile of Jesus,
Before ... well, before if someone had asked, "What province
        did you come from?", I could have said, "Ontario."
But that is not so easy now,
        and how can I tell you, brothers and sisters...
        how can I explain?

                I too have crossed an ocean
                my land is not the same

                    we have all come out of Egypt.

Elva McAllaster

To Ask, To Seek, To Knock

Kneeling on a flat cushion
Under vaulted stone arches
At gray dawn.

There's a big blue marlin on the line:
Three hundred pounds or more
Of fighting fish.

Reel in, reel out.
Let him dive toward the coral reefs
At the bottom of the ocean floor
When he will.
Steadily, steadily.

It may be muscle-straining hours
Before we can pull him in.

Praying while heels tap
Toward the tube stop.
Praying—eyes open,
Apparently reading the adverts—
In the rush hour train.
Praying on the up escalator
At Piccadilly Circus.

Hold the line firm.
Never mind the aching biceps,
The tug and strain, the tearing pain
In shoulder bones and
Vertabrae he jolts against
(Shock, leap, shock, leap)

As he fights toward the
Open sea.
Never mind the muscles' screaming;
They are bringing in
Blue marlin.

Grace before meat:
Grace asked for, yearned for, begged, besought,
And, like a dog that bays the moon,
Thought howls at heaven's gate
With every bite.
Sometimes, only the howling, and no bite taken.

The black bill flips above the surface
As the marlin pounds, twists, charges, pulls:
But more slowly now.
Black bill protrudes from shattered purple water
Followed by blue battling hulk.
Firm. Keep the line taut now.
Feel in, reel in.

Subconsciously while phones ring:
Praying.
A litany for typewriters.
A *sursum corda* for adding machines.
Oh, my God, my God . . .

Now. In he comes.
The fishermen sail back to port
Flying the marlin flag:
Triumphant, glad.

And thankful, thankful, thankful.
Kneeling on a flat cushion
Under vaulted stone arches
At gray dawn
To praise Him.

In tube stops,
On escalators,
At typewriters:
Forever:
To praise Him.

This Easter

Walk through the town:
Listen to all the daffodils
Blowing their new trumpets.

Greet the surrogate assembly of angels
Poised in serried tiptoe ranks
On the stalks of all the hyacinths.

Bulbs, buried in dark
Humus tombs,
Have risen in their
Resurrection cycle.

Now once for all
He flung the fastening stone
Aside.
Disposed of,
Brutally nailed to His death,
He still walked out from Joseph's
    private mausoleum
To offer every man alive,
Wilful, premeditating, with malice
    aforethought
(That's all of us),
A resurrection too.

We, dead in sin
(Dead, though frenetically alive;
Glib; giddy;
Swathed in this absorbing now),
May rise again by faith
To daily sainthood;
Diurnal miracle of
Deepened, heightened, glory-compassed,
Resurrected
Life.

Redeemer, King, my Sovereign Lord,
Dear Comrade Christ:
Now on Easter night I kneel to ask
What You would like to resurrect
This year,
This night,
From garden humus or from cave-cut tomb
Within my life.

As Your power, Creator God,
Fills bulbs with coming fragrance;
As You burst a Rome-sealed tomb,
Now send Your crucifixion, resurrection,
Rooting, sprouting, bursting, growing,
Where You will
This year,
This night.

Rehearsal

*"Lord, make my heart a place
where angels sing"—John Keble.*

This morning Abdiel came in first; while he
Began to strum a small guitar, he perched
On half a dozen bales of ragged hopes
And grimaced: "Surely these could be cleared out."

When Michael came, strange solemn trumpet notes
Sprang from the floor with every step he took,
And Gabriel, close behind, hummed shining tunes
While he looped back the drapes and pulled the chairs
To semi-circles. "Drab," he murmured. "Gray
And even dingy."

       "Open, though," said Michael.
"Available. Still listed in the ads
Up there. And fair acoustics. Abdiel,
Give us A. Now, Gabriel, ready? Unison—"

They sang.

From Jaffa

From Jaffa, Jonah once set sail
To find himself sole cargo bale
In a submarine with a muscled tail.

Coward and rebel, determined to fail;
Slack to obey, and pitched over the rail;
Chagrined when his teaching was found to avail.

Jonah from Jaffa: blood brother we hail.

The Next Morning: Twenty Songs for Twenty Voices

"If any man be in Christ, he is a new creature; old things are passed away; behold all things are become new" (II Cor. 5:17).

1

The scales say I'm still
Precisely 142 pounds.
I'd have guessed 102, this morning.

2

As though I had put my brain and
    all my nerves
Through the laundromat.
The fragrance:
The clean, clean washday fragrance.

3

Like having a bulldozer
push away ten tons of accumulated
Scrap iron—
And now they're planting grass seed.

4

His words were the jackhammers
Breaking up cracked old concrete
In a ruined pavement.

Thud, thud, thud, thud, thud.
Interminable.

The new street surface is open today,
And smooth.

5

Loving you, Mom
I couldn't, before.
You always seemed to have a beak
    and claws.

Last night I saw my own three-inch claws;
I watched them change
To clean pink fingernails,
Manicured.
Now I can see that you have hands to grip
And lips to kiss.

6

I finally found a city map
Right here in the glove compartment
After all those wrong turns
On wrong streets.

7

Like having livid scar tissue
All over my face
For years.
(No ears, seamed cheeks, bent nose.)
And now it's gone.

8

Same job, same house, same family.
Same cracked ceiling,
Same wrinkled draperies,
Same lumpy mattress.

But feeling as though
I'd been a guest last night
At a suite in the Hilton,
And knowing I'll always live there.

9

I'd been like a bashed-in car
With a cracked windshield
And rust-creased fenders.

Last night
The Factory repossessed
And reconditioned
Me.

10

In living color, now,
And the picture in focus!

11

Geraniums are being transplanted
Into a back yard
Where dented garbage cans have
   always stood
Patrolled by rats.

12

Yesterday,
Eczema and acne,
Scalp to toe.
Look: pink and firm
And clear.

13

Well, like a surprise visit
(By special invitation)
To Buckingham Palace.
Only more so.

14

Handcuffed by hymns.
Now, though, to find
The prison is no prison
But a gracious, spacious villa
That I have just inherited.

15

Major surgery
On my motives
And values.

16

From a bunk among attic trunks
and cobwebs
To picture windows
Facing the surf.

17

Growing in a weed-littered lot;
Wispy, withering,
With crackling brown leaves
On every twig.

Transplanted, now,
To moist dark humus.
Irrigated.

18

The boys will twirl and twirl and twirl
But they will find
That all the combinations
Have been changed on this safe.

19

A scummy lake
Full of old tires and dead fish.
Now,
Sparkles and ripples
Over white pebbles.

20

Bushels of rusty tin cans
Recycled
Into sculptured fawns
And seagulls.

The Lamp

To be
A wick:
Not self-sustained,
Fed by the oil that careful Hands
Keep pouring into the lamp.
Trimmed ruthlessly, sometimes.
Sharp snips of the shears
Must clip away
Charred edges.
Enduring, yet to be
Used up
In burning with
The Light.

The Faucet

He carries with him
A portable faucet.
Ice water is always instantly available
From that remarkable faucet
At the touch of a finger tip.

The town is parched by summer drought.
People loiter in the sultry air,
Dull-minded from the heat.
Their tongues are swollen from their thirst
Until their speech is thick and blurred.
Fevered faces;
Lips cracked, leathery, dry
With thirst and thirst and thirst.
Dust stirs and settles as they walk.

The man with the portable faucet
Sips coolness from time to time himself
But doesn't bother to offer anyone else
A drink.

They don't even know that they're thirsty,
He says—
And probably they don't.

Book Review

EPHESIANS 4:29

A smutty book, he said

Too calmly

He has never lived among the wheat fields
Has never seen heads of grain
Puffed, bloated, deformed,
Macabre, vile
All their wheatness gone

Grime on the hands
Filthy black spores to stifle the lungs

Profit gone, too
(No matter how grim the mortgage)
Ugly, stinking, foul
No flour from this

Parasitic
Contagious; spreading
To other fields and grain

Smut

Treasures of Darkness:
After Catastrophe

ISAIAH 45:3

And darkness, darkness, darkness for my heart.
Night-dark, starless. Blindfold-dark. Or blind.
I move in catacombs that stretch and wind,
Unendingly, through utter gloom... I start
Slow steps along a caverned street, where part
Unknown, unmarked, the alleys I must find...
And darkness, darkness, darkness.
                         Yet my mind
Laughs through layered shadows, for I hold a Chart
Braille legible to finger touch of faith
And One has promised treasures of the dark.
His wealth is vast. When every shadowy wraith
Of this my Stygian hour is gone, what mark,
What treasure found in darkness shall I hold?
My awed and grateful hands shall clasp His gold.

On Fragrant Hay

"Sweet infant," trills the smiling choir.
"He sleeps on fragrant hay."

And Christmas card madonnas
Smirk all thoughts of pain away.

How was it really when He came?

Did Mary moan and scream
And grind her teeth and retch
(Poor wretch!)
Before His star could gleam its gleam
Above that innyard barn?

He slept on fragrant hay?
Perhaps.
But sheep and cows
Were not made then of plastic,
Nor of styrofoam and paint.
Half-rotten straw and stinking wet manure
Were surely winter odors Joseph smelled,
Not sweet new hay
Nor clover blossoms.

No dainty crèche had been prepared
And kept detached
From stench of urine-mingled mud
Where ox feet stood,
Where ox teeth chewed or dribbled fodder.

God did not come
to antiseptic scented neatness
But to a winter barnyard's muck and filth.

He always comes:
To things as they are
And not to wished-for rearrangements
Of the facts.

Susan McCaslin

Manna

I live in time
Between infinities
Like one ever expecting
A letter.

I used to think it
A letter from a friend,
A love that held me by the gate.

Loveletters came and went
And I was waiting still.

Every day now
I wait for a letter from God
Every day
A new one.

Agon

Lion shall have his claws
And lamb her fleecy brow
Each gazing on the other's face
The warfare's name is AWE.

Fronted on a common shore
Before the two lie down
Lamb will don an armament
Lion a woolen gown:

Soft, wild eyes staring
Each to the other
His image bearing.

Elijah

The burn of the one who chariots me
Is not fire, Elisha

Breaks me, banks me up.
Sky's pathing shore
Ungolds, with me unfolds
Heart's hidden word

I am laughed, tossed, laboured
Lofted in cloud's car.
I am made stolen, whole from earth
Storied forth, Elisha

The break of the one who sorrows me
Is not death, Elisha

The Twin

I have heard you
Arguing with yourself over there
And now you can't even hear me.
You have made me an idea
So what can I do for you as a person?

Jacob had such a twin as yours
With whom he spent long nights
Agonizing, turning things over
Till I grew jealous (as they say)

Yanked him up by the hair
And gave him a good fight
A decent, a worthy combatant
"A run for his money."

For he was a good man, Jacob,
A tough number, and I couldn't
Stand to see those two wranglers
Wearing him down, wasting him.

Endtime

At the foot of the low hill
From where I stood, blind,
One of the ones who would not
Bear the stain of spittle
His hands on my eyes,
I felt the greenness of
The sapling that made his cross
Run vertical in my bones

And I would say his dying
Was a kind of music
Breaking in circles
From the marriage of
God and tree
His body a drum
Sounding from the base
Of the world

My ears had grown so keen
I needed no eyes
When I saw him:
Christ the drummer
Christ the tree
Pinned to the rock
At the edge of the world
Not far outside the gates of
   the city.

Later

We quickly forgot
The taste of bread and fish
When the crowd sat in even rows
And went home filled,
Singing down the hills.

Irascible in our flurry,
We rushed at the one who slept,
Languorous, below deck,
As if storm were but arms
To rock a cradle.

We turned from the stranger
Who confronted us on the road
Discoursing in appalling metaphor
On the firstfruits of the dead.

Afterwards we scurried to our boat
To fish the time, expecting nothing,
Desiring nothing but dark,
As if body as we knew it
Were an end term.

Come morning, relentless
He stood on the shore,
And again we did not recognize Him—
As if our death and this sweat
Were preferable to eternal life.

Song of the Lambs

You who make our black feet dance on blacker earth
And as at Thy birth our fleece burn bright
From rolling sea pure white draw us
And from the shattering light
Wring our sea-change.

The Beauty of the Law

1

God is no dull monarch
Dispensing arbitrary forgiveness
But Law himself, written into
The very structure of atoms,
The way we breathe,
The tables of our hearts.

Law is the invariable
Order of the world.

2

A righteous man comes
Among us to suffer
and to die

The magic unwinds
The code decodes, the
Spell unspells his name.

God has placed within us
A plumbline:
One straight tree.

Lamblike, matter
Explodes the tomb
Leaving the graveclothes
Undisturbed.

3

If the righteous man
By will walks through
The door of death:
He lives.

For Law is Justice
To those the Law
By Love makes just.

Master

Your face is always just beyond
Like a light in snow.
I cannot compare you, your hands
Your face to anything.
No symbol holds.

Yet you are no moth in frailty.
Your presence is flame and power.
And you are more solid than earth,
Your hands more serviceable
More human than mine.

Infinite gentleness, infinite power,
I love you like a fainting lover.
But my love poems are never enough.
For you are the poet, the lover,
And the poem.

Write Thou me.

The Gardener

I did not know
That light burned white
Where he had lain.
Nor did I grasp
The personal form
Of angels at his feet
And head.

I only saw a gardener
With strong brown hands
Who cut a furrow straight
And ploughed morning seed
Like rooted words
Into my soul.

Gladys McKee

Sing the Lord, Wisely

And so I sing—
Owls in emerald,
Gray house cats, stretching,
Streams in their pebbled beds
Sleepily slurring,
Vixens on velvet feet
Swift through the meadow,
Mice in the corncrib
Too sly for shadow;
Stars on a scale of sky
Steadily holding
In orbit, and oceans
Faithful tides keeping.
Sing the Lord, wisely—
Heart, do not worry,
You, too, are destined;
Cease your mad hurry.
You cannot alter
A summer, a spring,
Hold to this wisdom,
Sing the Lord, sing!

Diana Mee

Restaurant Conversation

I clink my fork against the china,
stir my coffee, salt the roast
and talk of God, and Christ,
    the Holy Ghost—my Word! how
words come hard.
No sentences can conjure up God's face
and faith is such a disappointing place
to start.

How could I hope
to mix Father God, like gravy, with the beef
or let the Holy Ghost flit
through my talk like sips of port?

And how can I
explain Christ?

I did not watch him
sand the wood or nail cross-beams
for his father's customers.
I did not see him fish or lace his sandals;
I did not memorize the fit of his robe
    or the way he mixed clay and spit for eyesalve.
I did not follow the cripples he told to walk
or stalk the devils he removed from writhing boys.

So,
why force such things at dinner?
or any time?
People nowadays want to keep their demons—
they don't beg wandering preachers for release
or follow Jews up mountaintops
to hear theology.

Yet—
As waitresses sail by with trays
filled with water in plastic cups,
    I half expect that water to turn wine
    or a broken slice of bread to feed the house.

John Meeter

Tree Thoughts

I'm like this dead tree
Prone, gnarled, twisted:
With a story untold, forgotten,
Prostrate on the sand and in the sun.

Don't think I'm altogether comfortless;
The sand is soft, supportive, evocative
Of good memories. From where I lie
I see shrubs, trees, life-giving water,
The green of cedar and the blueness of sky
And water; I see the white cliffs opposite,
The etched shoreline of the Manitou Islands.

There is hope for a tree, so I've been told,
That though prone it will sprout again,
That at the scent of water it will bud
And put forth branches like a young plant.
So also I'm sustained by a great hope.
There's more to me than dead branches
Reaching upward; the beauty and purity
Of a great love stroke and caress me,
Make me aware of an even greater love
From which I came and to which I shall return.

Just Before Dawn
on a Winter Morning

A snowy hillside, an upreaching tree,
Outline of our house, shadow of curling smoke,
Some small shrubs and trees
At the top of the slope where land and sky
Meet in the dim light of a new day;
And sitting, or resting, on the horizon
The full moon, round, perfect—
Within easy reach of a hungry rabbit—
Reluctant to disappear behind the hill,
Lingering over the gentle landscape,
Silvering God's creation of hill and tree,
Illumining the cross on the nearby church
With a softened light akin to glory.

The Deepest Apologetic

PSALM 65:2–3
(Today's English Version)

In a world of hail, tornado, hurricane,
Of airplanes disintegrated in the sky,
Of villages earthquaked out of sight,
Why do we keep talking about God,
About calm, peace, serenity?
Deep inside are awe and dread:
In puniness we contemplate the vastness
Of the universe, the wild eruption
Of storm and devastation out of law
And order and unvarying regularity,
The mystery of personality with memory
And expectation beyond the confines of our days.
There is a universe of order and purpose,
Of breathless beauty in snowflake and galaxy,
But there is also the mystery of mind
And memory and personality transcending
The star and the atom, reaching for God
In His greatness, wisdom, power,
At once the Origin and Goal of all things
Great and small. There is a beauty
Of the mind as well as of the blade of grass
Or the greening leaf or the spinning earth
That reaches outward and upward
For the God of glory, purpose, perfection.

But there is a deeper apologetic
Forever rising from the heart of man,
The hidden volcano at the center, what
Augustine calls a sea of restless waves.
Peace is no bauble or luxury but necessity
Inherent in our breath and every cell,
In guilt that needs and seeks forgiveness,
In brokenness that pleads for healing.
This remains the deepest apologetic,
Not the mind aware of the glory and greatness
Of God in the raindrop or the migrating bird
Or the encircling galaxies forever on the move,
But the heart of man with its pain and hurt,
Orbited by its deep despair and brokenness
To the God of grace, compassion, forgiveness:
It is our sin that drives us to God,
The God of love, the Cross, the Conquered Grave.

October Comes to Glen Lake

No birds,
No people,
A blow-me-over wind,
Clouds flying through the air
But not hiding the blue sky.
Birches and poplars bending,
Whitecaps pounding the shore,
A leaf sailing over the meadow.

A spot of yellow on the hills,
The Sleeping Bear motionless.

A man hurrying to his cottage,
To the warmth of a fireplace fire,
Memories blowing through his mind
Like leaves and clouds before the wind.

Lo, these are but the outskirts of His ways,
And how small a whisper do we hear of Him!

Grackle, Grackle, Grackle

There they are, fifteen or twenty of them,
Spread around on the freshly cut lakeside grass
Like a flock of sins belaboring my conscience.
I don't like the graceless half-backward way
They alight on the ground, nor their strut
So full of pomposity and mindless arrogance.
I don't like their noisy gregariousness,
Their raucous cacophonous squawking,
Their scolding me from the highest cedars,
Invaders reprimanding me as the intruder
And threat to a fresh generation of squawkers.
I don't like their dominating the birdbath,
Even breaking the necks of unsuspecting sparrows
That venture too close to their beaks or long tails.
Songless, graceless, obnoxiously aggressive,
Domineering, swaggering, completely lacking
In politeness or quietness or reverence,
Grackles annoy, disturb, and infuriate me.

I don't like myself for being so nettlesome,
But grackles ignore the Beatitudes, Lord;
And isn't one strident strutting swashbuckling
Lamech enough; do we need grackles besides?

Merle Meeter

Filling Out the Forms

The grey flowing flood of concrete
Fills the forms, as pulleyed cables
Draw the motored screed.
Six inches deep, the new concrete,
In sixteen-foot slabs by two hundred,
Glistens with water film and, later, sealer.

But first the old cracked blacktop
Must be broken up and bucketed away,
The hard-packed dirt and clay scraped down,
And a brown frosting of fresh moist sand—
Gauged carefully to depth—
Leveled by concrete hoe and shovel
In the bottom of each alternating bed.

Beauty is each calling of the Lord:
The practiced swinging of the truck spout,
Ten feet or more, to chute the wet "cement"
Precisely, gapless, before the relentless screed,
Not too turgid, not too shallow;
And the dexterous skimming of the long-handled float,
With fluent, sweeping, hidden-muscled motion,
Across a new span of the church parking lot.

Dissension

How it lances the chest,
Rasps the walls of the stomach:
    hacking,
    corrosive,
Rash and livid to slash,
Shrill and straining to crush.

Trust in the Lord and His Word
Flung away—wrathful ego rampant,
    murderous,
    suicidal—
The face of the King on the coin
Of the heart gouged and gashed.

The Game of Backsliding

The robins
rival
the starlings
for my seeds:
beans,
carrots,
peppers, melons,
radishes, pickles,
broccoli, and corn.

This morning
a quite contrary cat
fearlessly chooses
my garden—
how does it grow?—
to trampoline
in my tomatoes,
roll out the onions,
drag a dead rat
through the new strawberries.

I grin a wry
and guilty grimace
at the way
I too daily
sport with, spoil
the fragile shoots
of my May sowings,
His seeds of Christlike life.

Nevertheless,
I shoo the cat.

The Aim of Art

Should poetry
Rouse merely wonder
At the pearl and iridescent
Whorling of the abalone,
Or the gold and emerald pheasant
For the object's sake alone?

Or should it,
Like the rainbow,
Refracting from the prism
Of the poet's life and thought,
Show the Savior's grace and glory
In the object to praise God?

Today's Special

He was the intent type,
Stirring his red stew,
Steamingly tasting the future.

His hand on the ladle
Lurked in a sinewed talon-curve,
Remembering his tardy baby
Heelhold on borning brother Esau,

Who flopped in famished
From the hunt to beg, just then,
For lentils, "Soup, man!
I'm dyin' of hunger!"

So flit went honor for a bowl
Of beans, birthright of God
For a quick bellyful.

Chef Jacob served him smoothly.

Resurrection Rondeau

Let strident silver trumpets cry
And wind harps shrill with ecstasy,
For boulders burst at God's decree
When Christ their Molder bowed to die.

The hellish chant of "Crucify!"
Presaged the earthquake jubilee.
Let strident silver trumpets cry
And wind harps shrill with ecstasy.

Dark shrouded shame, crime shattered sky
As grave pods split and dead broke free
To hear the angel minstrelsy
Christ's resurrection certify.
Let strident silver trumpets cry
And wind harps shrill with ecstasy.

Literalist of the Gospel

MATTHEW 10:7–10

A cheerful little man
In rough brown tunic and hemp girdle,
Wedded to Jesus and poverty,
He proclaimed compassion and peace.

His voice was clear and sweet
And tunable as singing streams—
He spoke to wolves, dogs, cattle;
Birds flocked to his call.
He rebuked the wild, furious beasts,
Calmed the flurries of the tame.

Also, he preached Jesus Christ
In forest, hamlet, city, abbey.
No staff or sandals, scrip or coin,
No learning or papal license,
He feared no man or demon,
Forgave detractors, loved his persecutors.

Once playboy prankster,
Soldier, deserter, prodigal, thief—
His earthly father disowned him.

Francis of Assisi, at last, joyously commended
His wornout, pain-seared body to his Savior.

Travail Hymn

Make speed, you tidal waves,
　Your God commands.
Explode your vitals, earth,
　Your Lord descends.
Skies shall be torn away,
The stars shall blaze like hay
That cataclysmic day
　When Christ returns.

Sin warped the perfect world
　With wrenching groans.
Slick horrors scummed the ground;
　Man, abject, moans.
Again earth's frame disjoints
As God's just wrath appoints
Wild waters from His founts
　Of cloud and stone.

Old Egypt felt His rage;
　The Nile turned blood.
Cities dissolved in ash—
　Flame flowed from God.
But when Christ's cross touched heaven,
With joy we saw Him risen,
Then worked the Gospel leaven:
　God's ways are good.

Our Father on Earth
In Transit

He knew the library, the schools, the museum,
But he loathed the effluvium of a major city.
Yet it wasn't, all in all, a bad place to live
Once you were used to it, and he was,
Making ends meet, or better, with his relatives.

Then came the shake-up summons. He had to leave
The restaurants, fruit stalls, athletic events,
Concerts, entertainments, holidays, liturgies,
For a life of leather, wind and weather, war
And frustrations of multiple responsibilities.

Also, ecological problems you wouldn't believe!
Famines, neighbors who would poison your stock
For two tufts of grass or a trickle of water.
Still, the cities around were the greater risk—
When you'd seen a few vaporized by fire bombs.

The domestic trail was thorny too—women problems,
Feuding sons, separations, incest among your kin.
And then the day he set about to kill his son
For a God who'd never asked the like before!
Yet he trusted Him right up to resurrection.

Oh, he left the town of his birth, all right—
Though others have done as much, no question.
But the gladness he looked for he saw in a city,
A radiant cube with eternal foundations
Whose Builder and Maker is God.

Out of the Ruined Nursery

When Jack and Jill went up the hill,
They took a Humpty-Dumpty spill;
And waterless, with fractured crown,
They bent their way to mundane town
To buy an urban pumpkin shell.
With smog and rot the ceiling fell,
And, hopelessly, they left the heap—
A dazed Boy Blue, a gray Bo-Peep.

Beyond the garish city light,
They feel the dark and keen their sight
To find the star that points a cross.
Washed by a healing hillside floss,
They splash away their dust and sweat.
The King in radiant silhouette
Inclines to save with gracious will,
And Jack and Jill go up the hill.

Of Birds and Bards

The swallow darts
In graceful, azure beauty,
Floats, glides, swoops,
Rides out her rhythms
On the wings of the wind—
Unseen as the Spirit,
Who gives life, breath, all things—
Till she nests in God's altars.

Pecking at suet, grains,
Berries, bits of bread
Just outside the windows
Of everyday experience,
The sparrow hops, sorties,
Chirps, flirts, poses
To the inscape tune
Of Him Who upholds him.

Diving for fish,
The pelican scans the underwater,
Dim as embryonic symbol,
To bring up the brightest, best
Gulletful for him who waits
To receive the unpocketed prize,
His livelihood
And living gift from God.

Planing the thermals,
The eagle kingly soars
Above his conquered realm:
A richly scintillant metaphor,
He sentries for Jehovah,
Nobly oversees, yet stoops
For his Provident Creator
Who has taught him how to prey.

God in the Cave

One remembers the day he buried a father.
Two brothers, two nations, that struggled
Already in the womb of Rebekah,
Israel and Edom, met on a day
In the field of Machpelah.

Triple three-score years ended the sojourn
Of Isaac, and now their aged father
Was laid to wait the Woman's Seed,
The Dragon Scourge and Heaven Hero,
The King of Jacob's dreams.

There in the cave that Abraham
Had bought from Ephron the Hittite,
Those unlikely and portentous brothers stood.
But only Jacob bowed to bless in faith
The God Who sent the ram to free his father.

And Israel lived again those tales
Of heart-rejoicing truth: the well
Of Rehoboth, the romance of Rebekah,
Stone blasting of Sodom, the Flood
And the Rainbow, the Fall and the Promise.

In the darkness of the cave of death,
God, by His Spirit, moved the memory
Of Jacob His chosen, chastened
Anew His child to hope and love.
One remembers the day he buried a father.

Beth Merizon

The Crystal Hexagon

Out of the cloud a bright
   rosette
Out of the void, form.
Space and line,
A frost design
Tumbles from the storm.

Out of the timeless
   into time;
From pure Spirit, clay.
Out of the night
Imperial Light—
The Light, the Truth,
   the Way.

Reception

The candle throws a gentle light
Upon the darkening room:
A simple flame, like one that burned
To light the stable's gloom—

A wisp of fire to usher in
The Light that lights the world;
The Dayspring from on high received,
And one small flame unfurled.

Thomas Merton

Like Ilium

Is this the night the world must burn like Troy?
Is there no wise Aeneas
To look the Greek gift in its wooden teeth
Or fly the lovers of the hollow horse,
Loading his cross and sorrows
(With old Anchises) on his contrite shoulder?

Is there no priestly king
To crack the wooden wonder with his prophecy:
Does no one see the crowded sabres
Behind the lancets of those eyes?
The peace that sings like a muezzin
Upon that crenellated brow
Calls Troy to love a loaded citadel!

You who receive this idol full of pitch and matches,
Yet curse Christ-branch and Calvary
Because you hate the nails and Blood,
Refuse the peace price of that saving Wood,
Go, then, be deafened by the bonzes of your animal
Jumping and barking in the marble ruin
Too loud for you to hear the unborn armor
The steel heart bumping in that great
White horse's wooden drum.

Is this the night the world must burn like Ilium?

Messias

Stranger, the world expected You for long days.
We were all looking at the wrong horizon.
We came out and stood with our flags
In the gates of the wrong year.

We wanted to believe You with banners:
Our cannons prove us wrong.

God dwelt in our town without parades,
Stood with the poor men on the river bank,
Went down into the water before the blistered Baptist.

He came out of the river without armies and without money
But walked the red roads like a conqueror.
No man starved when thousands
Sat down around Him on the land.
But His miracles were without sin,
Without demonstration, without shame.

He did not despise the wild jasmine
Or turn His eyes away
From the young almond tree,
Yet He has refused the crumpled roses
You offered Him for your own pleasure.
And by that act I'll swear that He is true.

If He had been born of our sorrow,
He would have bombed the Samaritans with thunder,
Made of Jerusalem a solfatare.

Without revenge He blessed our country.
But we have praised the chastity of God
With our rotting lilies:

Those dirty trumpets turning brown,
Those wide, white mouths, painted with golden meal!
The musicians have sighed at His picture with the noise

Of circus angels.
Painters have praised Him with heresy.
We have not known You, virgin's Son!

He is the one clean King,
With weapons in His hands,
Rising in the night of our defeat,
Armed with a heart more burning than the sun.

Having ignored our ways, our gates,
He entered by the center of the ruined capital,
Stood like a giant in the smashed buildings,
And burned the long converging streets with the gentleness
    of His expression.

The children praised Him with the voice of orchards
And clung to Him like vines and surrounded Him like birds
While death was being destroyed.

O Emperor! When will You come again?
When will we all sit down in thousands underneath the trees?
Some who have washed their hands with their own tears
Have said: "How shall we know Him when He comes?"

He is the Light by which all Truth is understood,
The Light inside us,
Knowing His own Truth in the true world, the mountains
    and the stars.
He has locked the moon and stars in His treasury;
Can my eyes see my own eyes?
How can I seize the Light that knows me from within?

But we shall trace Him by the track of His own
    immortal music,
Nor count His wisdom by our own candlepower,
Yet find Him in our own mansions,
Catch Him in His own joy, and find Him in the echoes of
    His Father's feast.

Calvin Miller

The Brain

Gray-wrinkled, two-pound thing, I clearly see
I cannot trap you with an E.E.G.
You nervy organ, you! Skull-cased but free—
A brazen challenge to psychiatry.

Soft mass, I cannot help resenting you
Each time they search and probe for my I.Q.
Half of Einstein's lobe was two of you,
You joyless megavolt, computer shoe.

Be careful, Judas organ, or you'll find
God cauterizes every rebel mind.
You small gray lump, you always seek and grind,
Spend small electric currents, thinking blind,
Yet you're the only shabby place I see
That His great mind may come to dwell in me.

The Invader

I cannot fold the very breath of God
Into this chambered place I call my heart;
Great gales blow through my life, tornado shod,
As winds blow tides and sweep the stars apart.

Like Adam, I once lay, a small dead thing;
Then God breathed into me His breath of life.
And lips that never spoke, at once could sing—
A hungry peace devoured my surging strife.

Beloved Invader, it was really You
Who knew my strife and drew me on ahead
Till I could see the pit where gallows rose
And mercy clotted where the timbers bled.
Man murdered God but only loosed the wind
That fills my heart since I've been born again.

I Came Upon a Man

I came upon a man
Half-eaten by desire
But could not understand
A way to quench the fire
That raged within his soul.

Poor hating thing!
You must find help—
Some thorough cure
To heal malignant lust
That eats your reason,
Your spirits, in a coma.

Live... hate!... Work... hate!... Drive... hate!
(Feed negativity!)
Wake... hate!... Play... hate!... Eat... hate!
(Sleep objectivity!)
Grow carcinoma!

But you must hate, so die!
And never realize
The world floats in a sky of love,
While hate's sole prize
Is joy in contraband.

And hate within a sea of love
Is Satan's spell
For starving at a feast—
Love—stumbling into hell
By treading nail-pierced hands.

Love Story

She waits while over there he knocks. Again
Refused! Nor is there place throughout the town.
Be strong as steel lest Joseph sense the pain
You feel. It's yet a while till you lie down
To sleep. "There's nowhere else to go tonight,"
He said. She fought the burning in her eyes—
Rebuked her tears before they fell. Starlight
Crowned the cold, small town with fiery skies.
He took her in his arms and that embrace
Dissolved the desperation that they faced.
"I paid the stable rent," he said with shame.
"Your son will come tonight," she said. He gave
A kiss. Joy hushed the night! Salvation came—
An infant whimper from the shepherd's cave.

The Psalms of Nihilism Revisited

The Heavens declare the
  Glory of God
And the firmament showeth His
  handiwork
(Blind eyes never see His
  glory
And miss the declaration) . . .

In the beginning God created
  the heavens and the earth.
Unfortunately, there is no steno book
  of data dating to the first
  kinetic streak of light,
So it must be, we've made great
  yahweh sleep in slime with
  slithering protozoa crying to
  be multi-celled.
And tar-pits grew.

And ice in global tonnage
  came & buried mastodons,
And all of that which went
  before was raped by glacial flow,
And icy rivers washed their ways
  to shrouded seas,
And mist
  blew back,
And heavy-headed men
  painted cave walls,
Never dreaming that they
  once had been
The prisoners of the sea
  till their amphibian
Lusts had drawn them
  to the shore,
Where they grunted on the sand
  and only dreamed of walking
In the forest.

And a million years swarmed
  over all the moments that decayed,
And vegetation rotted,
And mountain rivers gouged
  the valleys with magnificent erosion.

And the evening and the
morning were the sixth day,
And just before sunset
On Friday afternoon
God made himself a bedroom
And terraced it with green,
And Adam stepped from his right hand,
And Eve stepped from his left,
And life caressed itself.
And they embraced
And slept in ecstasy
And cried in intimacy
  at the joy of their own
  creative night.

And God said,
  "That is good"—
The pair concurred.

Then a distant son of
  theirs named Moses
  wrote creation in the
  truth and beauty that
  would replace
this blind
and ugly psalm.
And what this Israelite
Egyptian wrote
denied to men
their Genesis of slime
and placed it in the stars.
And the Heavens no longer
cried in their absurdity
that they were born in the fiery
happenstance of near-colliding stars.

For in their gleaming
witness they had
issued from a womb of
black vacuity
and entered through
the birth canal of nothingness
and only dared to shine
when Yahweh said,
Eden shall not be dark
LET THERE BE LIGHT!

And light
was the gift
of his compassion,
for he knew we were
afraid of darkness.

But now we sleep uneasily;
we have lost the key to Eden,
and the light of science comes

and hangs horrendous
    reconstructions of hominoid
    beginnings in the family room
and then cries out:
"Man is happenstance—
let there be darkness!"
And we read their heavy books
and in our faithless times
we sleep in fear.

A Very Little Cross

Use me big or use me small, I said,
All the while believing it would be
Some ostensible, important place—
An elevated niche. But then instead,
He beckoned me away from dignity
To serve where men might see His face
And never mine.

Lord, raise some dais in the throng
Where fury crosses crowded ways—
There build Your theater of hope
Where many ears may hear my song.
I'll teach ten-thousand tongues to praise
And add to meaning greater scope.
Oh, use me splendidly!

It's strange I now hang by my hands
In crucifixion. Reason fails . . .
He gave me utter anonymity.
None see my sacrifice! The stands
Are empty now. These ugly nails
Were driven in obscurity—
A tragedy unseen.

I don't mind the dying, Lord,
But here, apart? Without impact?
No, please . . . give me a public stake
Much jeered and hooted, hatred stored
In some arena, scoffer packed . . .
Still You ordained that we must take
Our calvaries together, if apart.

Vassar Miller

Paradox

Mild yoke of Christ, most harsh to me not bearing,
You bruise the neck that balks, the hands that break you;
Sweet bread and wine, bitter to me not sharing,
You scar and scorch the throat that will not take you;
Mount where He taught, you cripple feet not bloody
From your sharp flints of eight-fold benediction;
Bright cross, most shameful stripped of the stripped body,
You crucify me safe from crucifixion:
Yet I, who am my own dilemma, jolting
My mind with thought lest it unthink its stiffness,
Rise to revolt against my own revolting.
Blind me to blindness, deafen me to deafness.
So will Your gifts of sight and hearing plunder
My eyes with lightning and my ears with thunder.

Bethlehem Outcast

Is there no warmth to heal me any more,
Straining to glimpse His manger, clutched by chills
Upon the lintel of the stable door;

Thawed by His breath, the oxen foul the floor,
While through my reedy bones the north wind shrills:
Is there no warmth to heal me any more?

Darkward His radiance reaches to explore
All nights but one whose shudder never stills
Upon the lintel of the stable door

Through which the gutturals of the shepherds soar
In flight with singing star-bursts from the hills.
Is there no warmth to heal me anymore?

Watching the magi yield Him royal store,
I wait held back and bound between two wills
Upon the lintel of the stable door.

Christ, save this wiseman without winter lore,
This bumpkin naked to the cold that kills!
Is there no warmth to heal me any more
Upon the lintel of the stable door?

To Jesus on Easter

You see the universe, as I see daylight,
opening to Your heart
like fingers of a little child uncurling.

It lies to You no more than wood to blade,
nor will You tell me lies.
Only fools or cowards lie. And You are neither.

Not that I comprehend You, who are simpler
than all our words about You,
and deeper. They drop around You like dead leaves.

Yet I can trust You. You resembling me—
two eyes, two hands, two feet,
five senses and no more—will cup my being,

spilling toward nothingness, within Your palm.
And when the last bridge breaks,
I shall walk on the bright span of Your breath.

Christmas Mourning

On Christmas Day I weep
Good Friday to rejoice.
I watch the Child asleep.
Does He half dream the choice
The Man must make and keep?

At Christmastime I sigh
For my Good Friday hope.
Outflung the Child's arms lie
To span in their brief scope
The death the Man must die.

Come Christmastide I groan
To hear Good Friday's pealing.
The Man, racked to the bone,
Has made His hurt my healing,
Has made my ache His own.

Slay me, pierced to the core
With Christmas penitence
So I who, new-born, soar
To that Child's innocence,
May wound the Man no more.

Oblation

I kneel,
my heart in my hands—
a cold fish,
a stale loaf.

What are these among so many?
Lord, Your business
is to know.

I rise,
my body a shell
heavy with
emptiness,

You whom
worlds cannot contain
not disturbing
one pulse beat.

My bones
being boughs aflame
with Your glory,
Lord, suffices.

William R. Mitchell

Epiphany on a Plot of Moonlight

Praise God for this little scrap of light—
No bigger than my windowed soul can frame,
No durance but a vision—just the same,
No whit less brilliant, that its scope is slight,
No more unseen, because its depth is sight.
Tear-wondered grace, how can that holy flame
Gloom to illumine shadow-haunting shame—
Scale down infinity to human plight?

Bewildered pilgrim in the awed reach of night,
My fretted mind shall blind itself and fall;
I shall lie swathed in dust, and grimly crawl
Through nightmare deserts of despair and blight.
Let me remember, from the error's thrall,
Praise God for this little scrap of light.

Theometry

I CORINTHIANS 15:56–58

Across the iron grid of destiny
I drive, striving to my visioned end.
I know, I know, at last this dizzy rush,
this mad careening consciousness, must yaw,
bend the arc hard, and hurtle back. And death
sits cocksure, out on that unplotted axis,
swings me like a plumbline for a toy.
Hope and fear are only x and y
    and every prayer is locked in centrifuge.

Well, but I strain against the closing curve:
and may some gift or benediction leap
a second further at the fatal pause.
My life, though wrenched into parabola,
yearns to describe a parable of One
who rammed the vertex through infinity
and strung all time and space in parallel.

Easter morning:
Romans 13:12

Pines wait in the gray light
no life in the dull stones
no sheen on the dull wet grass
no gloss on the jade branch.
Pines wait and the stones wait
and I stand in the gray light
stone heart and dull eyes
mind lulled, ears numbed, touch gone blind.

In the mere breath of the chill morning
the choked sob of the black brook, waiting,
blending with tremors of the pale aspens,
answering each other, whispering, murmuring.
Listen to their hushed, contending rhythms—
what are they rumoring, dark water and frail green leaves?
Is it only that the night pales?
only the cold east chafed to its daily glow,
only another of a million dawns, only another dawn?

Light, Light, they whisper, it is the light again—
brush of silver stroking the aspen leaves,
light woven silver in the dark brook's alloy—
light stirring in the black stems,
light from a million yesterdays,
warbling up through the dull roots,
seeping from the gray stones.
Oh, hear the ancient echoes, and reply.

The dawn calls, and the fire-born clouds call,
and the dumb clay-cumbered world struggles to say, to say—
the pines reach out, the spastic aspens gesture,
and slugs and creeping things clamber toward the day—
in alien tongues, in spasms of slow labor,
stammer "amen, amen," and scuttle to obey.

Weaker than all am I, more voiceless, graceless,
except in the lonely power to choose or shun—
and yet I wait, the solely conscious thing,
alone articulate, the only purposed one.
As the sun-fleck in the seed's heart yearns to its death,
bursts self, bursts the cold earth and grapples for the sun,
oh, Light bound frozen in my veins and in my bones,
rend the cold tomb of flesh and make a dawn.

A Requiem for Innocence

Out of the hurt left standing in his eyes
my face looks back in mocking disproportion.
His is a look I know, the look of one
who having trusted much has been in much
betrayed
                (face of a child, in mute surprise
at the cruelty of a laughlong friend, or such
as aging women wear for beauty gone,
or strong men, when death is a fact)
                                    and now,
sensing, in me, one who has guessed a portion
of his grim secret, comes with wound aclutch—
now he has come to try his trust on me.
Oh God, Oh God, in the name of sorrows how
shall I ever expiate those reddening hands?
Depart from me, I am a sinful man.

Depart in peace, be ye clothed and fed—
so I have sometimes said, in devious speeches.
But that way lies a fury, for their faces
look out at me from all the lonely places.
(Like a man I saw in Tokyo once, in the cold
    wind shivering wrapped in ropes and boards
    who looked me in the face as I went by—
    for I have memorized his dull brown eye,
    and a cold dirty wind howls like a cry
    through every snug pretense my life affords.)
Well, I have learned, when everything is said,
that when hurt pleads or when a sneer beseeches
(whatever prudence or the norms demand)
then one must try. For there's no reprimand
hurts half so deep as God's trust put aside.

So then, take up this wooden task of mine
with my more wooden hands, and once again
botch up my patchwork comfort as I can—
wisdom have I none, such as I have
I give you—though it's bound to come out lies,
words being only words, and I but man.

His pseudo-questions, spun with logic fine,
are but a game of shadows, where he tries
to stage the only question in his heart
and I bring pseudo-answers, for my part
and play my gestures in the center ring.
We labor to be pertinent and grave.
And yet, poor pilgrim, all this posturing
comes but to this: that you have been betrayed
and come to ask if you should be dismayed;
and I must answer, and I am afraid.

And all I know is, that your hurt and need
is grief to me—calls forth these fumbling ploys
because they are my version of the deed
that tried to play God's love in its own role.
Except I think you'd think it insolence,
I'd pray, after my fashion, for your soul
(and you may pray for mine); but that's an act
too awkward to confront the naked fact;
hurt-wise, you banter me adroitly there—
and my heart groans (the groaning is my prayer).

And yet, poor pilgrim, welcome to the sense
of hurt and outrage, for it is your grail;
now that you know the flavor of betrayal,
(and find it vinegar) perhaps you'll know
someday what urged that gesture long ago,
why He played out that vaudeville of outrage
with such crude props, on an ungainly stage;
and then you'll see why I must give, also,
   all a fellow-Iscariot can do—
   God knows I had to plead for comfort too.

Meditation on Psalm 139:7–12

Lie down in the vacant dark
let go the threads of day
let self go stark into oblivion—
even the stars go one by one their trackless way
till not a sextant of the memory
      can find a stay—
and yet the night is protestant of place.
Nor mind nor dark can finally erase
      the testament of grace.

Benediction

Let there be light in all the nightmare places,
in the millrace of license, in the stifled room;
let there be joy in starved and leaden faces,
in charred or sodden furrows, where no tears bloom.

Where stumbling feet, where fumbling hands are groping
against the scope of silence, in dumb primordial caves,
let chords of morning stars bring prismed hoping
and sing far up the slope, where mind blinds out and raves.

Say for me, God, their blessing I am seeking;
Lord, decree for them the sun, and Jesus speak aright
my scattered syllables—for past my yearning, past my speaking,
I have been stammering, let there be light.

Benediction for Danny

God bless little Danny, where his spirit runs
free in the fretted light of wooded suns—
whose Holy-Spirited heart loves briar,
    tree, stone, bird, fire,
    serpent, forest, hill and cove—
loves humbly unaware of love—
in perfect worship knows no worshipness;
God bless his hands, his feet,
    unprideful forehead sweet;
Let even night be gentle a caress.

Meditation on Psalm 142

Grief, the lean predator,
followed close in the dark
and neither spoke to me nor
    noted my prayers;
but stalked my fitful stages,
    counted my cares,
waited to shuck me stark,
    petal and leaf
    (old hunger of ages)

Almost he had his claws
slipped under my heart,
almost the subtle jaws
    gently laid hold;
but out of panic and need
memory snatched the old
    hearkening art
and the voice of Peace said "Day"
    and he cringed and scuttled away.

Light Giver

JOHN 9:25

Hands touch my lids, my tears;
through blears of hurt and lust
    through aching years of sin-smeared sight
my dim and random life now clears
    to searing light
      and the dark pales
      and pride and fears
      as it were scales
      fall to the dust.

Were one to ask of me
what face it is that shimmers like the day
    as yet I could not say.
I only know I see.

Stephen Mosley

The Story of the Turkish Bath

There once was a Turkish bath
that came to its own coming out
untowelled and wet behind the ears
He peeked around a wall
and looked at all the dirty people
Caked they were
not just stopping at the shirt sleeves
permeating
It seems that they had grown, eaten, slept,
and hoped
in enzyme-conquering, unwhiteintroduced
black gummy muck, dust, all kinds
and variety certainly didn't help
just complicated the filth
It was ingrained into every corner imaginable
The young bath was absolutely amazed
and they just went around blind to it all
nonchalantly reeking
Well everybody to them looked more or less
clean
no control comparisons
It hit him then
I'm going to have to take it all on
parading in the depths of me it will all come off
Repulsion
Me clean and never before bathed in
this is what I'm coming to?
all their horrible foreign substance
made me
and they'll probably laugh at my strange
brightness
The only way they'll ever see their caked-on
and the only way to get clean,
the Turkish bath
coming out
no longer hesitating.

Karl Neerhof

Reminder

DEUTERONOMY 11:14

dull raindrops fall
splattering
glazing my window in blotches
and blurring my view of the farmland

the colors converge
as the forms of white birches
seem twisted
refracted
deformed

dead grasses Rejoice
for the saturate Life from above
and whole fields Hosannah their Maker
with loud photosynthesis

After His Kind

A caterpillar's
Single overhaul proves
God's warranty best.

E. W. Oldenburg

In Canterbury Cathedral

On a day soft with April showers
the safe tires of our tour bus
had sung us south from London.

Sight-seer pilgrims, cameras slung,
no need or time on patient plodding
horses for long diverting tales.

We stood at last at Becket's shrine,
lost in architecture and dates,
confused by Norman and Gothic.

Our ancient tiny guide seemed shrunk
into his suit, dwarfed by his clothes
as we all were dwarfed by time.

His small precise English voice went on:
pronounced "Our Lord," and the words
fell on us like a benediction.

"Our"—incredible assumption of union
offered in passing to American strangers:
mortar for diverse motley stones.

Time and blood and history redeemed
from meaninglessness: two words
turned sight-seers into pilgrims.

Eutychus

*"And they brought the young man
alive and were not a little comforted"
(Acts 20:7–12).*

Eutychus saw light beams leap
From shining eye to eye
Across the wide room;
The lamps flared and exulted
As Paul talked on and on.
Images jumped from his tongue
Like flames from flaring wicks:
Panting runners racing,

Soldiers struggling into armor,
The rude cross, the empty tomb.
Eutychus saw wide eyes widen
As Paul's images spread
From concentrated points
To conceptual pools
Of light they loved,
Widening to flood all the world:
Of the attributes of love,
And of what love is not,
Of life, of what life is not,
Of life real, of life eternal,
Of life snuffing out death
Like a dark candle.

Eutychus in his window
Was wedged between the light
And the black Troas night;
Between his shoulder blades
The sharp window frame
Cut him in half: one ear
For the voice incessant
Speaking of life in pools of light,
One ear for voices from the dark:
A sailor's curses rumbling
Up like thunder from the harbor,
A woman's tipsy laugh,
Lilting, lingering, promising...
Life trembled and sang in the dark,
Stung in the night air with a bite of salt
From the sea that brought Helen to Troy.

And then the voices merged
For divided Eutychus—
The lights began to blur—
He dreamed his own dream,
United Eutychus dreamed his dream,
A wide-screen dream of youth,
Himself cast as Romantic Hero,
Fighting Achilles with Hector,
Putting on the whole armor...
Hacking beside Peter in the garden,
Winning first prize in the race,
Rescuing Helen (their love

Pure, of course, though she
Kissed him for reward), himself
Debating Pilate, rescuing Christ
From the mob, fighting Pharisees
With Paul, swashbuckling on a quest
For Immortal Life, like Jason's quest
For the golden fleece; Eutychus,
The one-man Church Militant,
Whirling-dervish force for right...
Just before he fell
His eyes half opened.
The lights were all whirling, whirling...
The night air half woke him
As he plunged, but then...
He was in the sea, diving
For Mycenaean treasure
In the Aegean... swimming
The Hellespont... swimming,
Swimming easily... floating,
Floating... until the earth
Struck him roughly—
Stamped his breath out.

When he awoke he seemed
To come from a deeper
And more silent dark
Than any he had known,
A dreamless dark
With no night sounds
Of cricket or distant owl;
No trumpet fanfare
For his grand reentry,
And no choirs of angels,
Only the quiet pool of light
And the circles of known faces
Breaking slowly into joy.
He had his own life back.
Not his gaudy life of dream,
But his common life of the real,
Life real, life eternal, his own life.
Really an everyday miracle
Without sound of rushing wind.
Eutychus, in the upper chamber,
Saw the tongues of flame burn steady.

Haman

*"So they hanged Haman on the gallows
that he had prepared for Mordecai" (Esther 7:10).*

"The Lovliest Lynchee was our Lord"—Gwendolyn Brooks

Haman, good provider, bought his own rope,
Arranged with care his own unique reward.
He has risen higher in public death
Than he dared hope to rise in public life,
High as the best carpenters of the realm
Could build, high as the best gallows-makers
He could afford to hire could lofty reach.
He twists slowly, slowly, at his rope's end,
Turning slowly, his gaze could see for miles
Around now if still his still eyes could see,
Turning slowly, could scan the capitol,
The ways and avenues that lead to power,
Turning slowly, South, East, North, West, search for
The junction where it all went somehow wrong.
    Always and only he had expected
Simple justice: just what he had coming,
Had served his king, had shirked no drudging task,
Kept his desk clean, filed all reports on time,
Learned decorum proper to high command—
Whose wife to flirt with and whom to avoid,
How to carve the roast, when to chill the wine,
How to serve up what the king wants to hear
At conference, and serve it up sincere.
Order, protocol, rank, degree, respect—
He knew his place and merely asked that those
Below know theirs; he wasn't asking much:
The easy bow, the bending of the knee
To rank, acknowledging the earned degree.
His wife at first had thought his ravings odd,
A petty egotistic fret; his friends
Had humored him and failed to understand
His point that so much more than wounded pride
Was on the line, that the whole nation reeled
When one small wretched Jew refused to kneel.
If order, rank, and rule were not for all,
None would have them—the gutted state would fall.
The king, poor blind mindless amorous fool,
Must be saved from himself, like it or not,
The state pushed back from the brink of chaos:

Blot out a people to save a nation,
Expunge a race for civilization.
The sentimental sops might call it cruel,
But realists would cautiously applaud
And see him clear: a man doing the job
That years of public life had trained him for.
He liked to think that the years had prepared
Him precisely to meet this Jewish threat:
A moment to shine high in the klieg lights
Of all the focussing historians.
History would give him simple justice:
The man who knew his job and got it done.
    Let the klieg lights of time affix him now
Twisting slowly, slowly, at his rope's end.
See him now in the bright harsh light of time
As man the butt of all ironic jokes,
Prickled on his own barbed wire, blown to hell
By his own bombs, gassed in the seclusion
Of his own chambers, and asking always
Only for what he has coming to him
And always, always, always getting it.
Man twists, slowly, slowly, at his rope's end,
Turning slowly, scanning, North, East, South, West:
History's avenues all lead to death.
The light winks, the bands play, the boots march on.
Man dances absurd at the end of his rope.
For life is a gala lynching party
Where every swinger brings his own rope:
It's bring your own rope and reap your reward.
    Except once: that grim party crashed by Him,
Intruding, who brought no rope of His own,
But borrowing man's He stole the scene
And died, took what wasn't coming to Him.
Look at Him, scene-stealer, on His hilltop,
Changing the rules, muddling simple justice
With mercy, redemption, something called grace,
And cheating man of his hard-earned reward:
Man's antic rope's end dance eclipsed at last
By the still shadow high on Golgotha.

Evangeline Paterson

Flat Person

Like some pressed flower
that has lost its color
she is a flat person

corpse-white, paper-thin.
She speaks other people's words
in whispers.

Her eyes
look out at you
from a long way back.

Passing winds flutter her.
I am afraid
that one might suddenly sweep her
away.

Lord, I want to see her
strike root in Your soil,
to see her colors brighten
and blaze

and I want to be sure
that no dark random wind
will ever be able to sweep her
away.

Deathbed

Now, when the frail and fine-spun
Web of mortality
Gapes, and lets slip
What we have loved so long
Out of our lighted present
Into the trackless dark

We turn, blinded,
Not to the Christ in Glory,
Stars about His feet

But to the Son of Man,
Back from the tomb,
Who built fire, ate fish,
Spoke with friends, and walked
A dusty road at evening.

Here, in this room, in
This stark and timeless moment,
We hear those footsteps

And
With suddenly lifted hearts
Acknowledge
The irrelevance of death.

Ashes

*Latimer to Ridley at the stake: "Be of
good cheer, Master Ridley. We shall
this day light such a candle in England as
shall not easily be put out."*

They are burnt out long ago, those fires,
Smithfield, Tyburn,
Reformer, Covenanter,
Movements and men.
Long ago

The smoke blew away
And we are disturbed no longer
By the cries and the conflict.
And is not the candle
Burnt out, Master Ridley?
How can a candle burn
In such heavy air?

And yet the ashes
Have never stopped blowing.
Grit in men's eyes,
Dust in their throats,
Vexation of spirit
Till they have groaned and cursed
All rakers of fires.
(Why, indeed,
Was that candle lit, Master Ridley?
We cannot remember.)

But when the frost comes
And no footing is sure,
And all safe ways
Are become a peril,
And a man can say no longer
"Here I stand"
With the ice underfoot
And the steep slope before him,
What will he not give
For a sure footing
And for the strewn ashes?

Though the cries have died away
With the smoke,
Though the flame reflected
In the eyes and the hearts
Has gone,
Sleep well, Master Ridley,
Your soul with God,
And with us, your ashes.

Miss Pettigrew and Tree

In her small single room
    Miss Pettigrew
        —bird bones and parchment skin—
        lives in a leaf world
            made by her pavement tree.

When the wind blows,
    the moving patterns dance
        across her walls
            and lift her heart like music

and when the wind is still,
    leaf shadows touch her face
        with Love that never reached her
            through humankind.

In stark-branched winter
    she feels companioned in
        adversity
and buds in April
    bring her a sign
        from that Far Country
            where she will flower, beyond
                this alien world.

Daily Miss Pettigrew
    —shrunk from life's jostling,
        frail essence in
            a birdcage skeleton—
                wonders why she should be
                    so recompensed

and lives, content, in shelter
    of Love enough for her
        beneath her tree.

163

For a Friend Dying

I JOHN 4:7–10

When light broadens behind the curtains, and I wake
      to my peaceful morning,
my thoughts go at once to you, setting out on your slow
      day's business of dying.

In the midst of my life I am living your death, seeing
      with your eyes the shining
of sun on the leaf. All day I am keeping pace
      with your slow journey

and wishing that those you love may be there to send you
      —from love into Love going—
and may you launch out gently into the dark
      like keel into water moving.

Exile

Yes, it is beautiful country,
the streams in the winding valley,
the knowes and the birches,
and beautiful the mountain's bare shoulder
and the calm brows of the hills,
but it is not my country,
and in my heart there is a hollow place always.

And there is no way to go back—
maybe the miles indeed, but the years never.

Winding are the roads that we choose,
and inexorable is life,
driving us, it seems, like cattle
farther and farther away from what we remember.

But when we shall come at last
to God, who is our Home and Country,
there will be no more road stretching before us
and no more need to go back.

Johanna Patterson

Primordial Pattern

And if I pulled
The red and crimson threads of sin
Out of the fabric of my life,
Would what was left
Be dull as winter rain
And fog at sea?
Be limp like faded flags
And seaweed beached?

O Lord, I should have known:
The red and crimson added to Your robe,
My tapestry reveals in green and gold
The boughs of Eden and the songs
Of birds of paradise.

The Pawn

White glow shining
In center board.
Left Right Front
Spears of bitter slaves
Foam-spewing horses
Knights steel-visored
A serpent-eyed queen
Impenetrable bastions
A black king, smiling.

Rear support deliberately withheld
He clears in death the opening
Through which his King
Will checkmate evil.

Ken Peeders

The Fly

In summer, fly, you'd be a pest, and I
With merciless dispatch would add you to
The list of dead—one missing in the war
For crumbs. But now because November's chill
Has marked you from the rest by driving you
Inside our door lethargically to buzz,
I wonder, should I let you winter with
That cricket in his basement niche? He'd be
A noisy evening friend. My daughter would
Create a home—a jar with punctures in
The lid and lettuce leaves (so many types
She's sought to save with her theology).
I feel like God, but will not act like Him.
I have no son to send who will adopt
The curse-of-flies and live and die and rise.
I have no grace which will forgive the times
That I've been wronged: your type on sandwiches,
A buzz that flips me off the edge of sleep,
Or farmyard swarms that commandeer my car.
I have no childlike love to see you through.
And you will fall. So I will walk away
Until some late November day I too
Go limp. Yet I believe, as you cannot,
The hand that brought you in, and me to you,
Does not in merciless dispatch just brush
Us both away, instead reveals a ruptured
Palm that ripped, and stretched, yet heals.

Eugene H. Peterson

Morning Prayers

"And he was given
much incense to mingle with the
prayers of the saints . . . and the smoke
of the incense rose up with the
prayers of the saints" (Rev. 8:3-4).

From this sunrise angle
the chipped cup rim
shapes coffee mist to an ellipse
holding the morning odor
in brief order to the eye
before my nostrils inhale
and make its rising incense
a part of morning adoration
to the Holy God who can
make me a hale fellow.

The Baptism of Jesus

Near Joshua's ford
old Triton gives one long last blast
on his horn and disappears for good
under the waters, just as Jesus,
lifted by John from the river font,
sees a schism in the sky,
hears God's soft cumulous voice
sound across the Jordanian drainage,
and feels the holy water rippling
with the breath of blessing.

John the Baptist

Raucous John skilled in epiplexis
pounds the pious ears of Pharisees,
stumps the desert to raise a righteous caucus
and clear the streets of unbelief for Jesus.

The locust/honey diet makes him lithe,
the rough leather jerkin shows him humble.
His lungs are purged of cant by desert air,
his Isaianic eyes alert to wonder.

Expert Messiah-watcher, he, not fooled
by desert sharpers greedy for miracles
and promising easy kingdoms, is faithfully
awake to give the inaugural word, "Behold!"

"He Is Not Here"

MARK 16:1–8

A mass of hewn rock entombs the Rock,
a Living Stone embedded deep among
the mythic mines where gnomes and trolls have dug

the dark past for moral money, the Pearl
of Great Price. Mourning miners come
in deep dawn to save the cached treasure

and find an empty hole, the loot plundered
and given away to God's poor and weak
who lose their lives and gain—a resurrection.

9 A.M. Sunday

These shouting bells that lash the vaulted air
above triangulated roof and light-washed campanile,
spreading concentric circled sound through city square
to eddy every bordering yard,
these rocking bells that leap defiant hedge,
gallop the water tower (that declares the town),
these beating bells that pulse the visible angelus hour,
arc the white-washed granary towers, then shinny
the shining parallels of railroad tracks.
These rapturous bells that throb their praise
above embroidered fields, embrace the sea-
green woodlot where the cattle clang
their early morning appetites, vibrate
the hawk that hangs above the nearest farm.
These flailing bells that tongue their time,
sounding the irrevocable summons,
striking the ground, swelling window and wall,
drum their cadence against membranes stretched
    beyond breaking,
beat and beckon from sleep-humped beds
to final reckoning.
These swinging carillons choired and chorused,
flinging the question,
tolling loud as a woodman's ax
knelling the tree's death, hollow echoed,
demand rocks shout and leaves
now dumb with greenness to call out.

Oasis

From over plain and desert bearded Magi came
athirst for some new knowledge; faces seared by flame
of sunswept sand and endless wind. Both flesh and soul
in need of one deep draught, one sight, to make them whole.
Here to the house they came, their burning need confessed,
Before the living water cupped at Mary's breast.

Ascension

Cock's crow and no wheel turning on the cobbled streets
    where night still clutches pocked walls
    and even beggars, sleep-spraddled in corners,
    but here, outside the gate, beyond centurion's stare,
    the shadows blue to light and dawn accentuates
    the farthest mountain tops.
What mission—this too early morning stroll?
    What lesson to be taught that could not be better said
    And translated in heavily curtained rooms?
    What need of hill-tiered seats and pulpit-rock?
Does this too steep ascent through admonition, charge, promise
    predict another (darker) day?
Now, in the morning clarity of mountaintop illumination,
    before light-dazzled eyes, the slow and sure withdrawal
    leaving nothing but explanations gently given.
And yet, as He said, He walks their downward road
    knowing too well their sad bewilderment,
    their baffled answers in marketplace and temple courts
Where disbelief and ridicule catch all their words in nets.

In the Beginning

No one who reads could pass
The message of this flower
Tucked carefully in this place
For this brief hour,

Knowing eternity
In seasonal rebirth,
Seeing the seed of beauty here
In the dark womb of earth.

Once so illiterate, I
Have been as gently led
To this starred open page
Where Genesis is spread.

Man Overboard

Staring as caught fish
they watched him slip along
the criss-crossed waves,
triumphant in his confidence
of faith,
mesmerized by the eyes of
Christ
until suddenly, as might be
expected,
he floundered
caught on the hook of his
own ego,
arms flapping like fins,
mouth gaping for help—
nothing more than a man
overboard!

From Behind Closed Doors

JOHN 20:19

His healing hands that blessed,
caressed,
are torn beyond all balm
and we could see
by the wound in His side
that He was no different from any man.

Were baptism sight and sound,
mountaintop experience,
vast hillside picnics,
tempest stillings
only hallucinations?

and what about the answers
to "Who do you say I am?"
the claims to "raise this temple
in three days,"
or "I and My Father are one"?
Certainly those were more than hyperbole.

"Follow Me," He said.
But those footsteps on Galilean dust
lead only to a cross.

and yet....

Anniversary

With man's acumen a brief time ago
they stepped the moon, a light ballet-like dance,
looked down the bleak, dark corridor they came
and marveled at this blessed circumstance.
And now, amid my garden's galaxies of bloom,
I touch a moon-flower, blurred against the night,
fragrant as all of summer, and I see
a moth (now birds have settled) in its flight,
and suddenly I wonder that we glorified
one little step man made up one more babel tower
with all this universe, the seasons, stars, myself,
    and moon-drenched flower.

Palm Sunday

Astride the colt and claimed as King
that Sunday morning in the spring,
He passed a thornbush flowering red
that one would plait to crown His head.

He passed a vineyard where the wine
was grown for men of royal line
and where the dregs were also brewed
into a gall for Calvary's rood.

A purple robe was cast His way,
then caught and kept until that day
when, with its use, a trial would be
profaned into a mockery.

His entourage was forced to wait
to let a timber through the gate,
a shaft that all there might have known
would be an altar and a throne.

Orchard View

"In the Beginning . . ."

Before the gathered harvest (ladder-pronged),
The blade turned, spring redolent earth
And always April's green and luminous light,
The branch—petaled with brief enameled flowers
(Bee-bristled), sun spread, wind sigh
And summer's echelons of rain,
Before wing-sound, petal-(sun)-drift,
   the thrum of thunder,
Fragrance and tart-sweet taste of fruit,
Before all these—Thou!

Te Deum Laudamus

High in the steepled church the shining bells
swing tongues unmuted to delight the air
with calls to praise, that anyone awake
might now begin this dawning hour with prayer.

Deep in the wood the hermit thrush,
in spiraled ecstasies to greet the dawn,
loops silver sounds for God's own sake alone,
flings his Te Deum now the night is gone.

If we, bell beckoned, should refuse to sing
Te Deum Laudamus to begin our days,
the very stars would ring, the rocks would shout
as now thrush, lark, and linnet spill His praise.

Assurance

Because he also knew
death's dark enclosures,
had passed immortally
from dark to light
[as his implausible birth]

he can explode this dark and
    isolated tomb,
swing open this barred cavern,
quicken by Lazarus' voice
this doomed and putrid flesh,
with but one touch dissolve
these self-forged bonds

and turn my face and soul
to celebrate the sun!

Psalm

Set stick to hide. Draw hair on string.
Place lip on metal, fingering notes.
Twist sound with tongue and lip to fling
Song from the unaccustomed throats.

Touch finger tips to ivory. Rout
Silence with bellows, reed, bone, and rod.
Clang gong. Lift flute. Purse whistle. Shout
Immoderate, joyous praise to God.

Catch

Fish-hooked, I knew no other way to come
(always a drifter in those depths I loved)
drawn up from stygian fathoms
along that pelagic path
to where light rippled, sunshot and surface splayed.
No other dictate heeded
but that urgency as one thin thread
straightened to tautness as a line of will,
drew tight, drew up.
Netted, tipped to sprawl,
to pulse gasp through spread gills,
the caught hook eased from gaping flesh,
the careful breathing in and out,
I lie as wonder bubbles shaken air
to new-found lungs heart larynx,
tongue.
Those past black days scuttled as a splintered boat,
He speaks the wind and wave for me
and charters all my breath.
Now lines are mine to hold.

Experience in April

I walk the April sodden fields
but find no solace in winter-worsened paths
where the headgear of God tears at limbs and cloth.
I see where droplets gather on scratched skin
and know a greater grief for sword-torn flesh
(myself the sword).
All heavy is this April air
now lachrymose with showers;
the shed salt tear still cannot lift
the chest weight of more grief unshed.

Then one bird's hymn of praise defies the gloom
by drawing heart and eye to this
messiah-twig of promise.
One imperceptible sip of faith,
one fingerling of hope, yeast risen,
(His words recalled)
and joy illuminates the April sky.

Confidence

Immunity is mine
   as your own twice-born heir,
   for etched on the lintels of my heart's door
   is that same message that marked hovels
   (neighbors to brick kilns)
   sheltering slaves' sons one black night
   when sudden wailing shattered silence.
Grained deep in wood, flooding down
   and stained as bright as blood
   burst grapes produce,
   this shining sign of life and love
   is my own proof of kinship claimed.
Named by you I wait
   the passing of death's angel
   nor fear my own safe crossing
   of the red divided sea.

At Galilee

Should never have come. At that hour fishing!
But had to be there arms bulging to move,
eyes straining the distance where shore lights diminished,
the reek of the boat and the nets long remembered

now needed. No syllables wanted between us
as sea splat on foredeck split silence apart.
Nets limp when we lift scatter stars as they settle.
We stare the darkness that goes back and in
seeing, not believing what can't really be there

yet is—now silhouetted against that first glimmer
tending a fire then turning to call.
Past nets silver spangled with O what a harvest
immersed then suspended in water, in space,

I rise to His voice myself hooked and drawn
as breath breaks on the edges I see light through night.

Eugene Rubingh

Some Thought
That It Was Merely Joy

Some thought that it was merely joy,
This journey, and the sweating drum,
The banging palms, the people proud
And laughing down the jungle trail.

It was not merely sweet to leap
The steaming swamps and tired, crouch
Around the evening fires, or say
That I had watched the witches die.

Such faces painted by the moon as these
Are all my own; my own progenitor
Was here and knelt about this ageless fire
And heard my words and cursed, incredulous.

For in these eyes there gleams such disbelief
As flashed through all the ancient denizens
Of my ancestral state, when round their fires
Some weary monk first told of Paradise.

The final bloody gift is lifted now,
But luckless, still uncomprehending gods
Will wield no death, will curse no womb;
The ancient weal lies shattered here.

There was a pain of birth, the crushing weight
Of this millenium for those who lay
Beneath the quiet stars and saw that Light,
The cataclysm, the redeeming flame.

These searing sparks of soul I took
And carried breathless down the sun-baked track
To strike this terror with a song of hope;
Some thought that it was merely joy.

In Memoriam

On April 19, 1975, Bill De Jong, missionary teacher,
drowned in Nigeria.

If this were all—the ink, the words,
The fragile deeds spun from his ready hands,
Tossed here upon the river of our lives,
Like bells still ringing in the saddened halls
Merely to soothe our weary eyes and ears—
If this his meager tale were etched—no more, I say—
Why, we should wait forever then, oblivion
His destiny, the silence but the heralder
Of death and Paradise. Within our ears
The world still shrieks, and were the ruined coasts
The only truth, were there no source
Beneath the shell, some racing wave
Would bruise and kill us lying here, looking
Dully at the quiet stars. Wait now!
I have to say that should you claw away
The words, the skin, the skeleton, and find
The heart's core naked now, there before you
Storms an argument with hell, and
Should no ships return, still see
Provisions here which we shall term
Our Christ-fired, raging dreams
And with this godly carpentry
We make from hope new boats to sail
And these will span the night.

in deserto vox clamantis

my home is desert heart, a barren night
whose pulsebeat hammers out the rage
to be and do, and i would leap
batblind under the dustfilled sky
to make a highway for the Lamb.

and shall i never speak for God, or say
He made me dull that i should crave
the secret of my paradise?
shall i not tie my shoes to stand
and go that damning mile tonight?

i am drunk with wanting—not mere glory
or some exotic herb to heal
my wearied head, not merely that,
but some great way to track, some sight
of houses on a hill or roaring sky.

for this flecked page, could i but read it well,
would tell me all of life, a hundred years
in every line, the twists of history,
the atoms' interplay, all clear at last,
if I could grasp one Word complete.

and this one meager hour of light could mark
the bounds of hate, could i but sense
that speech of stars, and empires rise
or fall with me, could i but ride
upon my dark horizon's rim.

then i would ride above these ruts of days
and splash these eyes with angel dreams,
then see at last the reach i lack,
or bend into the sleet, or write
that i had touched infinity.

if for such wanting, God, Thy dark left hand
will crumble my last essences,
then say that i yet saw one Height
where my own desert house was lit,
was waiting as i raced for home.

Discovery

tall, work-proud
we prayed for food:
at noon
the amber flames sighed
tenderly
across ripe fields

parched, white-lipped,
we prayed for rain:
at dusk
the dust storm sifted
orange dust
into dry souls

hot-eyed, wild
we prayed for love:
at midnight
Christ came passing by
and gave
a solitude

humbly then
we prayed for God:
at dawn
the burning cities
fanned by hate
prefigured hell

groping, blind
we searched for death:
and then at last
seared on our souls
we found
Immanuel

Reckoning

The loving hand of Christ was I,
It seemed, cupped there and bearing life,
Or in a darker mood, His fist
Raised to the angry sky to strike
A blow for God. A thousand tasks
Were lightly done, the grip yet steel:
Christ's hand would not so quickly tire;
His arm would thrust me through the years.

Yet I was wrong. The hand unclenched
Passed by old men but sped to friends,
And when my mind was wild with pain
I raised the fist at God—and now
The world is colder and my hate
Will rage across the night alone:
For I, who thought to be His hand,
I was the nail that pierced His palm.

Mary Ruch

Spring Song

Here's a limpid note from a song-bird throat
   Like a crystal drop in air;
And forsythian bells chime golden knells
   For winter's icy glare.
Here's a violet eye turned to the sky
   With a dew-drop for a tear;
And chuckling rills splash down the hills,
   And streams laugh cool and clear.
Here's a small green leaf on a wintry sheaf
   Of bare-twigged bush and bough;
And the sap runs free in the greening tree,
   And the brown earth clasps the plough.
And the song of spring makes the full heart sing
   God's praise in endless prayer,
For life flows again in the hearts of men
   When the spring song fills the air;
For the spring song's theme makes real the dream
   Of life after dark death's sleeping,
For a stone was rolled in a spring of old,
   And Christ found Mary weeping.

Feed My Sheep

We thirst,
And drink is offered us;
We hunger
And are fed:
We take
All that is proffered us
From Him
Who suffered, bled.
He feeds and cups
The starving soul,
Withholds no crumb or drop.

Yet for His hunger
All we give
Is husks, and sour sop.

Luci Shaw

Tithes

MATTHEW 23:23

All in bunches the furred leaves
are hung—narrow and stiff and
greyer than they grew
under the wall—
starred with a few
dry seeds. I've crushed and weighed
a small part of them into God's pot,
spikes, stalks and all.
The sun drained all the green
they'd ·got.
All they can give now is a tithe of death,
a thin spice in the air. But has God seen?
Has he the nose to savor
the last fine fragrance of their breath?
Will caraway mask my justice—
make it seem fair? Can mint
sweeten a meager mercy, or a hint
of dill improve the flavor
of my faith? Why ask? It's his affair—
and his prerogative to bless or not to bless.
The love he wants is too wide for my inches;
his righteousness
too heavy. And like the sun, not just a tenth
but "all," he says. "With all your heart,"
and that's nine-tenths too much!
(Such burdens and my good intention fails.)
I'll stick to weighing herbs on garden scales,
and my white-painted wall is thick enough,
I think, to keep out conscience, questions,
critics, seekers, friends, rough
beggars and itinerant carpenters,
though I suppose
God could leap it if I asked him to
or if he chose.

Angel Vision

Seeing Creation come, they know it well:
the stars, the shoots of green shine for them
one by one. They have eternity to learn
the universe, which once encompassing, angels
forget not. Clean as steel wires, shining
as frost, making holiness beautiful, aiming
at the Will of God like arrows flaming
to a target, earthy solidity presents no
barrier to their going. Easily they slope
through the rind of the world, the atoms
pinging in their celestial orifices. Matter
& anti-matter open before them like a bible.
Inhabiting the purposes of God, Who is
the Lord of all their Hosts, in Deep Space
their congregation wages war with swords of fire
& power & great joy, seizing from the
Hierarchies of Darkness Andromeda's boundaries
& all constellations. The rising Day Star
is their standard bearer, as on earth they stay
the Adversary's slaughter of the Sons of God.
                        .   Praise
is their delight also. Rank on rank they sing
circularly around the Throne, dancing together
in a glory, clapping hands at rebellion
repented of, or sheep returned. They who
accompany the bright spiriting up of a redeemed
swimmer from the final wave, who trace
the grey, heavy clot that marks the drowning
of the profane to his own place—how can we
think to escape their fiery ministry? We listen
for their feathers, miss the shaft of light
at our shoulder. We tread our gauntlet paths
unknowing, covered by shields of angels. (The ass
sees one & shames us for blindness.) "Fear not's"
unfurl like banners over their appearing, yet
we tremble at their faces.
                         Seraphim sing
in no time zone. Cherubim see as clearly on
as back, invest acacia planks with arkwood in
their certainty (whose winged ornamenting gilds
the tabernacle shade.) Comprehending the
compacted plan centered in every seed, the grown
plant is no more real to them & no surprise.
Dampened by neither doubt nor supposition,
they understand what happens to a worm. And if

we ask—Did he please God? Did he fulfill
the Eternal Plan for worms, drilling the soil,
digesting it? & his strange hermaphroditic
replication—did he do it well? & what will
happen to his wormy spirit when he shrivels back
to soil? heavenly Beings answer instantly,
giving God high praise for faithful worms.
The archangel sees with eyes quicker than ours &
unconfused by multiplicity. For him, reality's
random choice is all clear cause & effect:
each star of snow tells of intelligence; each
cell carries its own code; at a glance he knows
from whence the crests of all the wrinkles on
the sea rebound. He has eternity to tell
it all, & to rejoice.
                    But what is this
conjunction of straw & splendor? The echo of
sharp laughter from a crowd (of men bent from
the image of the firstmade man) as nails
pierce flesh, pierces the Bright Ones with
perplexity. They see the Maker's hands helpless
against Made Wood. The bond is sealed with
God's blood. Thus is Love's substance darkness
to their light. The Third Day sweetens the deep
Riddle. Heralds now of a new Rising, they have
eternity to solve it, & to praise.

Christ Risen Was Rarely Recognized

Christ risen was rarely recognized by sight.
They had to get beyond the way He looked.
Evidence stronger than His voice and face and footstep
waited to grow in them, to guide their groping
out of despair, their stretching toward belief.

We are as blind as they
until the open of our deeper eyes
shows us the hands that bless and break
our bread. Until we finger
wounds that tell our healing, or witness a miracle
of fish, dawn-caught after our long night
of empty nets. Handling His Word,
we feel His flesh, His bones, and hear
His voice saying our early-morning name.

To a Christmas Two-Year-Old

Child, and all children,
come and celebrate
the little one who came,
threatened by hate
and Herod's sword.
Sing softly and rejoice
in the reward
for all the baby boys
of Bethlehem
who died
in Jesus' place.

Small wonder when He grew
He wanted children by His side,
stretched out His arms, stood,
beckoned you,
called *Come to me*
and died
in your place
so that you could.

he who would be great among you

You whose birth broke all the
social and biological rules—
son of the poor who accepted
the worship due a king—
child prodigy debating with
the Temple Th.D.'s—you
were the kind who used
a new math
to multiply bread, fish, faith.
You practiced a
radical sociology:
rehabilitated con men and
call girls. You valued women
and other minority groups.
a G.P., you specialized in
heart transplants.
Creator, healer,
shepherd, innovator,
story-teller, weather-maker,
botanist, alchemist,
exorcist, iconoclast,
seeker, seer, motive-sifter,
you were always beyond,
above us. Ahead
of your time, and ours.

And we would like
to be *like* you. Bold
as Boanerges, we hear ourselves
demand: "Admit us
to your avant-garde.
Grant us degree
in all the liberal arts of heaven."
Why our belligerence?
Why does this whiff of fame
and greatness smell so sweet?
Why must we compete
to be first? Have we forgotten
how you took simply, cool water
and a towel for our feet?

Parable

riding easily
on the bright
unbroken sea—
bursting with a diversity
of lives—
a remnant salvaged
from a universal debris—
lifted by water above
the world's dark
muddy floor—
washed clean—
expecting the dove
and the sign of green
and light
from an opening door—
God's biggest parable:
· the ark

Royalty

He was a plain man
and learned no latin

Having left all gold behind
he dealt out peace
to all us wild men
and the weather

He ate fish, bread,
country wine and God's will

Dust sandalled his feet

He wore purple only once
and that was an irony

Getting Inside the Miracle

No, He is too quick. We never
catch Him at it. He is there
sooner than our thought or prayer.
Searching
backwards, we cannot discover "how"
or get inside the miracle.

Even if it were here and now
how would we describe the just-born trees
swimming into place at their green creation,
flowering upward in the air
with all their thin twigs quivering
in the gusts of grace? or the great
white whales fluking
through crystalline seas
like recently inflated balloons?
How can we
time the beat of the man's heart
as the woman comes close enough to fill
his newly-hollow side? Who will
diagram the gynecology
of incarnation, the trigonometry of trinity?
or chemically analyze wine
from a well? or see inside
joints as they loosen, and whole limbs?
Will anyone stand beside
the moving stone? plot the bright
trajectory of the ascension? and explain
the tongues of fire
telling both heat and light?

Enough. Refrain.
Observe a finished work. Think:
Today, another miracle—
the feathered arrows of your faith
may link
God's bow and target.

The Poet—
Silent After Pentecost

I who was thirsty, drank, was satisfied,
became myself a secondary source
of bubbling water, why
was my mouth still dry?

Brushed by dove's feathers
heart and winging mind—
I who had felt flight dared to ask
when will my words fly?

His burning oil from crown
to feet had covered me.
I was a torch for lighting, and for light,
yet was my throat still dark.

The overwhelming rush,
the mighty wind wide-spread the blaze.
Yet from my tinder tongue
came not one spark.

Breasting the gusts of praise,
filled with the singing Word
and words, and still
no sound would come.

That Holy Breath, promised,
to teach lungs, larynx, lips
in a needed hour, told mine
until today—"Be dumb!"

Enoch

crossed the gap
another way
he changed his pace
but not
his company

Power Failure

By what
anti-miracle have we
lamed the man
who leaped for joy,
lost ninety-nine
sheep,
turned bread
back to stone
and wine
to water?

The Singularity of Shells

A shell—how small an empty space,
a folding out of pink and white,
a letting in of spiral light.
How random? and how commonplace?
(A million shells along the beach
are just as fine and full of grace
as this one here within your reach.)

But lift it, hold it to your ear
and listen. Surely you can hear
the swish and sigh of all the grey
and gleaming waters, and the play
of wind with rain and sun, encased
in one small jewel box and placed,
by God and oceans, in your way.

The Groundhog

The groundhog is, at best, a simple soul
   without pretension, happy in his hole,
twinkle-eyed, shy, earthy, coarse-coated grey,
   no use at all (except on Groundhog Day).
At Christmastime, a rather doubtful fable
   gives the beast standing room inside the stable
with other simple things, shepherds, and sheep,
   cows, and small winter birds, and on the heap
of warm, sun-sweetened hay, the simplest thing
   of all—a baby. Can a groundhog sing,
or only grunt his wonder? Could he know
   this new-born Child had planned *him*, long ago,
for groundhog-hood? Whether true tale or fable,
   I like to think that he *was* in the stable,
part of the Plan, and that He who designed
   all simple wonderers, may have had me in mind.

Fire on the Berkshires, October 1974

ROMANS 1:20

Across these valleys roared the furnaces
of the Almighty, till all that was left of the leaves
(melted copper and ornamented brass and refined gold)
was a scattered heat that was partly Himself and
partly His sun and partly a glow of my own.

It was snow that slowly extinguished
the blazes of Fall on the flanks of the hills.
But His coals, searing the eyeballs, had kindled
an altar whose fires leap in the brain all this long
winter. They burn and will not be consumed.

To Dr. Clyde S. Kilby

on his 70th birthday, September 20, 1972,
*in love and gratitude**

It is a time when apples ripen,
friendships thicken,
maples kindle a Fall fire
west of Blanchard. Through the halls
scholars and students quicken
at a familiar voice,
and on the corner of Washington and Jefferson
squirrels and sparrows rejoice
because you're home. Like a hobbit
come back to the Shire
you're home again, our friend,
bringing Martha with you, and sunflower seeds,
a sackful of nuts, three score
years and ten worth of wisdom, under
your arm—letters and Lewis-lore—
your mind a well of distilled wonder.

It was your mind, your inner eye, that saw it
long before it happened—
the hierarchies of shelves
dusted obliquely by the late sun
behind old glass
in the narrow room once occupied
by a minority of one
and now inhabited by Inklings and elves.
Like a gardener raking grass,
piling the bright and varied leaves,
from far you gathered treasures, sheaves
of letters, papers ornamented
with the rich, crabbed English script,
searched out the volumes
burnished and precious with scholarship and age—
"fact shrunk to truth" speaking from every page.

Then you swung open for us all
the wardrobe door,
pushed us farther up and farther in
(accompanied by some favorite talking beast)
to Middle-earth, Narnia, and the Utter East.

---

*Dr. C. S. Kilby has been the moving force in the collection
of original mss., correspondence, and rare editions of C. S. Lewis
and a number of his friends and associates. Known as "The
Lewis Collection," it is housed in the Jonathan Blanchard Room at
Wheaton College.

In there, for us to re-explore,
is perfect Perelandra.
Treebeard is growing up the cornered wall.
In the Deep Space behind the rows of books
eldila elude us; Curdie
encounters Mr. Bultitude the bear.
There in that room
we smell the past, untainted by decay or death
but fragrant, for in there
the mallorns bloom
and all the blessed air
is warm with Aslan's breath.

Mustard Field

Small flowerhead in this blazing field,
pure lemonpale, poised over your
green gray stalk and leaves under the gray
green afternoon, my husband's camera
    prepares itself to tell one kind of truth
    about you.
Standing near, I have already found my
    focus: bright field to yellow patch to
    single plant to swaying flower to
    precise bud.
I see you as God sees me, come
from more than five thousand miles away,
picked, one-in-a-million (was it
chance, choice, destiny?) from the blur of
moving heads in a spring wind.

There is a mustard seed hidden in you!

Now I see you in reverse—retain the detail
of you, a color slide in the mind's eye,
enlarge the vision to a wide-angled view
of glory, multiplied from a few seeds.

It is a spring day in Switzerland:
the sun is hidden behind rain, but
light burns up like a promise
from the field, from the mustard flower.

Pneuma

". . . so it is with the Spirit" (John 3:8).

The wind breathes where it wishes.
The wind blows where it blows.

A flurry of starlings
scatter like lifted leaves
across the dark October field
driven against
their own warm, southward
impulse: winged instinct
thwarted by
a weight of wind.

The eye of Your storm
sees from the wild height.
Your air augments the world
tearing
away dead wood, testing,
toughening all trees
spreading all seeds
thawing a winter wasteland
sifting the sand, carving
the rock, the water,
in the end
moving the mountain.

Your wind breathes where it wishes,
moves where it wills, sometimes
severs my safe moorings. Sovereign gusts—
buffet my wings with your blowing,
loosen me, lift me to go
wherever you're going.·

May 20:
Very Early Morning

all the field praises Him/all
dandelions are His glory/gold
and silver all trilliums unfold
white flames above their trinities
of leaves all wild strawberries
and massed wood violets reflect His skies'
clean blue and white
all brambles/all oxeyes
all stalks and stems lift to His light
all young windflower bells
tremble on hair
springs for His air's
carillon touch/last year's yarrow (raising
brittle star skeletons) tells
age is not past praising
all small low unknown
unnamed weeds show His impossible greens
all grasses sing
tone on clear tone
all mosses spread a spring-
soft velvet for His feet
and by all means
all leaves/buds/all flowers cup
jewels of fire and ice
holding up
to His kind morning heat
a silver sacrifice

now
make of our hearts a field
to raise Your praise

Rib Cage

Jonah, you
and I were both signs
to unbelievers.

Learning the anatomy
of ships and sea animals the hard way—
from the inside
out—you counted (bumping your
    stubborn head)
the wooden beams and the great
curving bones
and left

your own heart unexplored.
And you were tough.
Twice, damp but undigested,
you were vomited. For you
it was the only
way out.

No, you wouldn't die.
Not even burial softened you
and, free of the dark sea prisons,
you were still
caged in yourself—trapped
in your own hard continuing rage
at me and Nineveh.

For three nights
and three days dark as night—
as dark as yours—
I charted the innards
of the earth. I too swam
in its skeleton, its raw underground.
A captive
in the belly of the world
(like the fish, prepared by God)
I felt the slow pulse at the monster's
    heart,
tapped its deep arteries, wrestled
its root sinews, was bruised
by the undersides of all
its cold bony stones.

Submerged,
I had to die, I had
to give in to it, I had to go
all the way down
before I could be freed
to live for you
and Nineveh.

The Joining

After reading Charles Williams and Romans 6

After the hours of restless
struggling through the waves
of fears, wounded, stroking against
gravity, treading water, stroking,
I choose to let go, to float
numbed, to trust myself to the words
sung across the lake: *Lay down*
your life, to trust my body to
the drifting wood—in weariness my bed,
my frame, the crux of all matters,
to which he was joined by force
but willingly, laid on it to be
what I have been
to gain my pain
(himself to drown in it).

          Thus
am I buoyed, and resting there
cruciform, new knowledge laps me
like a wave: *I* am the cross—
coarse grained and pocked with holes
of nails—to which he joins himself
(already joined to his deep baptism)
that he may join me to his strong escape,
his rising from the darkness of
the icy lake.

Phil Silva

To See How He Dwells Heartward

To see how He dwells heartward, the center, the crux
Of all that is, this is to be in unceasing prayer,
To know it is He Who breathes the very air
Which sustains us, and He the immortal flux.
How can we live within Him, and see Him not?
Hear His Spirit beneath feeling, thought, and will,
Deep as the deepest sleep, and deeper still;
To see Him only after death is too often our lot.
He is the rhythm of the hidden heart;
He is our axis; He is our nuclear being.
Without Him, seeing is not seeing;
All crumbles inward, and flies apart.
He who has a heart to love, let him love
The Christ within us, around us, above.

Sunlight, Splintered

Sunlight, splintered, sings on skin;
His grace, like birdsong, inward rings;
This the message nature brings:
Love's the rhythm fleshed within.
We are not clothed as one of those
Who beat the air, and air their songs,
But He loves us more, in all our wrongs,
And in His heart He holds us close.
Though I flay the air with words in vain,
I know He knows my inmost thought,
He Who has redemption bought,
Who hung on wood, betrayed and slain.
My unbelief has been cast out;
I live His love, past fear, past doubt.

Jesus! Flesh Torn

Jesus! Flesh torn, back scourged, thorn-crowned brow,
Nailed hands, pierced feet, now torture fresh urged:
Scorcher of cracked lips, sponged sour wine.
Fierce, the hour nine beneath God's hips!
History's poised tool: cruel Roman spear;
Bequeathed: God's voiced fear. Mystery's fool.
Plunged steel, blood-baptized, watered slit side;
Christ, again You cried out, realized
Your Father's will, made eternal life
For the Church, Your wife. Divine charade!
No whore, we lurch from darkness to light,
Confess Spirit-sight, though deaf and dumb,
Wander, ponder, bruised, Your timeless death,
The Comforter's breath, how we are used.

Lord, Let Me Recall the Fall

Lord, let me recall the fall and the flood
Whenever the tempter leads me to sin.
Let me remember I made You sweat blood,
That it was I who drove the nails in.
I was Pilate, Lord, impaled on the horns
Of a dilemma, and, like a coward,
Washed my hands of You, crowned You with thorns,
Though by Your Father I was empowered.
Yes, Lord, I was a fool, so bellicose
I scourged Your back with a sadist's whip.
Beneath the cross, I gambled for Your clothes,
And laughed as I watched holy blood drip
From Your flesh. By my spear, Your death was sealed.
Lord, I am not worthy; by Your stripes I am healed.

John W. Simons

Simeon's Light Remembered

Today is Candlemas, and by the light
Of feast and symbol I survey the night
Of this most tenebrous city of the dead,
Wherefrom all vision and all hope have fled.
I hold the shimmering candle in my hand,
And gaze on it, and seek to understand.

I, through the fetid city, see disease
Mistily rise from dead philosophies.
I see the dogmas shaken one by one
And hear the madmen cry in unison,
"Truth is truth, but truth is relative
And plastic to the age in which you live."

The danse macabre of brittle-phosphor bones,
Nocturnal revel on the graveyard thrones:
Here in the drunken polis of the blind
They celebrate the obsequies of Mind;
I hear the corpses of the city shout,
"We've gouged the eyes of reason out!"

Perplexed, and scarcely knowing what to do,
I look on Simeon to seek a clue.
The candle never wavered in his hand;
His eyes are fixed upon another land.
And through the luminous air the Spirit stirred,
Carrying the advent rumor of the Word.

Today is Candlemas. O holy Feast!
I hold my shimmering candle to the east,
And there I see the overthrow of night,
And there I see epiphany of light.
A City, like a bride adorned, descends.
Her tent is pitched. The reign of darkness ends.

The Whale and the Tiger

When Ahab saw his white leviathan
And Blake his burning tiger in the night,
They conjured metaphor from fevered sight
For that old sin which shadows everyman.

When Ahab wrestled with the monstrous whale
In the surging theater of liquid hell,
He traveled evil fathoms and he fell,
Opposing the white mirage to no avail.

When Blake endured his forest interlude
And eyed with dread God's blazing antonym,
No answer to his question came to him
Save echoes of subliminal solitude.

Dual projections of a self-disease
Contracted in the primal garden where
The search for good and evil shook despair
From that most blighted of all blighted trees.

Forest dilemma of marine defeat,
Shaper of tiger or leviathan,
Are crossed and canceled symbols to the man
Cleansed in the Lamb, purged by the Paraclete.

Edith Sitwell

Still Falls the Rain
THE RAIDS, 1940. NIGHT AND DAWN.

Still falls the Rain—
Dark as the world of man, black as our loss—
Blind as the nineteen hundred and forty nails
Upon the Cross.

Still falls the Rain
With a sound like the pulse of the heart that is changed
　　to the hammer-beat
In the Potter's Field, and the sound of the impious feet
On the Tomb:
　　　　　　Still falls the Rain
In the Field of Blood where the small hopes breed and the
　　human brain
Nurtures its greed, that worm with the brow of Cain.

Still falls the Rain
At the feet of the Starved Man hung upon the Cross.
Christ that each day, each night, nails there, have mercy
　　on us—
On Dives and on Lazarus:
Under the Rain the sore and the gold are as one.

Still falls the Rain—
Still falls the Blood from the Starved Man's wounded Side:
He bears in His Heart all wounds—those of the light that
　　died,
The last faint spark
In the self-murdered heart, the wounds of the sad
　　uncomprehending dark,
The wounds of the baited bear—
The blind and weeping bear whom the keepers beat
On his helpless flesh . . . the tears of the hunted hare.

Still falls the Rain—
Then—O Ile leape up to my God: who pulles me doune—
See, see where Christ's blood streames in the firmament:
It flows from the Brow we nailed upon the tree
Deep to the dying, to the thirsting heart
That holds the fires of the world—dark-smirched with pain
As Caesar's laurel crown.

Then sounds the voice of One who like the heart of man
Was once a child who among beasts has lain—
"Still do I love, still shed my innocent light, my Blood, for thee."

Leonora Speyer

House of Calvin

John Calvin was a man of God.
How did he dare to do this thing?
Thrust down the angels where they stood
Meek side by side with folded wing,
Remove the saints that all about
Praised God, and Mary, full of grace,
In that pure-candled place?

"Is not my word like a fire?
Like a hammer?" thundered John.
"Of what avail these carven sticks?
These images?" and lifted higher
His hands and dared to lay them on
The vast, inviolate crucifix,
The chalice, quickened wine and bread—
And yet he fell not dead.

Up on the altar dark and stripped,
He laid the Book, the great, bound Word,
Manifest evidence of the Lord.
Where once was light and chanted prayer,
Thuribles swinging in the air,
Rose a chill sound, the voice loud-lipped
Of mighty Calvin preaching there.

And like a hammer rose and fell
His voice, propounding line on line,
Driving them home:
      "Vengeance is mine!"
He cried. His listeners paled and shook;
He looked about and liked it well—
They say it was no pleasant look.
"Woe unto your pretense of prayer!
Vengeance is mine! Vengeance is mine!"
And held aloft the Book.

Fierce wolf of God, hungry and lean!
Down to the Church's very bone
He gnawed and crunched, licking it clean
Of ancient pomp and panoply;
There on the naked altar stone,
Imperishable and alone,
He placed the Book as on a throne.

And there it lies unto this day,
Vast Testament, the old, the new,
The two in one, the one in two;
I stood and watched it where it lay.

Bereft and wondering I stood,
Who loved the lovely things of God,
And suddenly a great wind came
And wrapped the altar like a flame,
Calling God's Name. Calling God's Name.

And this I heard and I saw this:
A light that leapt from Genesis,
And all of sound and all of sight
Were in the light; and this I heard:
"In the beginning was the Word!"

The Bible cried. It was one voice
From all the books within the Book;
Like wings outstretched its pages stirred:
"A tabernacle of the Word
Is this my Book. Where it doth lie
Am I. Am I."

And all the books within the Book
Cried out again. And I cried too.
I made no sound and yet I spoke—
There was a shouting in my side:
"In spite of all believers do,
I do believe!" I cried.

And all sound ceased and was no more,
Save for a sighing as of trees
From a far place where olives grew;
There was a Voice, a Face I knew—
I was aware of these.
And all light ceased and was no more,
Save for a light above the door,
Spectral and dim that found the gleam
Of fading Genesis:
                            they met—
To make a cross upon the floor.

On the bare board the Bible lay,
And I went out into the day;
And there were mountains all about,
They strode the valleys, soared the skies;
Sun glittered on each lofty slope,
And like the psalmist toward his hope,
I lifted up mine eyes.

Kathleen Speyers

David

david
is a miracle—the doctors say
His breath had brushed
the very dust of death
and swept it up in a cloud of choking life
that made me shudder
breathlessly.

david
is a miracle—I say.

I watched him spin
the dust cocoon around his green life
and count the minutes of living
one by one
until
minutes faded into the age
when he emerged
metamorphosed into a
fluttering butterfly
that soared high above us
—lizards scuttling across a dusty
earth.

david
was a miracle—the doctors say
His dust cocoon is
snug and dark again
breathless and still beneath the
scuttling of hurrying dry lizards' feet.

Perhaps he knew
how close
the trumpet sound
is
and once again
waits patiently
to be a butterfly
again

Northern Lights

the night engulfed us
we saw it

racing in and out
silently shouting across
the heavens
trembling and burning beneath
a cold flame

we saw it
interlocking in
        out
            spiraling
as though some
great unknown hand
beckoned
pulling it on through the night
        the lights
        weaving on dagger rivers
        of white
        locking us forever
        in place with our Maker

Ruthe T. Spinnanger

"In the Year that King Uzziah Died"

ISAIAH 6:1

Shut up as a leper,
Dead under a cloud,
Your royalty eclipsed:
And not till then
My vision dated.
Dated
That with certainty
I could look upon mortality
And know
When breath of kings and princes fail,
There would remain
That other vision burning,
Burning with a heat
Proportioned to its light.

No repetitious revelations
Come with such a vision.
It is enough to see
In each Uzziah dead,
In each disease, each shame,
Each royal claim eclipsed,
My Lord uplifted.
Surrounded with a host
Whose faces, feet and features
Are covered for that vision's errand,
To serve with nothing less
Than angel's wings;
And sing no other song
Save, Holy, Holy, Holy!

Whitewash
MATTHEW 23

I paint creation with a film of sense
Not indigenous. I overlay
Picassos deftly with small black and gray
Mondriaans in calculated defense
Of symmetry. I prize more innocence
Than virtue—prefer, though I never say
So, my canvas whitely primed, and kept away
From dangers of the pallet's influence.
I clarify the pointillistic earth,
Convert haphazard hues to straitened tones,
Make clear and sharp the pure aesthetic worth
Of *every*thing. I whiten in my mind my bones,
Render them fleshless, abstracted and clean.
I handle best the things I've never seen.

Elmer F. Suderman

When Will We Dance Again?

TO CHAD WALSH

after reading God at Large

when will we dance again
loosening our devotion
to compelling immediacy
total ecstasy
exultant
  d $_a$ ^{n} $_c$ ^{i} $_n$^{g}
with all our
mind
heart
soul
to the laughing god
cleansed by the dance triumphant
made whole again
by the r$_o$$_m$$_{p_i}$$_n$god
who has delivered us
into the madness
gladness
dash and
spontaneity
into the
awe
absurdity and
mystery
into the
gyrating
luminous
pulsing
celebrating life
that no death
has been able to kill
no grave
able
to hold?

Crucify Him!

The spine that cut the cattle
cuts the Christ
as men of rectitude
crown Him with thorns
deck Him in purple robes
and mock Him up the hill.

The tree that harbored robins
holds the Man of Sorrows
as soldiers sneer
and Pharisees cry out:
"Others he saved;
he cannot save himself!"

The nail that held the house
now tears His feet
and rips His hands
as soldiers mock
and people scorn
and helpless Mary
hopelessly stands by.

The spear that ripped the foreign foe
now rips the Christ
and slits His side,
and water, blood, and guts
splash softly down
and irrigate the earth.

The men that cried
"Hosanna to the King!"
in Jerusalem ages ago
and sang "Praise to the Lord!"
at First Church yesterday
(and we) here join the plea:
"Crucify, Crucify Him!"

Communion for the Aged

Hands that steered the tractor,
arranging properly the day's soil,
plowed autumn toward sundown,
grateful to hear darkness fall,
harvested wheat that read
forty bushels an acre,
talked to cows with milk pails,
filling with a steady swish
the empty bottom, then adding
three gallons more,
sweat tears as they knocked
against locked doors of life,
hungered and held silent communion
with chicken and fried potatoes;
knuckles now gnarled like the old oak
trunks they watered to green the prairies,
useless now except to dream of plow or udder
or of dying, bow and tremble as they take
bread and wine, body and blood
passed from one veined hand to another.

Thy Kingdom Come

The Lord's Prayer
   flows from facile worshipers
   like TV voices
   recounting the worries of the world
   and the wonder of anti-perspirants.

Lacking a congregation,
since all are
praying to themselves
or to impress the rest,
God seldom has a thing to do
or anyone to listen to.

Quietly he waits
to catch a man
who wants to find
but has not found

the meaning of
"Thy will be done."
One such is worth
a thousand dissembling
"Thine be the glories"
to an idol god.

Patiently God listens
for a troubled saint
with nothing
but a sense of sin
to lean heavily
on his pew
praying "Lord, have mercy!"
and yearning
for the Kingdom
that is yet to come.

Adam in the Garden

Adam in the suburban garden
Among the television trees,
Tasting the fruit of the Tree of Knowledge,
Carelessly tosses the core over his shoulder.

It explodes, brilliant as a million acetylene torches,
Deafening as a million sonic booms.
It shatters the picture windows and knocks
The cross of First Church out of the sky.

The sun hides his face behind a mushroom cloud.
The clock on the Federal Building and Loan Office
No longer reports the interest rate
Or flashes the time and temperature.

The net alert station is silent,
Huntley and Brinkley fail to report the flash,
Church bells are silent. Sermons on
Unilateral disarmament have been cancelled.

God, abandoned, lonely, obscured by smoke,
Stubs His toe on a steeple
Buried in the ashes of the garden and
Calls, "Adam, where are you?"

Robert D. Swets

In Memory of
E. William Oldenburg

(1936–1974)

we have seen him   as we have seen
faces passing in train windows
too briefly   but on numerous occasions
circling each other as if trains ran
in circles   waving at each others passing
or shouting through the open windows

we have seen him   coming & going
in sun & foul weather   our meetings
fell almost into a pattern
we had come to expect him

& now we are reminded
of something we had known
but had forgotten   setting aside
our certainty we are brought
to remember our frailty
this divine dust that
sticks to our bones that must
finally fall away

& now we do not see   he sees
& now we cannot know   he knows
now we have put him
into his grave
we leave quietly
we speak only in whispers

we remember as we remember
a train station   he has not
been switched off or abandoned
on some siding   this is not
his final destination   it is
no terminal station

it is only a waiting room

Grandfather

Grandfather sits & begins breakfast,
staring into his coffee cup...

"Grandfather, here, your slippers...."

but little moves him mornings: his glasses
slide slowly down his nose & threaten
to fall. He always frowns, & catches them
in time. He cocks his head, favoring
his good ear, as always, to listen
upstairs: what the snow is doing
to the roof: shushes to silence
grandma & his radio. Winters

always slow him down a bit. Arthritis.
& he, contrary, tests it, moving
out to the uninsulated porch, freezing
in his flannel shirt & baggy pants
reading the paper. Ask him,

"Grandpa, come in, it's warmer here."
"Only good chair's this one."
"Bring it in, why don't you."
"No room for it." & he turns
the page, & shoves his glasses back
with his thumb without slowing
the movements of his hand & eyes.

An explanation is in order. Grandpa
was an orphan immigrant at twelve; knew
only Dutch; worked hard, & went to school;
taught himself English, finished
college at seventeen, taught algebra,

geometry & catechism sixty years;
believes predestination; decries depravity;
is quick to find evidences
of gradual (but constant) degeneration.

His reading finds him sin: murder, rape.
He grunts. It hurts. But comes as no surprise.
Drunkenness. Divorce. Debauchery.
He has grown, now, almost to expect it.
He misses his dog, loves
his children, prays
humbly & unceasingly for them & their children.

He is a Calvinist, to be sure, sound & wise
if settled in his ways. He believes
in hell, & firmly in damnation, but
will not call it down. He sees himself
growing out of this world: trying hard
not to grow bitter. He folds
his glasses into his pocket, his paper,
& sets it aside. Rises. Stands
very still at the window, hands
on the ledge, looking out across the snow.

& when you see him, you remember
Christ in the weakness of His power
weeping over Jerusalem. & from the cross
praying a final forgiveness. Now,
seeing him, you have to believe
that this is not futile, what he does.
That here, at least, prayer is valid.
This once, & for this little while
you have to believe.

For Fifty Years of Music:
For Seymour Swets

for the wisdom of Yaroslav in deciding to fashion
in the broad fields the magnificent gates & then
the city Kiev & for its consecration choosing
the immense dark & gold & lovely Saint Sophia

for the apostolic coincidences that bring
dozens together into one   for the verity
that bread is indeed torn flesh   that wine
is blood   that we eat it & drink it & it is His

for after seven years the unexpected release
of the idiot   or the immense discovery of small
& slowly found out stars   or dreams that are not
rehearsed & cannot be written down or remembered

for the color of the apples & the taste of the sweet
milk   for the large grapes & cool waters   for the still
of the blue of the mountain that turns into the sky
or the small purple flowers that become honey

for slim wire bridges that grow down & thick & across
wide stretches of open sea   for the birds making
the great northern migration   for the lights
shimmering like thin icebergs in the crisp
   midnight & winter

for small red clay dolls   or colors that make up the light
that gives the face & portrait shadows & humanity   for this
& for the sound divinities that brood & govern here
for Zion that is coming & these latest years

for fifty years at least of music let us sing

A Hymn to God
the Holy Ghost

everything suffers by the comparison
a bird   shot down   how brown   how
much   how red the tie that grows   that covers
his chest   that binds his lungs
down & in.

whatever does not suffer out the blood forgets
or does not understand   or will not see
what cannot blend together   merge   for which
there can be no coming together
of elements.

the dew drops from the fingers
that reach the water in the baptismal font
the Father is the wetness of it   the Son
the dropping of it   the Ghost that moves
the water that once moved the wheel
that moves the rest the outside edge
so fast it spins away   that
brooded once & formed   & now
the cohesion that holds the atoms together that
elemental stuff that holds the neutrons
in the center   the protons   in the center
in the center   no still point   but the point
that holds the whole of creation
the center of attraction   the Ghost
the one without whom chaos at the best
and nothing or less than nothing otherwise.

Breaking Trinity

if there is to be rain
there first must be
the high falls of the yellowstone
& their thick mists   knocking
the edges from the colors of the rocks
rock into rock & breaking
water breaking water

things must break down
the fire pine   the cones
& seed that will not seed unless
the fire breaks the mountain
& the rocks   the ocean
that must break the rocks   breaking
waters breaking rock to land

that the blind pigs plunged that
the fig tree faded   if
the dinner is to mean anything first
there must be breaking break
the bread into moist
flesh & break the dark
red wine to blood

Star in the East

in this declining time & in this night
of achings of the bones & in the dark
the sound of wood or something that must break
breaks with the bones & overhead a star
fights for the right to shine with a streetlight
which wins because it's nearer where the roads cross

& its light doesn't have to in the night
go quite so far to get here or to cross
200 miles of rainy air at night
that not to mention fighting out the light
distractions on the way from now to daybreak
although there doesn't seem to be a star

besides this one to shine on this black night
& that bothers not a little one star
enough to poke light in the eyes & cross
the room & hope for sleep in darkness break
that bothers worries even in the dark
things far off seem much clearer in the light

it bothers more than simply that the night
obscures so much that shows up in the light
& this so little light one single star
uneasiness about it & the dark
unsettles thoroughly & not just cross
but genuinely fearful of the break

of mind that if it comes will come at night
the singleness that is intolerable will break
& consolation will not come with light
the border where the mind & terror cross
grows close in solitude unless the star
impossible to take would be the dark

& in this night & in this frightening dark
something must break & suddenly the star
& in its light the shadow of a cross

Fred W. Tamminga

Christmas Couplets
with Bells On

My bells, my tongues, my instruments of dust,
no longer need that tonal echo chamber,

that iron lung of spirits which possessed
my ding-dong mouthpiece, instrument of ramble:

making my dusty rattling into chi-
ming angel tongues—dust amplified by

dustbound electronics, made divine
by dustbound breath of demons—iambic lies!

No longer, no longer, no longer, Praise the Lord!
I hear it again: that dust-in-forming Word,

that stable sound transmitted from a stable
without the static stumblingblocks of babel,

without the spirits of the "air that kills,"
without the frothy unfulfilling fills

of supernoisy nothing. The Word is Flesh!
now hallelujahing through my hollowness

clear as an uncracked bell inside the lungs,
clear as a cosmos lingering on my tongue,

clear as a noiseless flame in wasteland trees,
clear as a cloud singing ahead of me . . .

Clear Tone, clear tone, making permissible
the touching of the Bell Invisible—

touch it and you are touched to chime
and shake with songs the spirits of this time

and clang the fog of ding-dong tongues away
that prophesy the night throughout the day

and keep you bound in chambers of pell-mell
full of the latest sound ... but not the Bell:

the Bell which calls you back to the Beginning
when our vibrating father stood there, ringing

the *name* of every Word-created thing,
giving it singing substance, making it sing

with Bell-toned modulations—as it must
to keep from being wildernessing dust.

I need a Bell to sound out jubilant Names
when I am busy ringing names in dust—

even my tongue-tied wilderness of dust
is ready now to wait upon its name.

The Messenger

A man has strolled into our quiet street.
He sees the tongue of fire above our houses:
a wind supreme comes on, surrounds him, rushes
majestically upon him—no retreat.

Above, around, heaven's vault now looses
its stench and smog and smoke: the sun depletes
herself in puffs of dark; thundering sheets
of stored-up fire spilling from their sluices.

"This is the day... !" his screaming voice is grim
and screams again. But who can hear his words?
Where are the people: children, men and women?

So with a howl that rips his vocal chords
(the trees are torches now, the parks are flaming)
he calls upon the mighty Lord of lords.

Quatrains for
a Christmas Card

The Christmas lines I write should be
like keenly cutting scimitars
that hack into the flummery
of angel hair and paper stars

of dainty shepherds crowding round
and kneeling by a stable birth
of singing voices that resound
of peace that shall fulfil the earth

of wise men who came riding high
on horse and camel from afar
their eyes upon the southern sky
in which they saw a falling star

of all deceitful sentiment
of candlelight and claret wine—
the birthday toast to Christ's descent
our purring way of feeling fine.

Because we feel as little guilt
as killers in the Herod horde
our hand sits ready on the hilt
our faith depends upon our sword

we want more blood upon demand
and war each Godforgotten day
and raging through each other's land
behead the child that's in our way.

O I can't go on. I have to sing
of starlight and a baby mild
and shepherds who come scurrying
to be still closer to the Child

of manna from an opened sky
above the town of Bethlehem
and wise men who came riding high
and angels' voices calling them.

He came! To give me love to give.
I know my shroud of death is torn—
what could I write, what could I live
if Jesus Christ had not been born?

Jan De Groot
trans. Fred W. Tamminga

about death and life

a kernel of wheat is sweet
and silences hunger
but a kernel of wheat must die
to give new kernels life

a kernel of grain is sweet
again and again
as long as new kernels appear
again

but for the kernel's life
a kind of death is needed

bread of life

a kernel of grain is hard
and tough as life
but death goes on
a kernel of grain stills hunger
even in those who die
like grain

there seems to be no end to this
life and death
death and life
death living on life
and life on death

but our lord was raised from the dead
this is the end of it
he does no longer die
he is bread
for the dead

whoever will eat
is filled with life:

hard and sweet
complete

about god with us

god is so great
he can become the size of a child

god is so mighty
he can become as helpless
as a human baby

god is so wise
he can lie on earth
without a sign of intelligence

god is so holy
he can come down
to dwell among men

god is so rich
he can become poor
and go in debt for us

god is so full of mercy
he lets jesus share his life with ours:
taking the guilt of ours into his
feeling the pain of ours in his
making the sadness of our life his

being with us
to be whipped for us
being with us
to be spit on for us

being crucified for us

Ballad of the Dragon

"For we are not ignorant of his devices."

The tale to be sung has a phantasy voice,
but it is as true as the sound
of brimstone rain and snakes on the brain
when the Dragon is stalking around.

Because of this tale the Dragon is bound—
the Dragon without a name,
for his name corroded the moment he sowed
his horrible seed of shame.

His name shall be fed to the ravening flames
that leap from his own spread jaws,
as soon as the song of right and of wrong
has cursed him before the Law . . .

For he goes on trial upon the white plain—
no shadows in which to disguise—
with his heart as the snare: for his heart will be bare
in all of its barbedwire lies.

For once in his life the Dragon must sing . . .
not whisper or sizzle or roar—
and the words he must say will burn him away
as a fraudulent troubadour.

Henrietta Ten Harmsel

Creation

The world is like a lute which God has strung
With strings invisible; the heavens around
Make up the ridged and arching board of sound,
The music-hole, the rhythmic moon and sun.
  The surging ocean and the moaning earth
Are giant basses both; the gentle breeze
Makes up the higher strings; the moving trees
And animals fill out the middle choir.
  This lute the Master struck with learnèd fingers,
The angels formed a band of skillful singers,
The mountains leaned to listen, floods stood still;
  But man alone hears neither strings nor voice
Unless the sovereign Lord makes him His choice
By His determined counsel and His will.

Jacob Revius
trans. Henrietta Ten Harmsel

Brazen Serpent

Swollen with venom of the deadly snake,
Hot as the hellish flames that never cease,
We dragged along the ground and found no peace
Until we saw Thee dying for our sake.
  O fangless serpent, hanging on the tree,
Soft'ning for us the grimness of God's face,
Thou giv'st the faith by which we dare embrace
Thy holy cure, and be embraced by Thee.
  Our sin, now sinless, Thou hast come to bury,
Our sickness loaded on Thyself to carry,
Become a worm down-trodden with the foot.
  O draw us up to Thee, teach us to feel
How Thou hast crushed the serpent with Thy heel
By offering for us Thy flesh and blood.

Jacob Revius
trans. Henrietta Ten Harmsel

Bloody Sweat

Lazy soul, why yawn so deep,
Gape and sleep?
Waken now and follow me.
See, your Bridegroom now has gone
To the lone
Garden of Gethsemane.

See how your Creator weeps,
Bends, and creeps
Underneath your load of sin.
A thousand-thousand crimson tears
Trickle here
From His tearing, bursting skin.

Ah, His sweat is really blood,
Like a flood,
Streaming forth from every limb.
All the earth can drink her fill,
If she will,
Of those drops that fall from Him.

When I look, I notice, too,
That this dew
Colors stem and leaf and bud.
That carnation once snow-white
Now is bright
With dark spots of crimson blood.

That white rose now shoots a bud
Red as blood,
Those pale tulips, in their turn,
Are transformed (Is it not so?)
Row by row,
And like bright flamboyants burn.

But what is that flower fair
Springing there
From this holy, bloody ground?
Lovely flower that will replace
By its grace
All the flowers that can be found.

"Jesus' goodness and His love
Spreads above
All who sorrow for their sin"—
In its name, surpassing sweet,
Rich, replete,
Healing balm for helpless men.

Sorry soul, which in me moans,
Grieves and groans,
Keep this flower in memory.
Do not seek it everywhere,
Only there:
Garden of Gethsemane.

Jacob Revius
trans. Henrietta Ten Harmsel

Suffering of Christ

From nothing to bring forth the round creation,
To force the raging sea to keep his bounds
The rising and the setting sun his rounds—
These are the signs of endless domination.
   But greater still, O Christ, that You should leave
The spotless halls of heaven for sinners' filth,
Debtless to pay their debts from Your great wealth
In hellish agony and deadly grief.
   O, could we rightly fathom this great feat!
What stony rock would then not melt with heat!
What heart would not with love be wounded through!
   But no; no man nor angel, Lord, can know it;
You, Lord, alone to us can ever show it,
For none has ever known this pain but You.

Jacob Revius
trans. Henrietta Ten Harmsel

He Bore Our Griefs

No, it was not the Jews who crucified,
Nor who betrayed You in the judgment place,
Nor who, Lord Jesus, spat into Your face,
Nor who with buffets struck You as You died.
   No, it was not the soldiers fisted bold
Who lifted up the hammer and the nail,
Or raised the cursèd cross on Calvary's hill,
Or, gambling, tossed the dice to win Your robe.
   I am the one, O Lord, who brought You there,
I am the heavy cross You had to bear,
I am the rope that bound You to the tree,
   The whip, the nail, the hammer, and the spear,
The blood-stained crown of thorns You had to wear:
It was my sin, alas, it was for me.

Jacob Revius
trans. Henrietta Ten Harmsel

Nancy Thomas

Hard God

Candles and rose light
through cathedral glass
poorly define Him.
No gentle picker of pale
violets in grass.
No wandering shepherd
breathing wisdom and hymns
in shaded vale.
Let it pass.

I serve a hard God.

Liken Him to a raging fire.

Remember Him
forcing Pharaoh higher
to cliff's edge,
then to churning sea;
see Him swallowing Korah
in an extemporaneous tomb;
recall His intended pyre
to be built
from His erring
but chosen sons,
quenched only by Moses' plea.

I serve a hard God.

He walks a stern path
through the earth.
His voice roars
in thunder,
giving birth
to terror;
oceans leap
in His wake
waves are hurled
mountains quake—
desolations are His footprints
in the world.

He is hard
and His way was stone,
tough and free
from gentility
   like nails
driven through bone
and splintered to a tree.

He thunders and kills
from below, in, above;
He consumes all dross.

He is stern
like love
and hard
like a cross.

Maranatha

Behind closed doors we crouched,
our fear, a festering sore;
no words to ease the agony
of a lost cause

when suddenly,
unhoped for and unheard of,
He simply
was there

alive
and love
and really God.

And still
His death lies dead;

His life
(defying all doors and doubts)
is ours.

Glory!

Individuation

There are no xeroxed copies in Your world.
Every grassblade wears its own private vein
pattern, though cast in a similar mold.
Each sunset and each drop of silver rain
is eternally original; each
leaf dances newly its own wind caper.
I give thanks in knowing Your creation
is not limited by plans on paper
schedules or inflexible charts, but free
You walk and touch this land. Not bound by Same,
each tiny babe is a first event, a
new thing, and all Your children wear Your Name
uniquely. For the multitude of ways
You fashion and fill and move and love—Praise!

The Leader

He comes, The Leader, with much applause
and turning of heads and scraping—
bring out the candles and celebrity damask!
(Color the carpet red,
the ride first class,
the bills paid.
Color his face smiley in the morning papers.)
For He's here our great our only
our venerated Christian VIP!
So spread the banquet rich and pungent
and politely munch and listen
to his poised and perpendicular words
on world poverty the whole man
healing helping loving feeding
(please pass the shrimp cocktail).
Render to Him His due acclamation.
    And meanwhile gently ignore the other—
the servant the sufferer the lowly lamb
watching in sorrow from behind
the potted geraniums.

Three Prophets

1. JONAH

Schooled in a strict tradition
of evenly positioned
high/low notes,
governed by definite rules,
Jonah's song had
few grace notes.
Wrath set the rhythm
all the way down
his short scale
with no room for change
once the pattern was set.
Is it any wonder, then,
he failed to understand
and grumbled at
the Musician's
last-minute reorchestration?

2. OBADIAH

Hear, proud people,
sequestered in your
high red rocks!
Your birthright bartered
centuries past,
think you yet to reign?
Did your wise men
so counsel you
to double-cross Jerusalem,
crush your once kinsman?
If so, duplicity
will yet
be Esau's bane.

3. AMOS

You dirty sheepherder!
How dare you
assault us with your verbiage,
hurl adjectives like garbage
at our coiffured heads!
We are the hope
of Israelite society,
making our homes
in the hilly
Samarian suburbs,
prodding our mates
to production,
gathering gold and glory
for our young.
"The poor," you rant,
"you crush the poor and needy!"
We say, "Let the poor
crush themselves!
Impediments to progress,
our land exceeds in such.
Stomp them out!
We are God's favored."
Why do you throw
your countrified insults
at us?
"Cows," you scream,
"fat cows of Bashan,"
jealous no doubt
for your own scrawny sheep.
Your metaphors wear the mood
of your meager background.
Be gone, pitiful prophet,
with your wild words
of meathooks and cattle.
God sees our sacrifices,
would not dare touch us.
We are His future.
We herald His kingdom
with wealth and wine for all.
Back to your mangers and mutton!
Your words are fare fit
for the fields you hail from
and foreign
to our spangled ears.

Defunct

You, Dagon!
Fainting, famished god
of Philistia's victory,
you've fallen from your throne,
trembling before the unbidden guest,
the gilded house
of the Hebrew Deity.
Palmless, you pay your obeisance.
Headless in Ashdod,
even you acknowledge Him
who is no usurper
but King and Lord
over Shiloh over Gaza and beyond,
who though captured,
cannot be contained
but spins and splinters
in and away from
your hapless temple,
who vindicates His holiness
on those who would steal
such strange booty.
Tell them, Dagon, how much better
to have lost the war!

Ezekiel Saw His Wheel

Ezekiel saw his wheel,
Daniel his clay-footed man.
Isaiah puzzled people
with words of stripes and lambs;
and woolly John
shouted his slant on the Light.
All Your children
have new eyes
and different
ways of
daring their dreams
into action.
And here am I, Lord.
Wipe the mist
from my eyes.
Roll back the stone
that blocks my mouth
and resurrect my voice.
Help me
to see and say
my own
my unique
vision.

Meditation on
I Peter 1:3–4

Rooted in red-rich dirt,
resurrection soil,
my hope is a green and living thing:
a wide willow
offering respite from summer's heat;
a blossoming sorrel
left to surprise squirrels and deer mice;
a licorice fern.
It has definite structure and hue,
real edges define it,
its roots are credible.
Tiny fingers stroke moisture/life
from the ground.
Each single cell drinks light and air,
releases an energy green and good.

My hope is a young sequoia.

Slender now,
its trunk will thicken
in a larger garden—
a sure inheritance.

My hope enriches Eden's slopes.

John H. Timmerman

Isaiah

An old man possessed by visions
in an age of dreamers, wandering
Isaiah called out to the winds:
  "Hear, O heavens, and give ear
    O earth,
  For the Lord has spoken."

The people would not hear the words
of the Lord, and Isaiah's voice
was lost at the silent center
of a raging world that spoke the
foreign tongue of misunderstanding:
  "Come now,
    let us reason together.
  Though your sins are like scarlet,
    they shall be white as snow."

In the desert no meaning roots
and flourishes. Here all was fire,
not the promise of snow. Here all
was wrath, not the promise of peace.

It was this emptiness between
fire and snow that Isaiah was called
to fill; his vision God's Word
to arrange the blank space into
promised joy: "The wolf
    shall dwell with the lamb,
    and the leopard shall lie down
    at ease with the kid,
    and the calf and the lion,
    the beasts of the wild with beasts of the field
    shall graze at ease on the meadows.

  And a child—
    a little child shall lead them."
A child, grasping real unicorns
in his arms, shall lead the lions,
shall give form to the impossible peace.

Isaiah, grown lean and tired in the desert,
  muzzy beard broken about the face,
  eyes blazed by the sun,
  temples hollowing and frail,
you taunt the pharaohs,
adjure the peoples,
lift that cracked voice in prophecy
that we still fail to understand.
We long to see its fulfilling, unable
to conceive of the child at ease with lions.

    "To us a son is given."
We are all the parents of Christ
according to your promise, Isaiah.
Time, you harsh midwife,
arrange our eternal validity
on the long awaited artwork of Isaiah's promise;
deliver anew this promise into fulfillment.
    Isaiah alone in the desert of time;
the voice cries in the wilderness
pointing to this impossible child
promising the peace of God.

Tracking Fields

From our back door the white fields roll
away against hills that tumble
into the sky. Along rills cold
snow-aged sycamores stumble
darkly into morning sun, gold
and glistening with frozen light.
    In his bobbing splash of red
    snowsuit my young son tramples
    down the tinder-weeds that lie
    hidden beneath the snow.
    I dash wildly in his footprints
    and seem to find the presence
    of another child going before me
    on this new morning. Like the sun
    he points the way on paths trailing
    through cold, wild fields. Lord,
grant to me
the power to fall in step
with this priceless child; reset
my hesitant steps to free
me in the glory of your dawning light.

Nancy Todd

Covenant Celebration

We drink the cup
Of clinging red—
Sin-stained glass
For God's blood.

As we stare into the clotted cup,
The wine becomes
Ancient pages
About
Garden and fruit
Serpent and sacrifices
Flood and rainbows
Jews and manna
An Exodus and a Cross—
About
A chosen race
The body of Christ
A peculiar people
Living stones

Gathered at the marriage supper of the Lamb
Feasting on the Living Bread and Wine
Offering praise
To a Lion
To a Shepherd
To a Rock
To a Morning Star
To Jesus Christ, the Son of God.

Smiling Eyes Approach All Pain

Smiling eyes approach all pain, all delusion, all death.
Bright sun, cool breeze, birds praise, flowers praise,
Tears praise, I praise. O Bright Morning Father of all
Glories, You are All-Suffering Father.
Sunshine lemon-light pain seeps, absorbs into the Creation
And we are it and we are in it,
Suffering, weeping, thirsting, starving, shivering, afraid,
Confused, angry, deluded, complacent.
Tear-stained, dirt-stained, hoping over the edge of a
Hillside, peering, squinting, fidgeting, watching.
Oh come. Come back! Please return!

Deep within, hard muscular contractions push out of the body
An agonizing whisper: "How long, O God, how long this
Futility, this absurdity, this slavery to corruption?
Birds balanced on branches look up, all insects and reptiles
peer around, all small furry and furless animals twitch
and fidget, all horned and hoofed, four-legged beasts watch,
And some humbled, hoping human beings long anxiously and
wait eagerly for:
THE REVELATION THE ADOPTION THE REDEMPTION OF
   BODIES.
Waiting, looking, watching anxiously, eagerly, with
Persevering rhythm we work and live.

Cornelius Van Bruggen

March Message

As March pours out a blend
Of sleet and baleful scuds,
Our maples twist and bend,
But hold their swollen buds.

Creation's God endows
These tough old dooryard trees
With spirit in their boughs
To burst with prophecies.

Shall He, Who brings to wood
The rich elixers of
Full life, not move to highest good
Our buds of faith and love?

Sandy Van Den Berg

Easter Morning 10:00 A.M.

God, do You ever
die inside, Your thoughts extending to
the person next to You
in the pew, calmly singing
of love that reaches up, but only echoes in
the anthem of
a thousand voices singing
"I serve a risen Savior,"
in the sanctuary tomb?

God, am I nothing
but dull wax
stopped mid-point and stuck
to the side of a burning candle
for You?

Then melt me,
God,
till I burn
strong again.

Sunset Crucifixion: Camera Shot

A tall reed in the wind sways slowly.
I will go home and take up the hammer,
Take up the nails and pound it to wood,
Pound it to wood, steadily, slowly—
A picture frame ready
To hang on the wall.

A bright crimson sun dries blood down slowly;
Clinging, it dies at the fading of day.
I will go home and take up the hammer,
Take up the nails and pound it in wood—
Steadily, slowly, a picture on wood,
Ready to hang on my living room wall.
Here by the sofa, high by the drapes,
Keep pounding, keep pounding
This picture called "Grace."

Debbie Vandenburg

Malnutrition

The bread became dry and stale,
The meat tough and rancid,
And the skimmed milk soured
By waiting too long.
We gorged on candies and pastries,
And, now, food vital for nourishment
Is no longer appetizing.
We need to change our eating habits,
For we are dying of malnutrition.
As hunger pangs increase,
Let the aroma of fresh-baked bread
And cooked choice cuts of meat
Fill the room once again.
Then we will eat to appease our hunger,
Drink the cold, refreshing milk,
And bow our heads in gratitude.

"Thy words were found, and I did eat them;
and thy word was unto me the joy
and rejoicing of mine heart" (Jer. 15:16).

Randall VanderMey

Easter

Nation after nation came
One by one, up the path,
Past the mailbox
And the picket fence, past the petunias,
Past the sign "Beware of Dog,"
Past the bulldog sleeping
With a smile on his face.
Each one came in turn
And stood on the welcome mat

And pounded in a nail, one at a time.
One through the foot, one through
The hand. A big shot from New York
Came and smacked one
Through the kidney. The kids came up
With sticky hands and took
Their licks. Bam. "Junior's got
Good hands, Marge, don't you think?"
Marge was busy pounding.
She bent the nail.
The policeman came up.

"Just one, lady. Get along."
He went away, up and down the long line
That stretched for centuries.
"Don't push. You there, come with me."
Etcetera.
Until only the sweeper was left.
Until what had been
A spread-eagled body
Lying whiter than a wedding invitation
Looked more like some kind of
Crazy iron armadillo,
There were so many nails.

Dark came and the winds came trampling
Out of the east
Like bulls. The moon looked
The other way. But then it grew,
Like an idea, huge and red,
Wavy with heat.   ►►►►

Everything panicked. Trees shrieked
And withered in the moon's heat.
Birds rose like helium balloons.
Telephone poles popped like corks.
The night was brighter than
A hamburg stand.
The night was hotter than
A hamburg stand.

At last
There came a popping sound
And nails were popping off
The crazy iron armadillo
Like buttons. All the nails.
Fizzing high into the air
Like Roman candles,
Until the spread-eagled body
Once again lay white,
Rising like bread.
And the world and all the nations
Peeled away.

Charles Van Gorkom

Be Still and Know That I Am God!

When the sun flaunts JEHOVAH'S Glory—
Flings a splash of color at the fleeced sky
That mounts in angry metamorphosis
Into glowering dragons swinging through the night;
When the buzzing roof-top ventilators
Of the tallest buildings burn out to shadows,
And descending solitude like falling rain
And nervous tobacco smoke bury the huddled day . . .

When dusty winds usher fits of frosted rain
Past hotel windows, torn curtains,
Faded prize-fight posters in the alley,
Blearing burning eyes with ice,
Flapping coattails as you wander,
While the city warmly curls her toes
Before her private fires
And the wind moans lonely . . . lonely . . . lonely
You creature of no place day or night,
Then come!

When busy lighted stores
Promise but evade
And you walk
And walk the shimmering sidewalks
In the fitful rain,
When your heart so cries
You suddenly run across the streets,
Blind, green light or red—
Then come, says the Word, to Me
    you know My address
And I will give you rest.

Joe Veltman

Love Looks

Serpent-haired
Medusa's stare
when returned
turned men
to stone.

God said, "Moses, make
a crossed snake,
bronze-cast
to cast the Serpent
out."

My father
the butcher
knew something
of slaughtering
lambs—

they stare.
But he who dares
to look
must love
the Lamb.

Eve 2

When brought at first this bride
from sleeping Adam's side
she was born of bone and flesh.

When bought again this bride
into Wounded Adam's side
she's born of blood and water.

On the Eve
of Snow White

The sign read
red-delicious apples
still-life red

she was deceived
to eat
then less naive
feared the worm

and shared the spoil.
The cross-section
was like a cloven hoof
unclean

she slept

and was transplanted
in time
to see
a cross implanted

in a skull
pitted with worms,
but undeceived saw
where the hill

was cloven
clean
through
the root of the tree

where hangs a sign
red, delicious apples
still life-red

she awakens

and is Christened
Snow White.

Upon Viewing

Upon viewing someone's remains, whose body, having turned into soap, lies on display at the Smithsonian Institute. His name has been changed to protect the innocent.

Was he, was he perhaps an old man, old
and fond of telling tales already twice retold?
And was it then for looking overmuch
behind that he was preserved in transit,
entranced by some devil-wizardly spell
that turned to soap the senile cells of his
arrested rot, the mottled brown of stale chocolate?

A Puritan perhaps, afraid the Lord
refused such clothed as he could afford—
his knee socks, still drawn to the proper height,
need one final washing; his abdomen
gives a faint blush, being thus exposed to sight.
Some half-wit sculptor, then, rewarded modest
virtue by soap-unsuiting him for either world.

We could resolve to take up this crude matter,
scrape, bleach, and wire his bones together,
dissolve, refine his mumified adipose,
compose a new improved John Ogaldon
and say indeed that he arose
just barely within the pale of resurrection
with all the veracity of white chocolate.

But having re-defined John Ogaldon,
there still remains the fine question,
What washing will resolve this same
John Ogaldon to his original blush
and not compromise his definite name—
Ogaldon, John: "beloved of God"?
Such washing, I fear, will call for blood.

Clarence Walhout

Wings

My father's pigeons opened
their white wings with joy
each morning when he took the stone
away from the opening of their cage.
Soaring overhead, now lost in the sun,
now floating downward, they held
their wings in blessing.
"Look at Keery," he said, holding out his hand,
"he comes when I call him."

Lament

A single piper shivers
    by the sea
A single gull circles
    listlessly
    in a sinister sky
A single lighthouse flings
    its intermittent call
    to silent ships slinking
    along the serrated knife-edge
    of the horizon

    In our sorrow, Lord, comfort us
    In our desolation, Lord, console us
In the chill of winter
    Be to us Immanuel
In the still of midnight
    Be to us Elohim

Then will we live as shriven souls
    Holding your wholly holy hand

Jacob

What fatherly foolishness
Wove itself into your aging brain
To fashion there a many-colored coat?
Did not the laddered steps to heaven
Burn their rungs into your feet?
Could you no longer see the dancing
Angels with their great white wings?
You held God in your youthful arms.
How could you lose the vision?
That coat, that rag, that unforgivable
Piece of earth, garb of an old man's folly.
The flesh and the world, Rachel and her children,
Meant more to you than millions
Of your God-obsessed descendants.
How could you let God slip through the slits
Of a blood-stained robe and die
In the cities of Egypt?
Deceiver to the end!
For how many centuries must we labor now
To find the God you lost?

I was a deceiver, yes, my son,
But let me tell you this:
That night I wrestled with God
He touched my side and lamed me.
That night I dreamed of heaven
I woke with a crook in my neck.
My weakness let me see
The beauty of the well-proportioned body.
I admired the buoyant limbs of my children,
The gracefulness of my lovely Rachel;
I saw the date palm sway in the wind
And the swallow dance in the sky,
The fig tree grow in the springtime
And the waters of Elah ripple under
The blue of the heavens.

No, I have not forgotten the white angels' wings
And the touch of angel flesh on mine,
But I see around me the touches
Of the hands of God that cripple the dreams of men
And turn them to the earth.
I did not betray you, my son.
You, too, shall come to know the love of wife and sons.
ou, too, shall discover your dreams
Wrapped in the folds of a many-colored coat.

New Moon

When the deft darkness
descends
into the small places
under the trees
and behind the careless stems
of ragweed
crowding out the light
and pushing vision back
till only the mind
can see,
when the stillness
of nightfall
quiets the robin's voice,
and leaves press silently
against the slate-grey sky
till only the mind
can hear,
when the mind folds inward
closed like a rosebud
till it can neither see
nor hear,
then Lord
give your sweet children peace.
Let no fond human voices
wrench unwilling ears.
Let no glad faces
smile in artificial light.
Let no foolish tinkers pry
at the sealed compartments of the mind.
Only let light return in the morning.
Only let birds begin again to sing.
Only let roses open to the warm
and rock-rending sun.

Jeanne Murray Walker

A Bestiary for the Birth of Christ

I. THE FROG

Ferns steam and boil beneath the sun.
The cypress tree lets down its hair.
The summer lull waits to begin
Till gold has fallen everywhere.

I sit beneath a leaf's dark toe
And listen to the apples swell.
Sprung from what bright, I do not know,
I ponder in this noon of cool.

I do not know what apples mean,
Why mosses foam upon the stones,
Nor why the man's eyes flame with sun,
Nor why his pulse blooms in my veins.

But still the garden fills my ear.
The apple nestles in the air,
Humming its color, sharp, gay, near,
Till silence loses poise and then

The night lies deep, but nagged by doom,
The gold cracks. And through that gap
Time pours its minutes. In a dream
I close my bottom eyelid up.

The swindle snake slips from his hole.
"Malice. Malice." It is done.
With that word, ferns turn into coal
And God becomes a man.

II. THE COW

The wind strolls and licks my bones
with its rough tongue as I lie dimming
in the moonlight on this desert.

All for me is desert now and I all bone:
A thigh whining like a piccolo
in the impartial, sliding sand.

➤➤➤➤

I am the sand's foundering ship.
It barks its shins on my skull.
I go down to drowning with my knowledge.

Five years ago, in the season when the locusts
split their skins, I stood lowing in the stall.
I tell you, He was the Son of God.

Now time buzzes through my bridge.
There is no heaven for cattle.
My collarbone arches, hollow, hollow.

III. THE RAVEN

I am a raven, most highly developed of birds,
            order *Passeras,*
            family *Corvidae,*
            a bird with a wingspan exceeding a yard
            and a well-tailored sense of irony.

I flew over the waters from Noah
and helped Flokki locate Iceland,
but since Poe my policy has been "Nevermore."

From my height I have surveyed the frog and the cow.

      The frog, natural enemy of the snake, has in his own way
      related the myth that says malice snapped the branch
      of eternity which, crashing end over end,
      scattered us off our perch into lurid time.

      The cow longs for salvation, believing that such exists.
      Not having been present in the stable myself,
      how can I authorize the reliability of a witness who was?

I, who am able to fly, know eternity when my wings slice it.
Time is the meat in the stubble between hedgerow and wire fence.
If the most capable of all birds cannot pick God out of the air,
we must learn to be satisfied with meat.

Only occasionally the wise, frail eyes of the
fieldmouse disturb me and
sometimes I grow
dizzy.

She Did

scheme of terrible softness
sleepier than her sandals, her home's rafters,
Joseph's beard, any rough child's bed
she had heard of.

she knew the clash and scratch of dirt
on her pretty ears and eyes and mind
(don't pray that she didn't)
and subtracting them swiftly she found

terrible softness gentling her senses so
she wished on that
sweet imagined something
for a place to lay the child

who flung and spun and
pulsed like wild blood
in her memory and her mother-mind
and her transformed body.

She did scheme. But some king
blew the bugle that started her down the road
to Bethlehem, and no dream
bore up under that brutal ride.

When she came to the time
where she thought softness waited
the place of her dream had changed, and she laid
her child in the clash and scratch of dirt

but knew what she forgot to scheme
when she looked at that night's humpbacked moon
   and crazy star:
that no old dream, no rafters, no ruin matters
   much when
God needs you to hold His hand.

Light, Everything Is Light

GENESIS 2:21-24

From bells to bells I progress into day.
The first bell falls upon the pale sidewalks
of sleep: jangle of newsboy's bike. I finish up
my dream (a midget eating the sun with a fork),
descend to my body where I find my tongue
cracked and stiff again. I wait. It moves. It swabs.
My arm comes to itself. I throw an absent-
minded leg across your thigh. Our thighs
together light the bell of the alarm,
which flares. Hello, body, flesh of my flesh.
The rosy morning starts, a palpitating
ring on growing ring. How could my body,
dumb as iron, articulate such light
unless its clapper were the very sun?

Holy Night

Chicago. This place may yet be Bethlehem.
Wheels unlace the streets all night,
silent on the strict ice. Listen. The hymn
of a drummer boy glistens and guts the neat
air. The shattered poor dream of God's clean
coming. The lake, shocked with cold
is torn, and the pocked buildings of Woodlawn
are torn. The ragged moon turns tired, old.

Yet briefly this place may be Bethlehem.
Chicago, two thousand years broken to peace,
waiting, wreathed and torn to be the home
of Christ. Christmas preys on this tired place.
Father, be with us in the ripping dark.
Send splints of angels, send the Child, and mark
the place we cheat the centuries, where we, weary,
kneel down in praise, arise in mended fury.

Sister Bertha

Who would guess that thin-breasted body
has wheezed Christ into three languages?
She walks down aisles to pews, an oddity
of God's redeeming grace; her sober thighs
are shut against all time and place and cause.
Who would guess her brambled hands held skies
matter-of-factly down to earth, spliced lengths
of heathen centuries to ours with their strength.

And who would guess that at night somewhere off in
a room where the loveliest thing is a fly that drones,
lying, her untouched body on a mattressed coffin,
she stares in the nervous dark, mad or blind,
a lover who primps her soul, and thinks whole poems
into a time and place out of mind.

Resurrection

Each time You go, I'm buried and I hear,
seething with honest worms, the truthful loam.
But coming again, You riddle at my ear
with promises of being in air, at home.
I'm comfortable enough, cupboarded in earth—
Oh, I would take the idiom of air:
sirens and chimes and mother's shrieks in birth
and silence in perpetual repair.
But repeated resurrection I can't bear.
Let me grow into death the way of a stone
Or let me wear the wind against my ear
eternally. I'm worried like a bone.
Above, I hear Your footsteps: in Your mouth
promises raucous as the sky when geese fly south.

Debbie Wallis

No Silent Night

It was not a silent night.
Men were questioning
what this strange starlight meant.
Others, roused in midst of their watch,
no longer questioned.
For their night was split
with the shock of a choir of angels
shouting, "Glory to God,
the Christ child comes!"

It was not a silent night.
It was a noisy confusing night.
The city was congested,
tempers were short,
the inns were crowded—all of them.
And Mary and Joseph—
what did their hearts cry
when they saw the lowly birth bed?

It was not a silent night.
His coming tore a woman's body.
His coming was hard—
dreadfully hard
for everyone involved.
His coming was not a mythical
anesthetized 20th century dream.
It was hard and cold.
It was heavy.

But it was not silent.
He forever split our darkness
with the proclamation of angels
that the Light of the world was shining.
That for all ages to come
we would know
that heaven is not silent.
For God has spoken.
He has come.

I'm Tired

i'm tired, so tired
i can't . . .
oh Lord, i can't go on.
i'm going down
and i'll never rise again.
what use am i
if i am lying in the dust?
if i am fallen in the pit?

are you tired indeed?
then come to me
for i am meek and lowly.
and if you would have rest,
then come to me
in lowliness of heart,
and i will give
an end of striving with yourself.
for i will give you
my precious burden
my easy yoke
for it is never you who till alone
nor carry by yourself.
so come to me
and i will give you a parched
and thirsty land to till
and i will give you rest.

Chad Walsh

The Stone Has Rolled Away

*"The Kingdom is
the Lord's" (Ps. 22:28).*

The stone has rolled away,
　The sun is bright and high
For colts and boys at play.
The stone has rolled away,
Make room for Easter Day.
　There's nothing left to die.
The stone has rolled away.
　The sun is bright and high.

Cereal Boxes

*"But as for me, I am a worm, and no man;
a very scorn of men, and the outcast of the
people" (Ps. 22:6).*

Cereal boxes and empty cans,
Corpses of dogs, and fleshless bones,
Chromium and rust of broken cars,
Shards of shattered bricks and stones

Be his garden, the last he will see,
A vertical beam for an olive tree.

Fires that Adam and Cain first lighted
Dully consume the shattered denials.
Here the rejected things of the earth
Come to the last of public trials.

Nailed to the sky in low relief
Thief and a God, God and his thief.

Hammer in hand, nails in my pocket
Here at the foot of the cross I stand.
Blood on the hammer, blood on my fingers.
Jesus, more blood, to dry my hand.

I Will Sing a New Song

"Thou art he that took me out of the womb" (Ps. 22:9).

I will sing a new song unto the Lord.
His glory has not worthily been spoken
Though every leafy tree and blade of grass
Whispers in wind to tell his hidden Name
And though the chipmunk, charged with sun and air,
Descends into his temple under earth

To say his prayers of praise. O choirs of earth—
Leaf, scale, feather, fur, hair—proclaim the Lord!
Set in movement the molecules of air.
Let the secret word openly be spoken,
Let the high echoes answer back the Name
And breath of angels furrow through the grass.

Though he has made me fleeting as the grass,
Though mole and I are shaped of brother earth
And to the earth return—O praise his Name,
All things that breed and die. Know he is Lord
Of the amino acids, and the word spoken
To dust raised Adam's eyes into the air.

For thou hast lifted me into the air
A little while, to tread the patient grass
With moving weight, and hear thy word spoken—
Eden, Sinai, the ends of any earth,
The cross into the skull. Speak the word, Lord,
The private word into my heart: thy Name.

O speak it now, and speak my hidden name
Planted in thee before birds broke the air.
Say who I am and introduce my Lord.
Ye little lives that nestle in the grass,
Slim creatures underground, wings above earth,
Be silent quickly, for the Lord has spoken.

Be clamorous quickly, for the Lord has spoken.
Sing in polyphony his public Name,
Descended out of heaven to the earth.
Say, sing, chant the Name of Jesus in air
kissing with Easter green the risen grass
That is the emerald carpet of the Lord.

The risen Lord has looked at me and spoken.
Though I am grass, he calls me by a name.
Sing high, bright air; praise him, brothers of earth.

Perhaps the Socrates

"Why hast Thou forsaken me?" (Ps. 22:1).

Perhaps the Socrates he had never read,
The Socrates that Socrates poorly understood,
Had the answer. From opposites, opposites
Are generated. Cold to heat, heat to cold,
Life to death, and death to life. Perhaps the grave's
Obscenity is the womb, the only one
For the glorified body. It may be
Darkness alone, darkness, black and mute,
Void of God and a human smile, filled
With hateful laughter, dirty jokes, rattling dice,
Can empty the living room of all color
So that the chromatic slide of salvation
Fully possesses the bright screen of vision.

Or perhaps, being Man, it was simply
He must go wherever man had been,
To whatever caves of loneliness, whatever
Caverns of no light, deep damp darkness,
Dripping walls of the spirit, man has known.

I have called to God and heard no answer,
I have seen the thick curtain drop, and sunlight die;
My voice has echoed back, a foolish voice,
The prayer restored intact to its silly source.
I have walked in darkness, he hung in it.
In all of my mines of night, he was there first;
In whatever dead tunnel I am lost, he finds me.
My God, my God, why hast thou forsaken me?
From his perfect darkness a voice says, I have not.

Fatherhood Is a School of Humility

FROM THE PSALM OF CHRIST

"My seed shall serve him" (Ps. 22:31).

Fatherhood is a school of humility, it corrects the soul.
Girls are the best school; I have four of them.
Sometimes when I look at them, I wonder where I fit in.
I might claim two noses, but their owners wouldn't
    thank me
For the gift. Alison's blond hair is hers, not mind;
When Demie plays the cello I cannot contend my poor
    recorder
Prenatally put music in her. Madeline dances ballet,
A straight queen, five foot three. My six feet stumble
    at a fox-trot.
And Sarah-Lindsay, when not shaking the house with her
    declarations
Does the serene acts of compassion and love with the grace
Of a soul that needs no schooling, forethought, or prompting.
In short, here they are, and I am glad. But where am I
    in them?
I was most in them at the start. The microscopic miracle—
Momentary, essential—was mine four times to assist.
It was as though four times I was able to help open
    a door,
And four bright spirits, assorted, entered from outer space.

Now they walk the four pilgrim paths, each in her own style.
What I have told and shown them of God is as transient
As the last year I could outswim Sarah in the race
    to the dock.
If they find God, or are found; if they have Him, or rather
If He has them, it is in four separate and secret ways.
Those doors are not mine to open. I do not knock.

Instead let me praise the fact. In any poem I write,
In my handwriting, or the way I build a bookcase
There is more of me than in Demie, Madeline,
Sarah, and Alison. They are a revelation
Not of me, but of the other Father. Glory and laud
Forever to Him who has given me more than a trinity
Of bright messengers, giggling with creation's first dawn,
In the ballet of a water fight between the float and the dock.

Two Hymns
Waiting for Music

1

Praise him loud and praise him lowly.
Sidewalks echo to his feet.
Praise him fast and praise him slowly,
Alley, avenue and street.
Praise the honking horns and whistles
Blaring forth the unknown God.
Praise the violets and thistles
Watered green by heaven's blood.

Praise him in the subdivisions.
Praise him in the city slum.
Praise him in the murdered redwoods
And the beating rains that drum
On the rooftops of our terrors
And the windows of our hopes.
Praise him in our truths and errors
And the ceaseless watch he keeps.

Praise him in the wolf and rabbit,
In the cockroach and the rat.
Praise him in the force of habit,
And the fires that level flat
All the suburbs of the manger
Till the kneeling kings are seen
Circled round the sleeping stranger
And the city streets blaze green.

2

London Bridge is falling down,
Empire State is lying flat.
All the works of hands and hammers
Lie in judgment at his feet.
Mortared stone in which we trusted,
Shafts of reinforced concrete
Prostrate on the earth before him
And the sky one crimson shout.

Shout of terror, shout of yearning
Rising from each city street.
Runways cracked and smoke from
    burning
Jets dissolving in their heat.
He is with us. Christ defend us
From the Christ of this return:
Savior, save us from your double,
From this Christ of burn, burn, burn.

See the sky's polluted evening
Washed to blue by crimson dyes.
See his hand that grasps the trowel,
See the rivets of his eyes.
In the debris of his judgment
Hear the fading moans and groans.
Rise into the air to meet him.
Be his temple's newfound stones.

David Waltner-Toews

If He Were Born Today

CHRISTMAS, 1974

winter night in palestine
clean and cold as polished steel

arabs rest their sheep
among rocks and thistles
like a patch of scruffy spring snow
on the hillside

somewhere behind them
in a desert cave
a small fire holds the vengeant night
at bay
men and women commune with clammy handshakes
and guns: the bread of death

below the shepherds
Israeli soldiers patrol the occupied city
stop to fidget at a small bar—
a sign at the city gate reads:
all arabs must register
with the military authorities
in the city of their birth

the shepherds, remembering the sign
joke about it;
they were born in tents
they do not leave their sheep

suddenly a rocket
sleek as a sacrificial blade
splits the belly of silence above them
exploding, shrieking into the streets below;
the streets answer with gunfire rattle
boots running on concrete
trucks
searchlights against the hills

the shepherds huddle behind a rock
their sheep are bleating, bleating

more rattle of guns

the bleating stops

lights out, motors choke into silence
boots stomp back to the bar
nervous laughter curls up like smoke
incense to the unspeaking
mask of night

down a cobbled alley
from the bar
in a small lean-to
anxious, calloused hands
are pushing some goats away
from their manger
nearby, on a bed of dirty straw
a palestinian woman groans
pushing with all her prayerful might
against the pain in her belly

Snowstorm

"I saw the Spirit coming down from heaven like a dove" (John 1:32).

A person could get lost
among these drifting cries and whispers,
the blinding purity of this vision, gift of a clouded heaven.

From his studio
the newsman says: no end in sight,
a bad night to be out,
stay home.

Under a swirling cone
of streetlamp
in the eye of a snow-curl
I find the four-pronged footprints.

The night is radiant with snow
white wings folding around me.
Somewhere, close at hand,
the sacred windbird,
kindly light of stormchildren,
is singing
peace
peace

Wald Heim

a poem to commemorate the centennial of the coming of a
large group of Mennonites to Canada in 1874

I

The Edens they carried with them
in a seed-bag of mother-tongue,
scattering, watering,
nurturing the past in a crop of names:
Rosenort, Grünthal, Waldheim.

Sometimes I can understand
their arrogance
their righteousness among the *English,*
the ungodly nonGerman speakers.
What man but a Philistine
would question: "Grunt thal?"
of "Forest Home you mean?"
Forest Home indeed!
The funereal moan of translation
could only be the work of godless men.

II

Waldheim: a cipher of aspen
bullrushes, foxtails—
green scrawl
of the inscrutable hand
on prairie parchment.
Ja, this is the place,
the old Prussia we carry with us
everywhere
like the doilies which make each sodhouse
and each suburban bungalow
home.
Here in this gulley on the high plateau
with the frogs
squawking Pintails and Canada Geese,
Low-German can flourish.
Here, our hearts can overflow with praise
even as the grain bins overflow.

III

They built churches,
stubborn wooden monuments
to the frailty of stomachs
and the inefficiency of horses,
brave witness to an overwhelming vision.

The coarse hands of brotherhood
joined here, the chapped hands of sisterhood.
Eyes, red with harvest dust,
turned inward,
traced fissures back into memory,
pored over frayed maps
in search of a lost vision.

The once-white churches
now flake under a scorching sun,
outposts in a long-forgotten war,
overgrown with Russian thistle.
Refugee souls huddle in church camps,
having once more failed to find
the land which was never promised.
In barb-enclosed pastures
the heifers kick up heels, impatiently,
and young bulls paw the ground.

But the vision—
where amid the wheat and raspberries,
the stubble, dust, and saskatoons,
the cold righteousness of snow—
where in all this was the vision?
Did they lift their heads, then,
and see? There were no hills—
but they were not abandoned.

IV

I have stood at the skirts
of stepmother city
to watch the holy ritual
of sun greeting horizon.
The primordial flame unleashes time,
throws the grey matter back into grey caves,
catacombs of the Ice Age
and the Thirty Years War   anabaptist cellars
of Friesland and Zurich   stakes where the Truth
branded our forbears indelibly:
And if I give my body to be burned,

➤➤➤

So be it.
The prairie sun is a laser,
burning through the vapour,
creating dazzling holographs:
icebergs   glowing gargoyles   blood on golden spearheads
colours are broken and scattered
upon the clouds   the piercing light creates
and destroys   the visions, enflamed,
shrivel to charred, enigmatic hieroglyphs
across the turquoise veil of evening.
No. No promises. Love demands Faith,
offers the terrifying possibility of everything,
the terrible possibility of nothing.

Did they worship this sun,
this giver of green life,
burning tongue of God?
They became children again—
I became a child again—
alone with the unspeakable Name,
pure voice of the wind at dusk.

Can you count how many stars
glitter in the vast, black dome?
They are the salt
which preserves us against Night.

Can you number the lonely children
in twilight wander-lost?
They are salt
drawing forth the flavour of earth's feast.

V

In Forest Home
they buried the seeds of history,
spread the compost of memory and righteousness
over semi-arid land.
Only if a seed empty itself to the black earth
will the children eat.   .
Oh, Parents, do not be afraid,
for we are the harvest.
We are the Wald Heim and the Grün Thal,
hybrid of clay and spring rain,
mutated by the Light of the World.
In a fellowship of seedlings
is the Kingdom born.

VI

The enlightening sun-borne vision
shall return us to the whole earth.
Morning like a Fräulein
shall gather each of us,
white and frail as eggs,
into her apron.
From the yoke of introspection
and a selfishness of blood
we shall be reborn,
radiant and vulnerable as new goslings.

Eugene Warren

Let Light Ride In
I JOHN 3:9

the divine *sperma*
verbal seed of
living light
        sown deep;
of that word
           born:

His seed remains
in you,
rooted, brancht
the foliage
        & harvest
of spilt Blood

          open
the gates
of yr skull / let light
ride in, conquer that
bone
      citadel   plant it
thick
      trees of healing
water from the throne
of split
        Rock

A Reason for Hammers
JEREMIAH 23:29

The strange beast
I used to be
         still hides
  in the back of a mirror
I find sometimes concealed
  in the pocket of
         my best suit.
  It is a dark & rusty
    mirror. I've had
  the pockets sewn shut
    but still feel an opaque
rectangle nicking my flesh
    with murky corner.
I smash the cloth with heavy steel
  but then the grains
  of dark reflection
    work thru my skin
  to become seeds of pain
    in my bloody garden.
These strange plants deceive no one.

On Bellini's
"St. Francis in Ecstasy"

The world under his bare feet
is shale, blue & gray,
rising to shine at the frame.

Beyond the walls of a distant city,
brown on a brown hill, a surf
of cumulus breaks against the towers.

At the hill's foot, a shadowy figure
guides a flock along a fence—
black brown grey and white;

Closer, a rock projecting from a bank
becomes a long-necked bird
that gazes across the fields

where a donkey stands listening
to the light. The saint's back
is to his cave; a rough frame of poles

canopied with vines encloses the door,
a plain desk holds a Bible and a skull.
Along the cliff's face a wall

of blue brick encloses a garden
of hardy plants, memorial
of the Garden walled with swords of flame.

Some small brown animal peers
from the bottom course of the wall,
looking astonied at the saint's bare feet.

Under the edge of Francis' rock shelf
a spout drains water from the cliff,
keeping the hermitage dry.

From this, Francis faces away:
head bared and tilted back,
his gaze goes beyond the frame,

beyond any visible focus;
but from that unseen point a light
falls to illuminate the whole scene
and pierce his open palms with joy.

A City to Come

FOR JACQUES ELLUL

Jesus on the road
    from Jerusalem
    to Jerusalem
bearing the mark
    of Wanderer

the mark Cain
    rejected, choosing to wear
    a city instead

Jesus casting the city
    behind him, choosing
    the road, hills, plain
    the sea & Jordan

    wearing dust & sunburn
    squinting at the sun
    for the time
      or lifting a finger
    to test the wind

Jesus fulfilling man's curse
    to wander, hearing
    the city's walls of noise
    shut against him

finding at last a place
    for his head
    a cross-taut chest
    for pillow

finding beyond the walls
a place
    where wandering ends
    where the curse
    is bled dry

    and out of the dust
    & stones, Abraham's
    children rise,

stones of light,
    raising a city
    unmarkt by Cain

Idols in a Museum

Skinny green goddesses
shrined in glass boxes—
incense-drencht, deep-carvd
temple walls
lit with hidden tubes—

a huge fresco of Buddha
& 10,000 flower worlds—
a weatherd statue
of a zen monk listening
to one foot passing—

before these bits of stone,
wood, fading paint,
pass the art students,
the noisy families who
don't hear the chants trappt
in old walls.

In their sterile air
the idols smell no
incense, devour no grain,
or blood . are fed
on the idle stares of tourists,
honord by the guide's lecture.

On another floor,
in a medieval chapel,
shadows genuflect
to a Christ fixt in wooden
agony—but the prints
of pierced feet lead out
to sunshine.

Christ Came Juggling

Christ came juggling from the tomb,
flipping and bouncing death's stone pages,
tossing those narrow letters high
against the roots of dawn spread in cloud.
This Jesus, clown, came dancing
in the dust of Judea, each slapping step
a new blossom spiked with joy.

Hey! Listen—that chuckle in the dark,
that clean blast of laughter behind—
Christ comes juggling our tombs,
tossing them high and higher yet,
until they hit the sun and break open
and we fall out, dancing and juggling
our griefs like sizzling balls of light.

All These Breads

all these breads—
matzo, rye,
tortillas, soft indian disks,
unbleached wheat—
broken, torn, snapped, crumbs
floating down from soft loaves
or popping up from the sheets
of perforated matzo—
these many grains
grown in red soils, black loam,
grey or yellow clay,
roots of wheat and oats
and barley and rye
probing dirt & rain,
the slender, parallel-veind leaves
arching in sun or lying
straightend in a strong wind—
crust, ground, rolld, sifted
at last becoming
all these breads—
one diverse loaf passing
from hand to hand,
dying into each mouth,
sprouting a new
& shining grain

Dancing the Rainbow

sharing covenant
with Rebecca,
grey December cat,
in downhill dance

lichens & moss
surrounded by sun
share covenant too,
afternoon spillings

of energy
oblations to the Creator
whose rainbow upholds
the scruboak

whose right hand uplifts
the ant
& feeds the zinging
wasp whose covenant

includes the poorest
stone, slowest beetle
& all the flaming nuclear
angels of the sun

among jackpine
& scruboak, we dance
within the rainbow-ring
of sure Promise

The Ironies of Love

The form is the track
of melody back-bent,
of words close-rankt
in orders meant to clothe
particular forces
in articulate forms.

The body's the soul
made visible, the outer dance
of identity, the glancing
self that darts and hides
where the trembling balance
decides for woe or health.

The infant Creator was
suckled by His created
mother—Deity conceived
in flesh and borne
by those He bore into Himself,
whom He received as He rose.

The face of Love shines
with irony that the world's
Sire became its child,
that the skilld Maker
was unmade, forsaken—through defeat
remaking self-broken Adam.

In exchanged glory shall
the blesst bodies be dresst,
each for each, each from
each, each in each shining
with lent light: Christ bright
in all, all in Him lucent.

Christographia XXIII

the tomato vines
still tied to their rough stakes
in november
        sprawl & hang
turn yellow, brown
their leaves shrink to brittle hands

victims
of the year's vegicide
they await the promise—
"today you will be with me"

today they are uprooted
& piled somewhere out of the way,
a last yellow blossom leaning
to catch the winter sun
faint among its roots

the blossom on the compost
reflects the coming Spring
even as its radial light
declines to dust

Darkness

The darkness exists;
it does not have to be imagined.
If I forget it,
it remains, a stain of shadow
under my feet,
at the nape of my neck,
leaking through my heart.

When we would lock the darkness
away from us with facsimiles of light,
we only feed its falseness.
Striking a match
on the wall of my flesh, I see,
after the pop and flare have dwindled,
after-images of my face
receding into night.

The darkness exists
and is more than our ignorance of light
and is more than the shadows cast
by our pride and fear.

Yet the True Star is kindled,
a straight blaze of sun
before which darkness flees
and gathers itself
into its own shadow.

A Conversion (1741)

Nathan Cole quit his plow
& hurry'd to hear Whitefield preach
& found his religion useless ash
before the stern words
"election" "grace"

"Hellfire   hellfire
ran Swift in my mind

"And while these thoughts
were in my mind
God appeared unto me
and made me Skringe: . . .
and I was Shrinked away
into nothing"

And in that nothing
Nathan Cole burst
with light, found
Farmington, Connecticut
ablaze with matter for praise:

all walls & common fences;
weeds, trees,
                and vines in special;
stones he'd earlier envy'd
for lack of soul—
now were new tongues to hymn
Election's glory,
Jehovah's sure salvation.
Selah.

Adam's Uncle

Adam's uncle
wasn't any monkey,
either...
our unnaveld Patriarch
was hoist
from the dust, enabled
to call his flesh & bone
his own/wife. Dark
doings, they did, under
a tree fruited
with loss: not dressing the Garden,
themselves they dresst
in It, a leafy evasion
but unpersuasive.

Once out,
they heard a
shout of triumph;
& saw the tempter fly up,
picking a coarse tune
on some splinterd rib.
Some music!
some dark hovering
concert! Abel's sib
beat the time,
set a shivering cadence
for man's scatterd
dance. (Hey, sleeping Adam:
be raised to Shine!)

As an Orchard, Sing

What we desire
is here:
the grass tips
seize the sunlight
& hide it
in dark roots.

The small stones
settle in dust;
our children's fingers
sprinkle tiny seeds
to ride the wind.

"The field
is the world"
where we root
& bud
bearing fruit
from limbs well-pruned
and roots manured
with daily joy.

Bareback in Kansas

The mare lathers the wind,
  her mane streams like light,
    my face is full of it;

I ride her like a lord of pastures,
  a meadow in each eye,
    stockpond deep in the center:

water down to mud, mud down
  to limestone colorless
    at those depths,
greasewhite until sun yellows it.

I am thinking of You
as her hooves bite the grass, spreading it;
I am thinking of Your face,
bearded & serene, of Your eyes like the pond on a clear day,
a double depth cloudless;
I am thinking of the mouth in Your side
that spoke the fountain,
of the dark bloodcaked eyes in Your hands and feet
  weeping,
I am thinking that You loved me as I mounted the ladder
& shoved the thorns around Your skull,
I am thinking that the palms of Your outspread hands
watched me as I turned from the hill
& went laughing back to the city
to spill wine like blood down my throat
& tell whores of the Fool.

I am thinking of the spearthrust
that brought the fountain from the rock;
I am thinking Your dead eyes held my image,
I am thinking You broke the darkness
& came after me,
I am thinking You tore the weeds from my flesh
& sowed good seed,
I am thinking of the nails driven into Love,

I am thinking of the governments raising steel helmets
against You, of the nails of denial in our mouths,
I am thinking of Your look that changes,
of the Light that sweeps from Your wounds.

And the mare races through the pasture,
   her mane flies in my face,
      I lie close to her neck,
the speed of her gallop is not more
than the speed of Your mercy:

And I know that You loved me
though the hammer was in my hand,
though the spear was registered in my name,
though I laughed and taunted—

You did not crush me, You hunted me,
& the swift arrow of Your mercy
shattered the swollen ball of my selfish eye
& Your kiss blossomed my sight anew;

And I know that You are the lamb,
that You are the tiger;
I know that Your love stands against all night,
that darkness' king has known the temper
of Your blade & fled;
I know that none evades You,
that death's shattered on Your rock.

And I know that this mare will rise with me,
that You will touch body as well as spirit,
that the blossom will have its stem,
that Your city stands forever,
that the tree bears in season & out,

I know that You know my name
& call it,
& my answering is to Life.

The Stones of the City

EXODUS 39:8–14

1. "the names of the children of Israel"

twelve tongues of flame
spoke these stones,
carved these names
on syllables of light

mouths of thunder
shouted this speech,
made this graph
of tribal glyphs
jeweled stair

of twelve stones,
each step a gate
to the City's
central season
blooms of flame

eyes of fire,
watch the cycles,
moon & sun,
                    stars' slow wheel,
constellated tongues
of light

2. "It was foursquare."

Patriarchal stone ladder,
12 starred constellation
of Aaron's bosom,
        stones hammered from earth
        by strokes of fierce light,
        stair & spectrum of ascent,
jeweled steps rise & endure,
each a name

Also, for the City,
these 12 stones,
foundations,
                    the gilgal by Jordan,
gates opening
into the Bride, the Body;

twelve mouths of praise
raised & tied to Aaron's chest—
gems weighting his breath,
foundations of the city,
rising / falling
in the cadence of his prayer

stones tribes apostles gates:
12 syllables for priestly prayer,
the chanted psalms of Sion

3. *"A bell and a pomegranate"*

a garment designed for a priest—
"a body you prepared for me"
the ephod of flesh
Jesus wore, inscribed
with all the tribes of Adam

the Son of Man's body
hammerd on the anvil
of Golgotha

the Son of God's body
transmuted
in the tomb's oven—

        that stone womb
        seald by Rome
        against theft

        or mystery

James E. Warren, Jr.

Parable

"And they did not receive him because his face was as though he would go to Jerusalem" (Luke 9:53).

I sought a human solace once
but found a door
(as He had done). What bitterness
I knew before

I knew that they could never dream
in that full place,
and feared the hunger that was fierce
upon my face!

Who knows? I might have tarried there
and come to harm
if I had found a look too sweet,
a hand too warm.

But I, who found no rest—no rest
for heart nor head,
have glimpsed at last the beautiful
bright town instead,

and on my journey have not ceased
to pray for them
whose kind unkindness kept me toward
Jerusalem.

Alston Chapel

NOVEMBER 22, 1963

Our hearts knelt down in wonder.
The darkness echoed, "Why?"
Our altar, like Golgotha,
heaved heavy toward a sky

of that resentful thunder
and whirlwind of our loss,
where shone from ancient shadows
the lightning of His cross.

The bread of grief was broken;
the tilted wine of tears
was sipped in sad communion.
And then—the prayers! the prayers!

O golden words of glory!
O silvery amen!
And then down aisles of silence
the Trinity swept in!

And we arose in splendor,
the first swift darkness gone;
and out of whispered hallways
we walked into the sun.

The Grave Grows Firm with Grasses

REVELATION 2:17

The grave grows firm with grasses;
the fevered leaves lie down.
Then even summer withers,
and we are left alone

in that insensate winter
which whitens all the mind
and drives us deep for moments
in hallways underground

to wait the many mansions
where avenues are full
of all the shining people
who loved and wished us well.

Till then, each gravestone naming
each name stands high and glad
and gleams—an April angel
that smiles and shakes his head.

Heed Not the Withered Gods

The mummied gods are set in stone
deep in the deserts terrible.
But One was wrapped in faith alone
and lay beneath a lighter spell.

The kingly gods in golden ways
lay down with scepter and with sword,
prepared to sleep a million days.
But One awoke upon the third.

So I, His roused and fortunate,
heed not the withered gods who bless
with silence where their temples wait
long in the moonlight motionless.

But journeying in joy instead
from cross to cross, from pain to pain,
I clutch Him in the broken bread,
I taste His wine within the rain.

Somewhere

*"And now, O Father, glorify thou me
with thine own self, with the glory
which I had with thee before the
world was"* (John 17:5).

A Glory and a Glory
before the clover came
or any sparrow murmured!
A Flame within a Flame

had flared and hung and pondered
O somewhere, O somewhere,
before a lip with music
leaned on the starless air,

before a dream or autumn
or thunder ever was.
And I have held that dwelling
more miracle because

when Labrador will kindle
and moonlight crash and sea
spill into stream and silence,
He will be there and He.

Before or After

REVELATION 8

What   great   clock   ticked
that   strange   half   hour?

The noiseless heart of God?
The soundless chanting of angels?
The silent tolling of aeons still to come?

At last the seven
angels were given
trumpets to peal through Heaven.
And one was shaking
incense upon the fire and making
thunder across the earth and quaking.

But only One knew
before or after the angels blew;

What   great   clock   ticked
that   strange   half   hour.

Today's Too Daft a Day

Today's too daft a day for Dante
to understand, who understood
(or felt) no man could be quite good
enough for Heaven if unManned,
if born before You, if without You.

What limits now Your Limbo, Lord?
Whom will they have for hero
who missed that roaring word
sung by Your minstrels under
Your torches nightly?
                    Will You tender
them cheap salvation who would shove
down tilted sidewalks into love?

Nuns walk frailly two by two.

Came Slowly Forth

REVELATION 6 AND 7

When first the sixth seal crumbled,
the moon became as blood;
and kings and captains trembled
with me and were afraid.

"Crash, mountains!" we were yelling,
and, "Crumble on us, crags!"
We saw the great stars falling
like summer-falling figs,

long in a long wind shaken,
saw heaven disappear,
and saw the fierce sun blacken
and felt the islands stir.

We crouched in ditch and den
and cloaked our eyes in shame
and fear from gazing on
the anger of the Lamb.

When we looked up, the earth
had knelt in robes of snow.
Then we came slowly forth.
Then we were kneeling, too.

Charles A. Waugaman

Over the Fields of Summer

How long since I remembered
The grainfield and the tares;
And how the blue-eyed grasses
In God's just thought compare
With man's ungainly person;
That Mackintosh in fall
And raspberries in summer
Assure His care of all
Creation? I'd forgotten
The neighbor who had died,
Although he built each autumn
New silos for his pride.

Pause by the burdened vineyard,
Watch the fall of a wren,
Stop for a drink at the pasture spring
And the Savior speaks again.
Now is the season to treasure
All that Love has brought,
For over the fields of summer
Returns the time for thought.

Thanksgiving in a Supermarket Line

For cardboard, boxing multipurpose foods,
Waxed paper, foil, self-service counters, soap
In decorator colors, interludes
Of piped-in music, Kleenex, plastic rope,
And all the ease of "open, brown, and serve"
I am quite grateful, Father. Even Dove,
Quick-frozen cherries, cellophane deserve
A mention when I'm thinking of Your love.
I can't imagine home without Scotch tape,
Nor man's inventiveness without Your gift
Of wisdom, somehow, bringing it to shape.
Man never gains advance without a lift.
    A little less than Puritan at heart,
    I count my blessings in a market cart.

The Lowly Eternal

Once more the pageant has been seen:
Once more the miracle has come.

We who donned burlap and gauze
Have worn silk:
We who are penniless
Have given gold.

Mere men,
We have been shepherds and angels,
Prophets and kings:
What is more,
We have mingled as friends.

Is there no end
To what the Child can do?

No end!

And Then God Spoke

The faithful doubted when our fields parched dun
And brittle; when emerald leaves, singed brown,
Had curled to shelter from the ceaseless sun.
Was ours the only harvest God turned down?
Had Pilgrims hilled up herring with their corn
To find it useless when the clouds blew dry;
Or Joseph's seven fat ears' wealth lay worn
To shadow when the seven lean drew nigh?
There was some prayer about our dust-veiled plain,
But more of cursing—more defeat than hope.
Softly, this morning, wind sang through the grain,
And from the slate clouds rain began to grope
　　For root-ribbed earth through tasseled golden spray
　　As God spoke to us through the corn today.

Laura Weller

Lord, Open Our Eyes

to the world
around us
Help us see
little things

    monarch butterflies
    unfolding their wings
    falling out of chrysalises

        bracket fungus—miniature shelves

        a wealth
        of insects and bees
        perching on poppies
        violets
        lilies

            dragonflies—feathery helicopters

                fawn eyes
                glittering like
                starlit skies

                    dandelion fluff
                    balls that puff
                    smoky spores

                ants scurrying
                carrying
                gold to build their castles

            lichens—pioneers on rocks

        a silent woodcock
        hiding in waves
        of goldenrod

        caterpillars
        going for walks

            corn stalks
            stretching
            their arms
            from the earth

➤➤➤➤

a mossy-shelled turtle
sleeping
seldom peeping
at his surroundings

Yes, Lord,
open our eyes
to the world
around us
help us see
little things

pussy willows—
tufts of gray fur

billows of clouds
lambs grazing
in the sky

geese flying
V-shape
high overhead

blue robin's eggs
lying on a bed
of mud and straw

starlings and sparrows
bickering
in the trees

black-capped chickadees
opening seeds
leaving shells
pitting the snow

apple blossoms like
a lone cloud or
mountain of snow

a shadow
of a fern
its ribs expanding
as it turns
in a breeze

rainbows
shining over dew
on leaves

wintergreen berries—
little cherries
on little trees

a squirrel standing
still
demanding attention
from nothing

ripples of water
tugging at weeds
waves that splash
then recede

Nancy Westerfield

Living Crèche

All day long, in the park,
Before the treadmill of onlookers
And ongoers, the dolls crouch,
Bundling their doll-child; and the doll-kings
Bend adoring under an askew star
Fixed to the shed. Only the living are
These creatures that munch their hay: sheep,
And a cow, a donkey walking his tether.
All night long, in the dark,
Before a host of others who are beholders,
The star floats, straightway, over
What most living seemed but doll-like:
Love at its birth, and adoration
Utmost gifts bringing; only doll-folk sleep;
The donkey and his brothers, whosoever
The living are, share light together.

Reading the Rites

Not for the lately dead, but for these
In the pit-site of a desert excavation,
Newly turned to light at pick's point,
Fish-hooked in the empty eye
And brought up for the reading of bones:
So many with yaws, so many cases
Of caries, rickets, so many arthritic hands,
Joints, spines, so many osteosarcomas
Told by the bones; so much accumulation of pain
In a midden, passed out of being
With the contents of skulls, past feeling
Except to these hands that turn the ancient sand,
Carefully turning the last rigidities of knotted bone,
Counting their ills.
What their own priests once said for them lost,
Lost in the tongue they said, yet
Not to be turned under again before some rite spoken,
Some pit-side prayer for their broken rest made
To the bone-reader's God, who walked with men
In the day of these bones, in another desert,
Counting the stricken, and promised an end
To ills, a place of wholeness, his heal to the pain shared
By these bones now reading and the bones lately read.

In His Sameness of Grace:
Our Church, Burning

FOR A CHURCH DESTROYED BY FIRE DECEMBER 25, 1969

God's arson has laid us our worship waste:
This place of our reverence late, late of our Christmasing,
That bell-towered peals for joy of His birth,
Reeks; in welters of smokes our altars blister
And break; like His flesh from the crossarms,
The hanged rafters char from the roof;
The great burning snakes in the steeple,
And its rent fabric fails, with a gnashing of bells.
Ah, Christ! Our singing is dead in our throats;
Were those false carols, false parables,
The canticles of ten lies that based our hopes?
What grace is this in God's gift of burning?
What is left is rubble.
What is left of us is God's rubble;
What is left is God's rubble His people:
We the broken bricks, the imperfect rocks of His
    building
And again His rebuilding: we are left, though He level,
And are not left graceless; in the stone of us
He yet towers. For this giving
Of us to ourselves, Our Father: thanks.

Placed by the Gideons

The landlord offers us his space for let
And it is scarred, by other loners
And losers: the split and peep-holed windowshade
Winking with garish signs, the sprung window,
Webs in the drawers, the mattress unsprung
And burns upon the counterpane, up the plumbing
A red spider running on infinitely painstaken wires,
Like a moving star cluster; and the landlord
Offers us his solace, his book of loving,
Left behind after Gideon and the others slept,
Passage fallen open for a sign, a sign:
How many mansions there are prepared
In that other house, beyond the landlord's room
He offers now, where every door closets the dark,
The spider threads an orrery, the plumbing perspires.

The Prisoner

First, it is said of him
That his own father did not marry his mother,
But left her this derelict to go the gutter-path
Tonight to a death-cell; and they say of him
That he was never at a loss for words:
Making speeches, making magical passes
Over sick persons and others, though tonight
He tongue-ties, after the decent rhetoric
Of judges and governors will have brought it well home
That the man who sits on the bench is not father.
Losing fathers, hunting for lost fathers
Is half the tale of those who bunk
A last night with us; listless and sunken-headed,
Face to face with tomorrow's infinite wordlessness,
As a rule they send messages—though this one listens
As if messages might still come from elsewhere to him.
I could say of him last: that his hopes are lies,
The messages out or in useless, that a man's flesh
Is the prisoner of its own wordedness, and we aim
To set this father's son free; and yet
He listens, but listens as one
Who holds the universe like a shell to his ear
And hears from afar off the roaring of created skies.

Unacceptables

Aged, infirm and incontinent,
They come to Sunday and to prayers
From ward behind recessed ward;
Buttoned to beds and chairs,
Buttoned to stiff upright clothes,
They come, not to see
Not to hear, not to respond;
Yet who knows what offering
Their ills make upon altars?
Eroded out of the world's way,
They have been folded, closeted,
Like old linens, old faces like embroidered linen
Folded in upon themselves, unacceptable
Longer to kin and to community;
Yet who knows in this communion
How they may be adequate
In the sight of One likewise unacceptable
To those He lived among, the outcast
Buttoned to crossed hoists and spat upon?

Urban Churchyard

The package store cater-cornered
Cries Burning Up With Specials
For the Fourth; and blazing across
Its parking lot, the supermarket
Will pay to next week's lucky winner
In the lottery an easy thousand.
Thoroughfare and strident sidewalk draw
The heavy traffic past this narrow
Watered place of grass and Virginia creeper,
Three hackberry trees, two evergreens,
One ash, and the grace of leaves ceaselessly
Shadows down a tuck-pointed wall.
Seed and cone straw the ground
Not here concretely sealed; a squirrel talks;
A robin admonishes its young;
And dim behind vandal-proof bars,
The window with cross and crown offers
What neither is easily won, nor bought.

Christ Writing in the Sand

The woman stands, pinioned, between her accusers
And her judge: the grave man writing with his finger
Upon the ground. What stoning will the hand speak,
Or the tongue? Still he has not given them
The word of punishment for her crime, given
The sign of God's righteous judgment that all wait for,
Herself included. Under their waiting scrutiny,
He only draws strange lines, and the frown
Of his abstractness lines his brow.
How can they know that now they have pursued him
To the brink of their own knowing, and of his saying
In answers such as they can understand
His different world-view, of an infinite mercy?
Still they surround him, his inquisitors,
And do not know how he surrounds them
With his solitary heart. Only the woman knows
Herself surrounded, overcome. One after one, the others
Leave them there solitary: the woman grown
Silent and thoughtful, thrown upon herself
For her own punishment, and the silent writer.
The sand has blown, erasing what he wrote.
Go forgiven, he has spoken; but still she keeps there,
Close and closer still, reading what only she has known.

Dorann Williams

Whiteheat

Joy comes,
consuming my soul like dry tinder—
an ecstatic bonfire,
reaching,
limitless,
feeding on invisible fuel.

I feverishly
try to tend it alone
   but—
my touch brings only
choking smoke.

Oh Christ,
hold me back, to watch and wait
   while
   you take charge
   and stoke my soul
with grace.

Sherwood E. Wirt

John in Gethsemane

The grass is pleasant here
rains have given the earth a chance to soften
I wonder we have not come to Gethsemane
        more often.

We are worn out from the Temple crowds
I can hardly stay awake
I wish he would join us and get some rest
        for his own sake.

But ever since supper he has seemed strange—
something on his mind— .
I expect it will all work out tomorrow
        and we can all unwind.

How drowsy it all seems this evening
        and the earth
                how kind.

Heaven Harvester

God gave me grapes great
clusters of them
then he picked them and took them away
naturally I sulked
it hardly pays to be a branch
    I muttered
and wouldn't you know it my next grapes
    were bitter
so God said you can keep them
I can't use them
so they went to the birds.

Pruning time
and the sweetness of the Lord came
pouring in from the Vine
and I said
Father take this branch it's all yours.
He said back to work son
    give me grapes.

Turnabout

Say I was there
taking it in,
where would you put me?
Standing and weeping with
  Mary,
    Mary
      and John?
Sitting in the bleacher section
with the clowns
hurling insults at holiness?
Kneeling by the upright
waiting my turn at dice?
You're wrong.
I would have been streaking down the road,
robe aloft, elbows like pistons,
cutting toward a Roman culvert
and diving into it.
Which makes it all the more
you see
a work of supernatural Grace
for a faithful, saving Lord
to pull me out
and spin me round
and send me back.

The Roman Lock

The rock . . .
The Roman lock . . .
What is there to it?
How did he do it?

They tell me he is risen
out of death's prison
but how can that be?
What did they see?

O terror of that daybreak hour
O rapture of the Savior's power
O Life that broke but did not bend
O grave that burst from end to end!

On the Resurrection

If Christ remained but six hours on the cross
after a few years of sorrow and affliction,
which he suffered willingly for humankind
that heaven might be purchased forever,
why is He everywhere to be seen
painted and preached only in torments?—
which were light compared with the joy that followed
when the wicked world's cruel blows were finished.

Why not talk and write about the majestic Kingdom
He enjoys in heaven and soon will bring to earth
to the glory and praise of His worthy Name?
O foolish crowd, because you are so earthbound
and have eyes only for the day of His ordeal,
you see His high triumph shorn of its true worth.

*Tommaso Campanella**
trans. Sherwood E. Wirt

Tommaso Campanella (1568–1639), Italian philosopher and poet, became a Dominican monk
as a youth. Later he was accused of heresy and spent twenty-six years in a Naples prison.
This sonnet's uniqueness lies in its protest against the overwhelming medieval emphasis
on the crucified Jesus, and the comparative bypassing of the Resurrection.

Norberto Wolf

A Psalm for Today

PSALM 22

My God, my God. Why have You forsaken me?
I am a caricature of a man
and despised by the people.
They laugh at me in all their newspapers.
I am surrounded by armored tanks,
machine guns take aim at me,
and I am surrounded by wires
—barbed, electrified wires.
All day long they call roll,
and a number is tattooed on me.
They take pictures of me by the wire fences
and all my bones
can be counted, as in an x-ray.
I have been denied all identity,
pushed naked into the gas chamber,
and they have parted my clothes among themselves.
I scream asking for morphine and nobody listens—
I scream bound by a strait jacket.
I scream all night in the asylum for the demented
in the pavilion for the terminal patients
in the infectious-sickness wing,
in the old folks' home.
I agonize, drenched in sweat, in the psychiatric clinic
I gasp in the oxygen tent.
I weep in the police station
   in the prison yard
      in the torture chamber
         in the orphanage.
I am tainted by radioactivity
and nobody comes near me for fear of contamination.
But I will declare Your Name to my brothers;
I will praise You in the midst of our meeting people.
My hymns will ring out among many people.
The poor will have a banquet,
Our people will celebrate a great feast,
The new people who will be born.

Ernesto Cardenal
trans. Norberto Wolf

Mildred Zylstra

Summer

A stream of amber light
a rain of liquid gold
a flood of honey warmth
pours down from the sky's blue bowl.

The sand is hot to my hands
warm fingers of sun stroke my back
dazzled by sparkles of light
I am meshed in a web of gold.

On the tawny ridge of the dune
the yellow grasses wave
sway out from the rooted stems
bend gently down and return.

Light-poised on a driftwood branch
a butterfly opens orange wings
opens and shuts like a fan
dances on motionless feet.

I have reached the center of peace
suffused with ambient fire
absorbed in the radiant light
that pours from the Son beyond suns.

PART TWO
Historic American and English Poets

Anne Bradstreet

As Weary Pilgrim

As weary pilgrim, now at rest,
  Hugs with delight his silent nest,
His wasted limbs now lie full soft
  That mirey steps have trodden oft,
Blesses himself to think upon
  His dangers past and travails done.
The burning sun no more shall heat,
  Nor stormy rains on him shall beat.
The briars and thorns no more shall scratch,
  Nor hungry wolves at him shall catch.
His erring paths no more shall tread,
  Nor wild fruits eat instead of bread.
For waters cold he doth not long,
  For thirst no more shall parch his tongue.
No rugged stones his feet shall gall,
  Nor stumps nor rocks cause him to fall.
All cares and fears he bids farewell
  And means in safety now to dwell.
A pilgrim I, on earth perplexed
  With sins, with cares and sorrows vext,
By age and pains brought to decay,
  And my clay house mold'ring away.
Oh, how I long to be at rest
  And soar on high among the blest.
This body shall in silence sleep,
  Mine eyes no more shall ever weep,
No fainting fits shall me assail,
  Nor grinding pains my body frail;
With cares and fears ne'er cumbered be
  Nor losses know, nor sorrows see.
What though my flesh shall there consume,
  It is the bed Christ did perfume,
And when a few years shall be gone,
  This mortal shall be clothed upon.
A corrupt carcass down it lies,
  A glorious body it shall rise.
In weakness and dishonor sown,
  In power 'tis raised by Christ alone.
Then soul and body shall unite
  And of their Maker have the sight.
Such lasting joys shall there behold
  As ear ne'er heard nor tongue e'er told.
Lord, make me ready for that day;
  Then come, dear Bridegroom, come away.

In Memory

of My Dear Grandchild
ANNE BRADSTREET
Who Deceased June 20, 1669,
Being Three Years and Seven Months Old

With troubled heart and trembling hand I write,
The heavens have changed to sorrow my delight.
How oft with disappointment have I met,
When I on fading things my hopes have set.
Experience might 'fore this have made me wise,
To value things according to their price.
Was ever stable joy yet found below?
Or perfect bliss without mixture of woe?
I knew she was but as a withering flower,
That's here today, perhaps gone in an hour;
Like as a bubble, or the brittle glass,
Or like a shadow turning as it was.
More fool then I to look on that was lent
As if mine own, when thus impermanent.
Farewell dear child, thou ne'er shall come to me,
But yet a while, and I shall go to thee;
Meantime my throbbing heart's cheered up with this:
Thou with thy Savior art in endless bliss.

Occasional Meditations

By night when others soundly slept,
And had at once both ease and rest,
My waking eyes were open kept
And so to lie I found it best.

I sought Him whom my soul did love,
With tears I sought Him earnestly;
He bowed His ear down from above,
In vain I did not seek or cry.

My hungry soul He filled with good,
He in His bottle put my tears;
My smarting wounds washed in His blood,
And banished thence my doubts and fears.

What to my Savior shall I give,
Who freely hath done this for me?
I'll serve Him here whilst I shall live
And love Him to eternity.

In Thankful Remembrance

What shall I render to Thy Name
  Or how Thy praises speak?
My thanks how shall I testify?
  O Lord, Thou knowest I'm weak.

I owe so much, so little can
  Return unto Thy Name,
Confusion seizes on my soul,
  And I am filled with shame.

O Thou that hearest prayers, Lord,
  To Thee shall come all flesh,
Thou hast me heard and answered,
  My plaints have had access.

What did I ask for but Thou gav'st?
  What could I more desire?
But thankfulness even all my days—
  I humbly this require.

Thy mercies, Lord, have been so great
  In number numberless,
Impossible for to recount
  Or any way express.

O help Thy saints that sought Thy face
  To return unto Thee praise
And walk before Thee as they ought,
  In strict and upright ways.

Upon the Burning
of Our House

In silent night when rest I took,
For sorrow near I did not look;
I wakened was with thundering noise
And piteous shrieks of dreadful voice.
That fearful sound of "Fire!" and "Fire!"
Let no man know is my desire.
I, starting up, the light did spy,
And to my God my heart did cry
To strengthen me in my distress
And not to leave me succorless.
Then, coming out, beheld a space
The flame consume my dwelling place.
And when I could no longer look,
I blest His Name that gave and took,
That laid my goods now in the dust.
Yea, so it was, and so 'twas just.
It was His own, it was not mine,
Far be it that I should repine;
He might of all justly bereft,
But yet sufficient for us left.
When by the ruins oft I passed,
My sorrowing eyes aside did cast,
And here and there the places spy
Where oft I sat and long did lie:
Here stood that trunk, and there that chest,
There lay that store I counted best.
My pleasant things in ashes lie,
And them behold no more shall I.
Under thy roof no guest shall sit,
Nor at thy table eat a bit.
No pleasant tale shall e'er be told,
Nor things recounted done of old.
No candle e'er shall shine in thee,
Nor bridegroom's voice e'er heard shall be.
In silence ever shall thou lie,
Adieu, Adieu, all's vanity.
Then straight I 'gin my heart to chide,
And did thy wealth on earth abide?
Didst fix thy hope on mold'ring dust?
The arm of flesh didst make thy trust?
Raise up thy thoughts above the sky
That dunghill mists away may fly.
Thou hast an house on high erect,
Framed by that mighty Architect,
With glory richly furnished,

Stands permanent though this be fled.
It's purchased and paid for too
By Him who hath enough to do.
A price so vast as is unknown,
Yet by His gift is made thine own;
There's wealth enough, I need no more,
Farewell, my pelf, farewell, my store.
The world no longer let me love;
My hope and treasure lie above.

As Spring the Winter

MAY 13, 1657

As spring the winter doth succeed
And leaves the naked trees do dress,
The earth all black is clothed in green.
At sunshine each their joy express.

My sun's returned with healing wings,
My soul and body doth rejoice,
My heart exults and praises sings
To Him that heard my wailing voice.

My winter's past, my storms are gone,
And former clouds seem now all fled,
But if they must eclipse again,
I'll run where I was succoréd.

I have a shelter from the storm,
A shadow from the fainting heat,
I have access unto His throne,
Who is a God so wondrous great.

O hath Thou made my pilgrimage
Thus pleasant, fair, and good,
Blessed me in youth and elder age,
My Baca made a springing flood.

O studious am what I shall do
To show my duty with delight;
All I can give is but Thine own
And at the most a simple mite.

Elizabeth Barrett Browning

The Look

The Savior looked on Peter. Ay, no word,
No gesture of reproach: the heavens serene,
Though heavy with armed justice, did not lean
Their thunders that way: the forsaken Lord
Looked only on the traitor. None record
What that look was, none guess; for those who have seen
Wronged lovers loving through a death-pang keen,
Or pale-cheeked martyrs smiling to a sword,
Have missed Jehovah at the judgment-call.
And Peter, from the height of blasphemy—
"I never knew this man"—did quail and fall,
As knowing straight *that* God, and turnéd free,
And went out speechless from the face of all,
And filled the silence, weeping bitterly.

The Meaning of the Look

I think that look of Christ might seem to say,
"Thou Peter! art thou, then, a common stone
Which I at last must break my heart upon,
For all God's charge to His high angels may
Guard my foot better? Did I yesterday
Wash *thy* feet, my beloved, that they should run
Quick to deny me 'neath the morning sun?
And do thy kisses, like the rest, betray?
The cock crows coldly. Go, and manifest
A late contrition, but no bootless fear;
For, when thy final need is dreariest,
Thou shalt not be denied, as I am here:
My voice to God and angels shall attest,
'Because *I know* this man, let him be clear.'"

John Bunyan

Who Would
True Valor See

Who would true valor see,
  Let him come hither;
One here will constant be,
  Come wind, come weather;
There's no discouragement
Shall make him once relent
His first avowed intent
    To be a pilgrim.

Whoso beset him round
  With dismal stories,
Do but themselves confound—
  His strength the more is.
No lion can him fright;
He'll with a giant fight,
But he will have a right
    To be a pilgrim.

Hobgoblin nor foul fiend
  Can daunt his spirit;
He knows he at the end
  Shall life inherit.
Then fancies fly away,
He'll fear not what men say;
He'll labor night and day
    To be a pilgrim.

John Byrom

A Hymn for Christmas Day

Christians awake, salute the happy morn
Whereon the Savior of the world was born;
Rise to adore the Mystery of Love,
Which hosts of angels chanted from above:
With them the joyful tidings first begun
Of God incarnate and the virgin's Son.
Then to the watchful shepherds it was told,
Who heard the angelic herald's voice: "Behold!
I bring good tidings of a Savior's birth
To you and all the nations upon earth;
This day hath God fulfilled His promised Word;
This day is born a Savior, Christ the Lord:
In David's city, Shepherds, ye shall find
The long-foretold Redeemer of mankind;
Wrapped up in swaddling clothes, the Babe divine
Lies in a manger; this shall be your sign."
He spake, and straightway the celestial choir
In hymns of joy, unknown before, conspire:
The praises of redeeming Love they sung,
And Heaven's whole orb with Hallelujahs rung:
God's highest glory was their anthem still;
Peace upon earth and mutual good will.
To Bethlehem straight the enlightened shepherds ran,
To see the wonder God had wrought for man;
And found, with Joseph and the blessed maid,
Her Son, the Savior, in a manger laid.
Amazed, the wondrous story they proclaim,
The first apostles of his infant fame.
While Mary keeps and ponders in her heart
The heavenly vision which the swains impart,
They to their flocks, still praising God, return,
And their glad hearts within their bosoms burn.

Let us like these good shepherds, then employ
Our grateful voices to proclaim the joy:
Like Mary, let us ponder in our mind
God's wondrous love in saving lost mankind.
Artless and watchful as these favored swains,
While virgin meekness in the heart remains,
Trace we the Babe who has retrieved our loss,
From His poor manger to the bitter Cross;
Treading His steps, assisted by His grace,
Till man's first heavenly state again takes place:
Then may we hope, the angelic thrones among,
To sing, redeemed, a glad triumphal song.
He that was born upon this joyful day,
Around us all His glory shall display;
Saved by His love, incessant we shall sing
Eternal praise to heaven's almighty King.

My Spirit Longs for Thee

My spirit longs for Thee
Within my troubled breast,
Though I unworthy be
Of so divine a Guest.
Of so divine a Guest
Unworthy though I be,
Yet has my heart no rest
Unless it come from Thee.

Unless it come from Thee,
In vain I look around;
In all that I can see
No rest is to be found.
No rest is to be found
But in Thy blessed love:
O let my wish be crowned
And send it from above!

Thomas Campion

De Profundis

Out of my soul's depth to Thee my cries have sounded:
Let Thine ears my plaints receive, on just fear grounded.
Lord, should'st Thou weigh our faults, who's not confounded?

But with Grace Thou censur'st Thine when they have erred;
Therefore shall Thy blessed Name be loved and feared.
E'en to Thy throne my thoughts and eyes are reared.

Thee alone my hopes attend, on Thee relying;
In Thy sacred Word I'll trust, to Thee fast flying,
Long ere the watch shall break, the morn descrying.

In the mercies of our God who live secured,
May of full redemption rest in Him assured;
Their sin-sick souls by Him shall be recured.

Seek the Lord!

Seek the Lord, and in His ways persever.
   O faint not, but as eagles fly;
   For His steep hill is high;
Then striving gain the top, and triumph ever.

When with glory there thy brows are crowned,
   New joys so shall abound in thee,
   Such sights thy soul shall see,
That worldly thoughts shall by their beams be drowned.

Farewell, World, thou mass of mere confusion,
   False light, with many shadows dimmed,
   Old Witch, with new foils trimmed,
Thou deadly sleep of soul, and charmed illusion.

I the King will seek, of kings adored;
   Spring of light, tree of grace and bliss,
   Whose fruit so sovereign is
That all who taste it are from death restored.

G. K. Chesterton

A Hymn for the Church Militant

Great God, that bowest sky and star,
Bow down our towering thoughts to Thee,
And grant us in a faltering war
The firm feet of humility.

Lord, we that snatch the swords of flame,
Lord, we that cry about Thy car,
We too are weak with pride and shame—
We too are as our foemen are.

Yea, we are mad as they are mad,
Yea, we are blind as they are blind,
Yea, we are very sick and sad
Who bring Good News to all mankind.

The dreadful joy Thy Son has sent
Is heavier than any care;
We find, as Cain his punishment,
Our pardon more than we can bear.

Lord, when we cry Thee far and near
And thunder through all lands unknown
The Gospel into every ear,
Lord, let us not forget our own.

Cleanse us from ire of creed or class,
The anger of the idle kings;
Sow in our souls, like living grass,
The laughter of all lowly things.

William Cowper

Longing to Be with Christ

To Jesus, the Crown of my Hope,
  My soul is in haste to be gone;
Oh bear me, ye cherubims, up,
  And waft me away to His throne!

My Savior, whom absent I love,
  Whom not having seen I adore,
Whose Name is exalted above
  All glory, dominion, and power,

Dissolve Thou the bond that detains
  My soul from her portion in Thee,
And strike off the adamant chains
  And make me eternally free.

When that happy era begins,
  When arrayed in Thy beauty I shine,
Nor pierce anymore, by my sins,
  The bosom on which I recline,

Oh then shall the veil be removed
  And round me Thy brightness be poured.
I shall meet Him whom absent I loved;
  I shall see whom unseen I adored.

And then never more shall the fears,
  The trials, temptations, and woes,
Which darken this valley of tears,
  Intrude on my blissful repose.

Or, if yet remembered above,
  Remembrance no sadness shall raise;
They will be but new signs of Thy love,
  New themes for my wonder and praise.

Thus the strokes which from sin and from pain
  Shall set me eternally free
Will but strengthen and rivet the chain
  Which binds me, my Savior, to Thee.

Light Shining out of Darkness

God moves in a mysterious way
  His wonders to perform;
He plants His footsteps in the sea
  And rides upon the storm.

Deep in unfathomable mines
  Of never-failing skill
He treasures up His bright designs,
  And works His sovereign will.

Ye fearful saints, fresh courage take;
  The clouds ye so much dread
Are big with mercy and shall break
  In blessings on your head.

Judge not the Lord by feeble sense,
  But trust Him for His grace;
Behind a frowning providence,
  He hides a smiling face.

His purposes will ripen fast,
  Unfolding every hour;
The bud may have a bitter taste,
  But sweet will be the flower.

Blind unbelief is sure to err
  And scan His work in vain;
God is His own Interpreter,
  And He will make it plain.

Old-Testament Gospel

Israel in ancient days,
Not only had a view
Of Sinai in a blaze,
But learned the Gospel too;
The types and figures were a glass
In which they saw the Savior's face.

The paschal sacrifice
And blood-besprinkled door
Seen with enlightened eyes
And once applied with power
Would teach the need of other blood
To reconcile an angry God.

The Lamb, the Dove, set forth
His perfect innocence,
Whose blood, of matchless worth,
Should be the soul's defence;
For He who can for sin atone
Must have no failings of His own.

The scape-goat on his head
The people's trespass bore,
And to the desert led,
Was to be seen no more.
In him, our Surety seemed to say,
"Behold, I bear your sins away."

Dipped in his fellow's blood,
The living bird went free;
The type, well understood,
Expressed the sinner's plea,
Described a guilty soul enlarged
And by a Savior's death discharged.

Jesus, I love to trace
Throughout the sacred page
The footsteps of Thy grace,
The same in every age!
Oh grant that I may faithful be
To clearer light vouchsafed to me!

Walking with God

Oh, for a closer walk with God,
  A calm and heavenly frame,
A light to shine upon the road
  That leads me to the Lamb!

Where is the blessedness I knew
  When first I saw the Lord?
Where is the soul-refreshing view
  Of Jesus, and His Word?

What peaceful hours I once enjoyed!
  How sweet their memory still!
But they have left an aching void
  The world can never fill.

Return, O holy Dove, return,
  Sweet messenger of rest;
I hate the sins that made thee mourn
  And drove thee from my breast.

The dearest idol I have known,
  Whate'er that idol be;
Help me to tear it from Thy throne
  And worship only Thee.

So shall my walk be close with God,
  Calm and serene my frame;
So purer light shall mark the road
  That leads me to the Lamb.

Praise for the Fountain Opened

ZECHARIAH 13:1

There is a fountain filled with blood
   Drawn from Emmanuel's veins,
And sinners, plunged beneath that flood,
   Lose all their guilty stains.

The dying thief rejoiced to see
   That fountain in his day;
And there have I, though vile as he,
   Washed all my sins away.

Dear dying Lamb, Thy precious blood
   Shall never lose its power
Till all the ransomed Church of God
   Be saved, to sin no more.

E'er since, by faith, I saw the stream
   Thy flowing wounds supply,
Redeeming love has been my theme
   And shall be till I die.

Then in a nobler, sweeter song
   I'll sing Thy power to save,
When this poor lisping, stammering tongue
   Lies silent in the grave.

Lord, I believe Thou hast prepared
   (Unworthy though I be)
For me a blood-bought free reward,
   A golden harp for me!

'Tis strung and tuned for endless years
   And formed by power divine
To sound in God the Father's ears
   No other Name but Thine.

My Soul Thirsts for God

I thirst, but not as once I did,
The vain delights of earth to share;
Thy wounds, Emmanuel, all forbid
That I should seek my pleasures there.

It was the sight of Thy dear Cross
First weaned my soul from earthly things
And taught me to esteem as dross
The mirth of fools, and pomp of kings.

I want that grace that springs from Thee,
That quickens all things where it flows,
And makes a wretched thorn like me
Bloom as the myrtle or the rose.

Dear Fountain of delights unknown!
No longer sink below the brim,
But overflow and pour me down
A living and life-giving stream!

For sure, of all the plants that share
The notice of Thy Father's eye,
None proves less grateful to His care
Or yields him meaner fruit than I.

Richard Crashaw

Crucifixion Hymn

Now is the noon of sorrow's night,
High in his patience as their spite.
Lo, the faint Lamb with weary limb
Bears that huge tree which must bear Him.
That fatal plant, so great of fame
For fruit of sorrow and of shame,
Shall swell with both for Him and mix
All woes into one crucifix.
Is tortured thirst itself too sweet a cup?
Gall and more bitter mocks shall make it up.
Are nails blunt pens of superficial smart?
Contempt and scorn can send sure wounds
    to search the inmost Heart.

Easter Day

Rise, Heir of fresh eternity
    From Thy virgin tomb.
Rise, Mighty Man of Wonders, and Thy world with Thee;
    Thy tomb, the universal east,
    Nature's new womb,
Thy tomb, fair immortality's perfumed nest.

Of all the glories making noon gay
    This is the morn.
This rock buds forth the fountains of the streams of day.
    In joy's white annals live this hour
    When Life was born;
No cloud scowl on His radiant lids, no tempest lower.

Life, by this Light's nativity
    All creatures have.
Death only by this day's just doom is forced to die.
    Nor is death forced, for he may lie
    Throned in Thy grave;
Death will on this condition be content to die.

Matthew 22

*"Neither durst any man from that day
ask Him any more questions."*

Midst all the dark and knotty snares
Black wit or malice can or dares,
Thy glorious wisdom breaks the nets
And treads with uncontrolled steps.
Thy quelled foes are not only now
Thy triumphs, but Thy trophies too;
They both at once Thy conquests be
And Thy conquest's memory.
Stony amazement makes them stand
Waiting on Thy victorious hand,
Like statues fixed to the fame
Of Thy renown and their own shame.
As if they only meant to breath
To be the life of their own death.
'Twas time to hold their peace when they
Had ne'er another word to say;
Yet is their silence unto Thee
The full sound of Thy victory.
Their silence speaks aloud and is
Thy well-pronounced panegyris.
While they speak nothing, they speak all
Their share in Thy memorial.
While they speak nothing, they proclaim
Thee with the shrillest trump of fame.
   To hold their peace is all the ways
    These wretches have to speak Thy praise.

On Our Crucified Lord
Naked and Bloody

They have left Thee naked, Lord, O that they had;
This garment too I would they had denied.
Thee with Thyself they have too richly clad,
Opening the purple wardrobe of Thy side.
   O never could be found garments too good
For Thee to wear, but these of Thine own blood.

John Donne

Good Friday, 1613, Riding Westward

Let man's soul be a sphere, and then, in this,
The intelligence that moves, devotion is,
And as the other spheres, by being grown
Subject to foreign motions, lose their own,
And being by others hurried every day,
Scarce in a year their natural form obey;
Pleasure or business, so, our souls admit
For their first mover, and are whirled by it.
Hence is't that I am carried towards the West
This day, when my soul's form bends towards the East.
There I should see a Sun, by rising, set,
And by that setting endless day beget:
But that Christ on this cross did rise and fall,
Sin had eternally benighted all.
Yet dare I almost be glad I do not see
That spectacle, of too much weight for me.
Who sees God's face, that is self-life, must die;
What a death were it then to see God die?
It made His own lieutenant, Nature, shrink;
It made His footstool crack, and the sun wink.
Could I behold those hands which span the poles,
And tune all spheres at once, pierced with those holes?
Could I behold that endless height which is
Zenith to us, and to our antipodes,
Humbled below us? Or that blood which is
The seat of all our souls, if not of His,
Make dirt of dust, or that flesh which was worn
By God, for His apparel, ragg'd and torn?
If on these things I durst not look, durst I
Upon His miserable mother cast mine eye,
Who was God's partner here, and furnished thus
Half of that sacrifice which ransomed us?
Though these things, as I ride, be from mine eye,
They're present yet unto my memory,
For that looks towards them; and Thou look'st towards me,
O Saviour, as Thou hang'st upon the tree.
I turn my back to Thee but to receive
Corrections, till Thy mercies bid Thee leave.
O think me worth Thine anger, punish me,
Burn off my rusts and my deformity,
Restore Thine image so much, by Thy grace,
That Thou may'st know me, and I'll turn my face.

Batter My Heart

Batter my heart, three-personed God; for You
As yet but knock, breathe, shine, and seek to mend;
That I may rise and stand, o'erthrow me, and bend
Your force to break, blow, burn, and make me new.
I like an usurped town, to another due,
Labor to admit You, but O, to no end;
Reason, Your viceroy in me, me should defend,
But is captived, and proves weak or untrue.
Yet dearly I love You, and would be loved fain,
But am betrothed unto Your enemy.
Divorce me, untie or break that knot again;
Take me to You, imprison me, for I,
Except You enthrall me, never shall be free,
Nor ever chaste, except You ravish me.

Thou Hast Made Me

Thou hast made me, and shall Thy work decay?
Repair me now, for now mine end doth haste;
I run to death, and death meets me as fast,
And all my pleasures are like yesterday.
I dare not move my dim eyes any way,
Despair behind, and death before doth cast
Such terror, and my feeble flesh doth waste
By sin in it, which it towards hell doth weigh.
Only Thou art above, and when towards Thee
By Thy leave I can look, I rise again;
But our old subtle foe so tempteth me
That not one hour myself I can sustain.
Thy grace may wing me to prevent his art,
And Thou like adamant draw mine iron heart.

Hymn to God My God
in My Sickness

Since I am coming to that holy room
   Where, with Thy choir of saints for evermore,
I shall be made Thy music; as I come
   I tune the instrument here at the door,
   And what I must do then, think here before.

Whilst my physicians by their love are grown
   Cosmographers, and I their map, who lie
Flat on this bed, that by them may be shown
   That this is my southwest discovery
   Per fretum febris, by these straits to die.

I joy, that in these straits, I see my West;
   For, though their currents yield return to none,
What shall my West hurt me? As West and East
   In all flat maps (and I am one) are one,
   So death doth touch the resurrection.

Is the Pacific Sea my home? Or are
   The Eastern riches? Is Jerusalem?
Anyan, and Magellan, and Gibraltar,
   All straits, and none but straits, are ways to them,
   Whether where Japhet dwelt, or Cham, or Shem.

We think that Paradise and Calvary,
   Christ's cross, and Adam's tree, stood in one place;
Look, Lord, and find both Adams met in me;
   As the first Adam's sweat surrounds my face,
   May the last Adam's blood my soul embrace.

So, in this purple wrapped, receive me, Lord;
   By these His thorns give me His other crown;
And, as to others' souls I preached Thy Word,
   Be this my text, my sermon to mine own:
   Therefore that He may raise the Lord throws down.

316

Oh My Black Soul

Oh my black soul! now thou art summoned
By sickness, death's herald and champion;
Thou art like a pilgrim, which abroad hath done
Treason, and durst not turn to whence he is fled,
Or like a thief, which till death's doom be read,
Wisheth himself delivered from prison;
But damned and haled to execution,
Wisheth that still he might be imprisoned.
Yet grace, if thou repent, thou canst not lack;
But who shall give thee that grace to begin?
Oh make thyself with holy mourning black,
And red with blushing as thou art with sin;
Or wash thee in Christ's blood, which hath this might
That being red, it dyes red souls to white.

If Poisonous Minerals

If poisonous minerals, and if that tree
Whose fruit threw death on else immortal us,
If lecherous goats, if serpents envious
cannot be damned, alas, why should I be?
Why should intent or reason, born in me,
Make sins, else equal, in me more heinous?
And mercy being easy and glorious
To God, in His stern wrath why threatens He?
But who am I, that dare dispute with Thee,
O God? Oh! of Thine only worthy blood,
And my tears, make a heavenly Lethean flood,
And drown in it my sins' black memory.
That Thou remember them, some claim as debt;
I think it mercy if Thou wilt forget.

A Hymn to God the Father

Wilt Thou forgive that sin where I begun,
  Which was my sin, though it were done before?
Wilt Thou forgive that sin through which I run,
  And do run still: though still I do deplore?
    When Thou has done, Thou hast not done,
      For I have more.

Wilt Thou forgive that sin which I have won
  Others to sin, and made my sin their door?
Wilt Thou forgive that sin which I did shun
  A year or two, but wallowed in a score?
    When Thou hast done, Thou hast not done,
      For I have more.

I have a sin of fear, that when I have spun
  My last thread, I shall perish on the shore;
But swear by Thyself that at my death Thy Son
  Shall shine as He shines now and heretofore;
    And, having done that, Thou hast done,
      I fear no more.

At the Round Earth's

At the round earth's imagined corners, blow
Your trumpets, angels; and arise, arise
From death, you numberless infinities
Of souls, and to your scattered bodies go;
All whom the flood did, and fire shall, o'erthrow,
All whom war, dearth, age, agues, tyrannies,
Despair, law, chance hath slain, and you whose eyes
Shall behold God, and never·taste death's woe.
But let them sleep, Lord, and me mourn a space;
For, if above all these, my sins abound,
'Tis late to ask abundance of Thy grace
When we are there. Here on this lowly ground,
Teach me how to repent; for that's as good
As if Thou hadst sealed my pardon with Thy blood.

Annunciation

Salvation to all that will is nigh,
That All, which always is All everywhere,
Which cannot sin, and yet all sins must bear,
Which cannot die, yet cannot choose but die,
Lo, faithful Virgin, yields Himself to lie
In prison, in thy womb; and though He there
Can take no sin, nor thou give, yet He will wear
Taken from thence, flesh, which death's force may try.
Ere by the spheres time was created, thou
Wast in His mind, who is thy Son, and Brother,
Whom thou conceived; yea thou art now
Thy Maker's maker, and thy Father's mother;
Thou hast light in dark, and shuttest in little room
Immensity cloistered in thy dear womb.

Why Are We By All Creatures?

Why are we by all creatures waited on?
Why do the prodigal elements supply
Life and food to me, being more pure than I,
Simple and further from corruption?
Why brookest thou, ignorant horse, subjection?
Why dost thou, bull and boar, so sillily
Dissemble weakness, and by one man's stroke die,
Whose whole kind you might swallow and feed upon?
Weaker I am, woe is me, and worse than you;
You have not sinned, nor need be timorous.
But wonder at a greater wonder, for to us
Created nature doth these things subdue,
But their Creator, whom sin nor nature tied,
For us, His creatures, and His foes, hath died.

John Dryden

Veni Creator Spiritus

Creator Spirit, by whose aid
The world's foundations first were laid,
Come visit every pious mind;
Come pour Thy joys on humankind;
From sin and sorrow set us free,
And make Thy temples worthy Thee.
O Source of uncreated light,
The Father's promised Paraclete!
Thrice-holy Fount, thrice-holy Fire,
Our hearts with heavenly love inspire;
Come, and Thy sacred unction bring
To sanctify us while we sing!
Plenteous of grace, descend from high,
Rich in Thy sevenfold energy,
Thou Strength of His almighty hand,
Whose power does heaven and earth command!
Proceeding Spirit, our Defence,
Who dost the gift of tongues dispense,
And crownst Thy gift with eloquence!
Refine and purge our earthy parts;
But, O, inflame and fire our hearts!
Our frailties help, our vice control,
Submit the senses to the soul;
And when rebellious they are grown,
Then lay Thy hand and hold them down.
Chase from our minds the infernal foe,
And peace, the fruit of love, bestow;
And lest our feet should step astray,
Protect and guide us in the way.
Make us eternal truths receive,
And practise all that we believe:
Give us Thyself that we may see
The Father and the Son by Thee.
Immortal honor, endless fame,
Attend the Almighty Father's Name:
The Savior Son be glorified,
Who for lost man's redemption died;
And equal adoration be,
Eternal Paraclete, to Thee.

Giles Fletcher

Palm Sunday: Good Friday

It was but now their sounding clamors sung,
"Blessed is he, that comes from the Most High,"
And all the mountains with "Hosanna" rung,
And now, "Away with him, away," they cry,
And nothing can be heard but "Crucify!"
   It was but now the crown itself they save,
   And golden name of King unto Him gave,
And now no King but only Caesar they will have.

It was but now they gathered blooming May,
And of His arms disrobed the branching tree
To strew with boughs and blossoms all Thy way,
And now, the branchless trunk a Cross for Thee,
And May, dismayed, Thy coronet must be:
   It was but now they were so kind to throw
   Their own best garments where Thy feet should go,
And now, Thyself they strip, and bleeding wounds they show.

See where the Author of all life is dying.
O fearful day! He dead, what hope of living?
See where the hopes of all our lives are buying.
O cheerful day! They bought, what fear of grieving?
Love love for hate, and death for life is giving:
   Lo, how His arms are stretched abroad to grace thee,
   And, as they open stand, call to embrace thee.
Why stay'st thou then, my soul? O fly, fly thither haste thee.

Felicia Hemans

The Agony in the Garden

He knelt, the Savior knelt and prayed,
   When but His Father's eye
Looked through the lonely garden's shade
   On that dread agony;
The Lord All above, beneath,
Was bowed with sorrow unto death.

The sun set in a fearful hour,
   The stars might well grow dim,
When this mortality had power
   So to o'ershadow Him!
That He who gave man's breath, might know
The very depths of human woe.

He proved them all!—the doubt, the strife,
   The faint perplexing dread,
The mists that hang o'er parting life,
   All gathered round His head;
And the Deliverer knelt to pray—
Yet passed it not, that cup, away!

It passed not—though the stormy wave
   Had sunk beneath His tread;
It passed not—though to Him the grave
   Had yielded up its dead.
But there was sent Him from on high
A gift of strength for man to die.

And was the sinless thus beset
   With anguish and dismay?
How may *we* meet our conflict yet
   In the dark narrow way?
Through Him—through Him, that path who trod—
Save, or we perish, Son of God!

George Herbert

Jordan (I)

Who says that fictions only and false hair
Become a verse? Is there in truth no beauty?
Is all good structure in a winding stair?
May no lines pass, except they do their duty
   Not to a true, but painted chair?

Is it no verse, except enchanted groves
And sudden arbors shadow coarse-spun lines?
Must purling streams refresh a lover's loves?
Must all be veiled while he that reads, divines,
   Catching the sense at two removes?

Shepherds are honest people; let them sing:
Riddle who list, for me, and pull for prime:
I envy no man's nightingale or spring;
Nor let them punish me with loss of rhyme,
   Who plainly say, *My God, My King*.

The Reprisal

   I have considered it, and find
There is no dealing with Thy mighty passion,
For though I die for Thee, I am behind:
   My sins deserve the condemnation.

   O make me innocent, that I
May give a disentangled state and free;
And yet Thy wounds still my attempts defy,
   For by Thy death I die for Thee.

   Ah! was it not enough that Thou
By Thy eternal glory didst outgo me?
Couldst Thou not grief's sad conquests me allow,
   But in all vic'tries overthrow me?

   Yet by confession will I come
Into Thy conquest. Though I can do nought
Against Thee, in Thee I will overcome
   The man who once against Thee fought.

The Windows

Lord, how can man preach thy eternal Word?
  He is a brittle, crazy glass;
Yet in thy temple thou dost him afford
  This glorious and transcendent place,
  To be a window, through thy grace.

But when thou dost anneal in glass thy story,
  Making thy life to shine within
The holy preachers, then the light and glory
  More reverend grows, and more doth win,
  Which else shows waterish, bleak, and thin.

Doctrine and life, colors and light, in one
  When they combine and mingle, bring
A strong regard and awe; but speech alone
  Doth vanish like a flaring thing,
  And in the ear, not conscience, ring.

The Jews

Poor nation, whose sweet sap and juice
Our scions have purloined and left you dry:
Whose streams we got by the apostles' sluice,
And use in baptism, while ye pine and die:
Who by not keeping once, became a debtor,
  And now by keeping lose the letter—

  Oh that my prayers! mine, alas!
Oh that some Angel might a trumpet sound,
At which the Church, falling upon her face,
Should cry so loud until the trump were drowned,
And by that cry, of her dear Lord obtain
  That your sweet sap might come again!

The Collar

I struck the board and cried, "No more;
                    I will abroad!
What? Shall I ever sigh and pine?
My lines and life are free, free as the road,
Loose as the wind, as large as store.
                    Shall I be still in suit?
Have I no harvest but a thorn
To let me blood, and not restore
What I have lost with cordial fruit?
                    Sure there was wine
Before my sighs did dry it; there was corn
                    Before my tears did drown it.
Is the year only lost to me?
                    Have I no bays to crown it?
No flowers, no garlands gay? All blasted?
                    All wasted?
Not so, my heart; but there is fruit,
                    And thou hast hands.
Recover all thy sigh-blown age
On double pleasures; leave thy cold dispute
Of what is fit and not. Forsake thy cage,
                    Thy rope of sands,
Which petty thoughts have made, and made to thee
Good cable, to enforce and draw
                    And be thy law
While thou didst wink and wouldst not see.
                    Away! Take heed;
                    I will abroad.
Call in thy death's-head there: tie up thy fears.
                    He that forbears
To suit and serve his need,
                    Deserves his load."
But as I raved and grew more fierce and wild
                    At every word,
Me thought I heard one calling, *Child!*
                    And I replied, *My Lord.*

Easter

Rise heart; thy Lord is risen. Sing His praise
                     Without delays,
Who takes thee by the hand, that thou likewise
                     With Him mayst rise:
That as His death calcined thee to dust,
His life may make thee gold, and much more, just.

Awake, my lute, and struggle for thy part
                     With all thy art.
The cross taught all wood to resound His Name,
                     Who bore the same.
His stretchèd sinews taught all strings what key
Is best to celebrate this most high day.

Consort both heart and lute, and twist a song
                     Pleasant and long:
Or, since all music is but three parts vied
                     And multiplied,
O let Thy blessed Spirit bear a part,
And make up our defects with His sweet art.

Easter Wings

Lord, Who createdst man in wealth and store,
Though foolishly he lost the same
Decaying more and more,
Till he became
Most poor:
With Thee
O let me rise
As larks, harmoniously,
And sing this day Thy victories:
Then shall the fall further the flight in me.

My tender age in sorrow did begin;
And still with sicknesses and shame
Thou didst so punish sin,
That I became
Most thin.
With Thee
Let me combine
And feel this day Thy victory;
For, if I imp my wing on Thine,
Affliction shall advance the flight in me.

Redemption

Having been tenant long to a rich lord,
  Not thriving, I resolved to be bold
  And make a suit unto him, to afford
A new small-rented lease, and cancel the old.

In heaven at his manor I him sought;
  They told me there that he was lately gone
  About some land, which he had dearly bought
Long since on earth, to take possession.

I straight returned, and knowing his great birth,
  Sought him accordingly in great resorts;
  In cities, theaters, gardens, parks, and courts;
At length I heard a ragged noise and mirth
  Of thieves and murderers; there I him espied,
  Who straight, *Your suit is granted*, said, and died.

Paradise

I bless Thee, Lord, because I grow
Among Thy trees, which in a row
To Thee both fruit and order owe.

What open force or hidden charm
Can blast my fruit or bring me harm
While the enclosure is Thine arm?

Enclose me still for fear I start.
Be to me rather sharp and tart
Than let me want Thy hand and art.

When Thou dost greater judgments spare
And with Thy knife but prune and pare,
Even fruitful trees more fruitful are.

Such sharpness shows the sweetest friend,
Such cuttings rather heal than rend,
And such beginnings touch their end.

The Storm

If the winds and waters here below
        Do fly and flow,
My sighs and tears as busy were above,
        Sure they would move
And much affect Thee, as tempestuous times
Amaze poor mortals, and object their crimes.

Stars have their storms, ev'n in a high degree
        As well as we.
A throbbing conscience spurred by remorse
        Hath a strange force;
It quits the earth, and mounting more and more,
Dares to assault Thee and beseige Thy door.

There it stands knocking, to Thy music's wrong,
        And drowns the song.
Glory and honor are set by, till it
        An answer get.
Poets have wronged poor storms: such days are best;
They purge the air without, within the breast.

Sin's Round

Sorry I am, my God, sorry I am
That my offences course it in a ring.
My thoughts are working like a busy flame,
Until their cockatrice they hatch and bring;
And when they once have perfected their draughts,
My words take fire from my inflamed thoughts.

My words take fire from my inflamed thoughts,
Which spit it forth like the Sicilian hill.
They vent the wares and pass them with their faults,
And by their breathing ventilate the ill.
But words suffice not; where are lewd intentions,
My hands do join to finish the inventions.

My hands do join to finish the inventions:
And so my sins ascend three stories high,
As Babel grew before there were dissensions.
Yet ill deeds loiter not, for they supply
New thoughts of sinning: wherefore, to my shame,
Sorry I am, my God, sorry I am.

The Altar

A broken altar, Lord, Thy servant rears,
Made of a heart, and cemented with tears:
  Whose parts are as Thy hand did frame;
  No workman's tool hath touched the same
        A   heart   alone
        Is   such a   stone
        As   nothing but
        Thy power doth cut.
        Wherefore each part
        Of my hard heart
        Meets in this frame
        To praise Thy name:
  That, if I chance to hold my peace,
  These stones to praise Thee may not cease,
O let Thy blessed sacrifice be mine,
And sanctify this altar to be Thine.

Let All the World in Every Corner Sing

Let all the world in every corner sing, My God and King!
  The heavens are not too high,
  His praise may thither fly;
  The earth is not too low,
  His praises there may grow.
Let all the world in every corner sing, My God and King!

Let all the world in every corner sing, My God and King!
  The Church with psalms must shout,
  No door can keep them out;
  But, above all, the heart
  Must bear the longest part.
Let all the world in every corner sing, My God and King!

Aaron

Holiness on the head,
  Light and perfections on the breast,
Harmonious bells below, raising the dead
  To lead them unto life and rest:
    Thus are true Aarons dressed.

Profaneness in my head,
  Defects and darkness in my breast,
A noise of passions ringing me for dead
  Unto a place where is no rest:
    Poor priest thus am I dressed.

Only another head
  I have, another heart and breast,
Another music, making live not dead,
  Without Whom I could have no rest:
    In Him I am well dressed.

Christ is my only head,
  My alone and only heart and breast,
My only music, striking me e'en dead
  That to the old man I may rest
    And be in Him new dressed.

So holy in my head,
  Perfect and light in my dear breast,
My doctrine tuned to Christ (Who is not dead,
  But lives in me while I do rest)
    Come, people; Aaron's dressed.

Trinity Sunday

Lord, who hast formed me out of mud,
  And hast redeemed me through Thy blood,
  And sanctified me to do good,

Purge all my sins done heretofore:
  For I confess my heavy score,
  And I will strive to sin no more.

Enrich my heart, mouth, hands in me,
  With faith, with hope, with charity,
  That I may run, rise, rest with Thee.

Love (III)

Love bade me welcome: yet my soul drew back,
    Guilty of dust and sin.
But quick-eyed Love, observing me grow slack
    From my first entrance in,
Drew nearer to me, sweetly questioning
    If I lacked anything.

"A guest," I answered, "worthy to be here":
    Love said, "You shall be he."
"I, the unkind, ungrateful? Ah, my dear,
    I cannot look on thee."
Love took my hand, and smiling did reply,
    "Who made the eyes but I?"

"Truth, Lord; but I have marred them; let my shame
    Go where it doth deserve."
"And know you not," says Love, "who bore the blame?"
    "My dear, then I will serve."
"You must sit down," says Love, "and taste my meat."
    So I did sit and eat.

Prayer (I)

Prayer, the church's banquet, angels' age,
    God's breath in man returning to his birth,
    The soul in paraphrase, heart in pilgrimage,
The Christian plummet sounding heaven and earth;

Engine against the Almighty, sinner's tower,
    Reversèd thunder, Christ-side-piercing spear,
    The six-days' world transposing in an hour,
A kind of tune, which all things hear and fear;

Softness, and peace, and joy, and love, and bliss,
    Exalted manna, gladness of the best,
    Heaven in ordinary, man well dressed,
The Milky Way, the bird of Paradise,

    Church bells beyond the stars heard, the soul's blood,
    The land of spices; something understood.

Gratefulness

Thou that hast given so much to me,
Give one thing more, a grateful heart.
See how Thy beggar works on Thee
       By art.

He makes Thy gifts occasion more,
And says, If he in this be crossed,
All Thou hast given him heretofore
       Is lost.

But Thou didst reckon, when at first
Thy Word our hearts and hands did crave,
What it would come to at the worst
       To save.

Time

Meeting with Time, "Slack thing," said I,
"Thy scythe is dull; whet it for shame."
"No marvel, sir," he did reply,
"If it at length deserve some blame;
       But where one man would have me grind it,
       Twenty for one too sharp do find it."

"Perhaps some such of old did pass,
Who above all things loved this life,
To whom thy scythe a hatchet was,
Which now is but a pruning knife.
       Christ's coming hath made man thy debtor,
       Since by thy cutting he grows better."

Death

Death, thou wast once an uncouth hideous thing,
        Nothing but bones,
    The sad effect of sadder groans:
Thy mouth was open, but thou couldst not sing.

For we considered thee as at some six
        Or ten years hence,
    After the loss of life and sense,
Flesh being turned to dust, and bones to sticks.

We looked on this side of thee, shooting short;
        Where we did find
    The shells of fledge souls left behind,
Dry dust, which sheds no tears, but may extort.

But since our Savior's death did put some blood
        Into thy face,
    Thou art grown fair and full of grace,
Much in request, much sought for as a good.

For we do now behold thee gay and glad,
        As at doomsday;
    When souls shall wear their new array,
And all thy bones with beauty shall be clad.

Therefore we can go die as sleep, and trust
        Half that we have
    Unto an honest faithful grave,
Making our pillows either down or dust.

Gerard Manley Hopkins

The Starlight Night

Look at the stars! look, look up at the skies!
O look at all the fire-folk sitting in the air!
The bright boroughs, the circle-citadels there!
Down in dim woods the diamond delves! the elves'-eyes!
The gray lawns cold where gold, where quickgold lies!
Wind-beat whitebeam! airy abeles set on a flare!
Flake-doves sent floating forth at a farmyard scare!
Ah, well! it is all a purchase, all is a prize.
Buy then! bid then!—What?—Prayer, patience, alms, vows.
Look, look: a May-mess, like on orchard boughs!
Look! March-bloom, like on mealed-with-yellow sallows!
These are indeed the barn; withindoors house
The shocks. This piece-bright paling shuts the spouse
Christ home, Christ and His mother and all His hallows.

Carrion Comfort

Not, I'll not, carrion comfort, Despair, not feast on thee;
Not untwist—slack they may be—these last strands of man
In me or, most weary, cry *I can no more.* I can;
Can something, hope, wish day come, not choose not to be.

But ah, but O thou terrible, why wouldst thou rude on me
Thy wring-world right foot rock? lay a lionlimb against me?
   scan
With darksome devouring eyes my bruisèd bones? and fan,
O in turns of tempest, me heaped there; me frantic to avoid
   thee and flee?

Why? That my chaff might fly; my grain lie sheer and clear.
Nay in all that toil, that coil, since (seems) I kissed
   the rod,
Hand rather, my heart lo! lapped strength, stole joy, would
   laugh, cheer.
Cheer whom though? The hero whose heaven-handling flung me,
   foot trod
Me? or me that fought him? O which one? Is it each one?
   That night, that year
Of now done darkness I wretch lay wrestling with (my God!)
   my God.

Barnfloor and Winepress

"And he said, 'If the Lord do not help thee,
whence shall I help thee? Out of the barnfloor,
or out of the winepress?'" (II Kings 6:27).

Thou that on sin's wages starvest,
Behold we have the joy in harvest;
For us was gathered the firstfruits,
For us was lifted from the roots,
Sheaved in cruel bands, bruised sore,
Scourged upon the threshing floor;
Where the upper millstone roofed His head,
At morn we found the heavenly Bread,
And, on a thousand altars laid,
Christ our Sacrifice is made!

Those whose dry plot for moisture gapes,
We shout with them that tread the grapes;
For us the Vine was fenced with thorn,
Five ways the precious branches torn;
Terrible fruit was on the tree
In the acre of Gethsemane;
For us by Calvary's distress
The wine was rackèd from the press;
Now in our altar-vessels stored
Is the sweet Vintage of our Lord.

In Joseph's garden they threw by
The riven Vine, leafless, lifeless, dry;
On Easter morn the Tree was forth,
In forty days reached Heaven from earth;
Soon the whole world is overspread;
Ye weary, come into the shade.

The field where He has planted us
Shall shake her fruit as Libanus,
When He has sheaved us in His sheaf,
When He has made us bear His leaf.
We scarcely call that banquet food,
But even our Savior's and our blood,
We are so grafted on His wood.

As Kingfishers Catch Fire

As kingfishers catch fire, dragonflies draw flame;
As tumbled over rim in roundy wells
Stones ring; like each tucked string tells, each hung bell's
Bow swung finds tongue to fling out broad its name;
Each mortal thing does one thing and the same:
Deals out that being indoors each one dwells;
Selves—goes itself; *myself* it speaks and spells;
Crying *What I do is me: for that I came.*

I say more: the just man justices;
Keeps grace: that keeps all his goings graces;
Acts in God's eye what in God's eye he is—
Christ, for Christ plays in ten thousand places,
Lovely in limbs, and lovely in eyes not His
To the Father through the features of men's faces.

The Lantern Out of Doors

Sometimes a lantern moves along the night,
That interests our eyes. And who goes there?
I think: where from and bound, I wonder, where,
With, all down darkness wide, his wading light?

Men go by me whom either beauty bright
In mould or mind or what not else makes rare:
They rain against our much-thick and marsh air
Rich beams, till death or distance buys them quite.

Death or distance soon consumes them: wind
What most I may eye after, be in at the end
I cannot, and out of sight is out of mind.

Christ minds; Christ's interest, what to avow or amend
There, eyes them, heart wants, care haunts, foot follows kind,
Their ransom, their rescue, and first, fast, last friend.

That Nature Is a Heraclitean Fire
and of the Comfort of the Resurrection

Cloud-puffball, torn tufts, tossed pillows flaunt forth,
    then chevy on an air-
built thoroughfare: heaven-roysterers, in gay-gangs they
    throng; they glitter in marches.
Down roughcast, down dazzling whitewash, wherever an
    elm arches,
Shivelights and shadowtackle in long lashes lace, lance,
    and pair.
Delightfully the bright wind boisterous ropes, wrestles,
    beats earth bare
Of yestertempest's creases; in pool and rut peel parches
Squandering ooze to squeezed dough, crust, dust; stanches,
    starches
Squadroned masks and manmarks treadmire toil there
Footfretted in it. Million-fuelèd, nature's bonfire burns on.
But quench her bonniest, dearest to her, her clearest-selvèd
    spark
Man, how fast his firedint, his mark on mind, is gone!
Both are in an unfathomable, all is in an enormous dark
Drowned. O pity and indignation! Manshape, that shone
Sheer off, disseveral, a star, death blots black out;
    nor mark
            Is any of him at all so stark
But vastness blurs and time beats level. Enough! the
    Resurrection,
A heart's-clarion! Away grief's gasping, joyless days,
    dejection.
            Across my foundering deck shone
A beacon, an eternal beam. Flesh fade, and mortal trash
Fall to the residuary worm; world's wildfire, leave but ash:
    In a flash, at a trumpet crash,
I am all at once what Christ is, since he was what I am, and
This Jack, joke, poor potsherd, patch, matchwood, immortal
    diamond,
    Is immortal diamond.

Pied Beauty

Glory be to God for dappled things—
   For skies of couple-color as a brinded cow;
     For rose-moles all in stipple upon trout that swim;
Fresh-firecoal chestnut-falls; finches' wings;
   Landscapes plotted and pieced—fold, fallow, and plow;
     And all trades, their gear and tackle and trim.
All things counter, original, spare, strange;
   Whatever is fickle, freckled (who knows how?)
     With swift, slow; sweet, sour; adazzle, dim;
He fathers-forth whose beauty is past change:
     Praise Him.

God's Grandeur

The world is charged with the grandeur of God.
   It will flame out, like shining from shook foil;
   It gathers to a greatness, like the ooze of oil
Crushed. Why do men then now not reck His rod?
Generations have trod, have trod, have trod;
   And all is seared with trade; bleared, smeared with toil;
   And wears man's smudge and shares man's smell: the soil
Is bare now, nor can foot feel, being shod.

And for all this, nature is never spent;
   There lives the dearest freshness deep down things;
And though the last lights off the black West went
   Oh, morning, at the brown brink eastward, springs—
Because the Holy Ghost over the bent
   World broods with warm breast and with ah! bright wings.

The Leaden Echo
and the Golden Echo

MAIDENS' SONG FROM ST. WINEFRED'S WELL

The Leaden Echo

How to keep—is there any any, is there none such, nowhere
    known some, bow or brooch or braid or brace, lace, latch
    or catch or key to keep
Black beauty, keep it, beauty, beauty, beauty, . . . from
    vanishing away?
O is there no frowning of these wrinkles, rankèd wrinkles deep,
Down? no waving off of these most mournful messengers,
    still messengers, sad and stealing messengers of grey?
No there's none, there's none, o no there's none,
Nor can you long be, what you now are, called fair,
Do what you may do, what, do what you may,
And wisdom is early to despair:
Be beginning; since, no, nothing can be done
To keep at bay
Age and age's evils, hoar hair,
Ruck and wrinkle, drooping, dying, death's worst, winding
    sheets, tombs and worms and tumbling to decay;
So be beginning, be beginning to despair.
O there's none; no no no there's none:
Be beginning to despair, to despair,
Despair, despair, despair, despair.

The Golden Echo

      Spare!
There is one, yes I have one (Hush there!);
Only not within seeing of the sun,
Not within the singeing of the strong sun,
Tall sun's tingeing, or treacherous the tainting of the
    earth's air,

Somewhere elsewhere there is ah well where! one,
One. Yes I can tell such a key, I do know such a place,
Where whatever's prized and passes of us, everything that's
 fresh and fast flying of us, seems to us sweet of us and
 swiftly away with, soon done with, and yet dearly and
 dangerously sweet
Of us, the wimpled-water-dimpled, not-by-mourning-matchèd
 face,
The flower of beauty, fleece of beauty, too too apt to, ah!
 to fleet,
Never fleets more, fastened with the tenderest truth
To its own best being and its loveliness of youth: it is an
 everlastingness of, O it is an all youth!
Come then, your ways and airs and looks, locks, maiden gear,
 gallantry and gaiety and grace,
Winning ways, airs innocent, maiden manners, sweet looks,
 loose locks, long locks, lovelocks, gaygear, going gallant,
 girlgrace—
Resign them, sign them, seal them, send them, motion them
 with breath,
And with sighs soaring, soaring sighs deliver
Them; beauty-in-the-ghost, deliver it, early now, long
 before death
Give beauty back, beauty, beauty, beauty, back to God,
 beauty's Self and beauty's Giver.
See; not a hair is, not an eyelash, not the least lash lost;
 every hair
Is, hair of the head, numbered.
Nay, what we had lighthanded left in surly the mere mould
Will have waked and have waxed and have walked with the
 wind whatwhile we slept,
This side, that side hurling a heavyheaded hundredfold
What while we, while we slumbered.
O then, weary then why should we tread? O why are we so
 haggard at the heart, so care-coiled, care-killed, so
 fagged, so fashed, so cogged, so cumbered,
When the thing we freely forfeit is kept with fonder a care,
Fonder a care kept than we could have kept it, kept
Far with fonder a care (and we, we should have lost it) finer,
 fonder
A care kept.—Where kept? Do but tell us where kept,
 where.—
Yonder.—What high as that! We follow, now we follow.—
 Yonder, yes yonder, yonder,
Yonder.

The Windhover

TO CHRIST OUR LORD

I caught this morning morning's minion, king-
    dom of daylight's dauphin, dapple-dawn-drawn Falcon, in
      his riding
    Of the rolling level underneath him steady air, and striding
High there, how he rung upon the rein of a wimpling wing
In his ecstasy! then off, off forth on swing,
    As a skate's heel sweeps smooth on a bow-bend: the hurl
      and gliding
    Rebuffed the big wind. My heart in hiding
Stirred for a bird—the achieve of, the mastery of the thing!

Brute beauty and valour and act, oh, air, pride, plume here
    Buckle! AND the fire that breaks from thee then, a billion
Times told lovelier, more dangerous, O my chevalier!
    No wonder of it: sheer plod makes plough down sillion
Shine, and blue-bleak embers, ah my dear,
    Fall, gall themselves, and gash gold-vermilion.

Spring and Fall

TO A YOUNG CHILD

Margaret, are you grieving
Over Goldengrove unleaving?
Leaves, like the things of man, you
With your fresh thoughts care for, can you?
Ah! as the heart grows older
It will come to such sights colder
By and by, nor spare a sigh
Though worlds of wanwood leafmeal lie;
And yet you will weep and know why.
Now no matter, child, the name:
Sorrow's springs, are the same.
Nor mouth had, no nor mind, expressed
What heart heard of, ghost guessed:
It is the blight man was born for;
It is Margaret you mourn for.

The Caged Skylark

As a dare-gale skylark scanted in a dull cage
Man's mounting spirit in his bone-house, mean house, dwells—
That bird beyond the remembering his free fells;
This in drudgery, day-laboring-out life's age.

Though aloft on turf or perch or poor low stage,
Both sing sometimes the sweetest, sweetest spells,
Yet both droop deadly sometimes in their cells
Or wring their barriers in bursts of fear or rage.

Not that the sweet-fowl, song-fowl, needs no rest—
Why, hear him, hear him babble and drop down to his nest,
But his own nest, wild nest, no prison.

Man's spirit will be flesh-bound when found at best,
But uncumbered: meadow-down is not distressed
For a rainbow footing it nor he for his bones risen.

Spring

Nothing is so beautiful as spring—
    When weeds, in wheels, shoot long and lovely and lush;
    Thrush's eggs look little low heavens, and thrush
Through the echoing timber does so rinse and wring
The ear, it strikes like lightnings to hear him sing;
    The glassy peartree leaves and blooms, they brush
    The descending blue; that blue is all in a rush
With richness; the racing lambs too have fair their fling.

What is all this juice and all this joy?
    A strain of the earth's sweet being in the beginning
In Eden garden. —Have, get, before it cloy,
    Before it cloud, Christ, Lord, and sour with sinning,
Innocent mind and Mayday in girl and boy,
    Most, O maid's Child, thy choice and worthy the winning.

Thou Art Indeed Just, Lord

Justus quidem tu es, Domine, si disputem tecum:
verumtamen justa loquar ad te: Quare via impiorum
prosperatur?

Thou art indeed just, Lord, if I contend
With thee; but, Sir, so what I plead is just.
Why do sinners' ways prosper? and why must
Disappointment all I endeavor end?
Wert thou my enemy, O thou my Friend,
How wouldst thou worse, I wonder, than thou dost
Defeat, thwart me? Oh, the sots and thralls of lust
Do in spare hours more thrive than I that spend,
Sir, life upon thy cause. See, banks and brakes
Now, leavèd how thick! lacèd they are again
With fretty chervil, look, and fresh wind shakes
Them; birds build—but not I build; no, but strain,
Time's eunuch, and not breed one work that wakes.
Mine, O thou Lord of Life, send my roots rain.

Hurrahing in Harvest

Summer ends now; now, barbarous in beauty, the stooks arise
    Around; up above, what wind-walks! what lovely behaviour
    of silk-sack clouds! has wilder, wilful-wavier
Meal-drift moulded ever and melted across skies?

I walk, I lift up, I lift up heart, eyes,
    Down all that glory in the heavens to glean our Saviour;
    And, eyes, heart, what looks, what lips gave you a
Rapturous love's greeting of realer, of rounder replies?

And the azurous hung hills are his world-wielding shoulder
    Majestic—as a stallion stalwart, very-violet-sweet!—
These things, these things were here and but the beholder
    Wanting; which two when they once meet,
The heart rears wings bold and bolder
    And hurls for him, O half hurls earth for him off under
      his feet.

The Wreck of the Deutschland

To the happy memory of five Franciscan Nuns, exiles by the Falk Laws, drowned between midnight and morning of December 7th, 1875

I   Thou mastering me
        God! giver of breath and bread;
     World's strand, sway of the sea;
       Lord of living and dead;
  Thou hast bound bones and veins in me, fastened me flesh,
  And after it almost unmade, what with dread,
     Thy doing: and dost thou touch me afresh?
Over again I feel thy finger and find thee.

II   I did say yes
       O at lightning and lashed rod;
    Thou heardest me truer than tongue confess
       Thy terror, O Christ, O God;
  Thou knowest the walls, altar and hour and night:
  The swoon of a heart that the sweep and the hurl of thee trod
     Hard down with a horror of height:
And the midriff astrain with leaning of, laced with fire of stress.

III   The frown of his face
       Before me, the hurtle of hell
    Behind, where, where was a, where was a place?
       I whirled out wings that spell
  And fled with a fling of the heart to the heart of the Host.
  My heart, but you were dovewinged, I can tell,
     Carrier-witted, I am bold to boast,
To flash from the flame to the flame then, tower from the grace
    to the grace.

IV   I am soft sift
       In an hourglass—at the wall
    Fast, but mined with a motion, a drift,
       And it crowds and it combs to the fall;
  I steady as a water in a well, to a poise, to a pane,
  But roped with, always, all the way down from the tall
     Fells or flanks of the voel, a vein
Of the gospel proffer, a pressure, a principle, Christ's gift.

►►►►

V   I kiss my hand
           To the stars, lovely-asunder
       Starlight, wafting him out of it; and
          Glow, glory in thunder;
     Kiss my hand to the dappled-with-damson west:
     Since, tho' he is under the world's splendour and wonder,
       His mystery must be instressed, stressed;
For I greet him the days I meet him, and bless when I understand.

VI   Not out of his bliss
          Springs the stress felt
       Nor first from heaven (and few know this)
          Swings the stroke dealt—
     Stroke and a stress that stars and storms deliver,
     That guilt is hushed by, hearts are flushed by and melt—
       But it rides time like riding a river
(And here the faithful waver, the faithless fable and miss).

VII   It dates from day
          Of his going in Galilee;
       Warm-laid grave of the womb-like grey;
          Manger, maiden's knee;
     The dense and the driven Passion, and frightful sweat;
     Thence the discharge of it, there its swelling to be,
       Though felt before, though in high flood yet—
What none would have known of it, only the heart, being hard at
      bay,

VIII   Is out with it! Oh,
          We lash with the best or worst
       Word last! How a lush-kept plush-capped sloe
          Will, mouthed to flesh-burst,
     Gush!—flush the man, the being with it, sour or sweet,
     Brim, in a flash, full!—Hither then, last or first,
       To hero of Calvary, Christ's feet—
Never ask if meaning it, wanting it, warned of it—men go.

IX   Be adored among men,
          God, three-numberèd form;
       Wring thy rebel, dogged in den,
          Man's malice, with wrecking and storm.
     Beyond saying sweet, past telling of tongue,
     Thou art lightning and love, I found it, a winter and warm;
       Father and fondler of heart thou hast wrung:
Hast thy dark descending and most art merciful then.

X   With an anvil-ding
    And with fire in him forge thy will
  Or rather, rather then, stealing as Spring
    Through him, melt him but master him still:
Whether at once, as once at a crash Paul,
Or as Austin, a lingering-out sweet skill,
  Make mercy in all of us, out of us all
Mastery, but be adored, but be adored King.

PART THE SECOND

XI   "Some find me a sword; some
    The flange and the rail; flame,
  Fang, or flood" goes Death on drum,
    And storms bugle his fame.
But we dream we are rooted in earth—Dust!
Fresh falls within sight of us, we, though our flower the same,
  Wave with the meadow, forget that there must
The sour scythe cringe, and the blear share come.

XII   On Saturday sailed from Bremen,
    American-outward-bound,
  Take settler and seamen, tell men with women,
    Two hundred souls in the round—
O Father, not under thy feathers nor ever as guessing
The goal was a shoal, of a fourth the doom to be drowned;
  Yet did the dark side of the bay of thy blessing
Not vault them, the millions of rounds of thy mercy not reeve
  even them in?

XIII   Into the snows she sweeps,
    Hurling the haven behind,
  The *Deutschland*, on Sunday; and so the sky keeps,
    For the infinite air is unkind,
And the sea flint-like, black-backed in the regular blow,
Sitting Eastnortheast, in cursed quarter, the wind;
  Wiry and white-fiery and whirlwind-swivellèd snow
Spins to the widow-making unchilding unfathering deeps.

XIV   She drove in the dark to leeward,
    She struck—not a reef or a rock

➤➤➤➤

But the combs of a smother of sand: night drew her
    Dead to the Kentish Knock;
  And she beat the bank down with her bows and the ride of her
    keel:
  The breakers rolled on her beam with ruinous shock;
    And canvas and compass, the whorl and the wheel
Idle for ever to waft her or wind her with, these she endured.

XV   Hope had grown grey hairs,
      Hope had mourning on,
  Trenched with tears, carved with cares,
      Hope was twelve hours gone;
  And frightful a nightfall folded rueful a day
  Nor rescue, only rocket and lightship, shone,
      And lives at last were washing away:
To the shrouds they took—they shook in the hurling and horrible
  airs.

XVI   One stirred from the rigging to save
      The wild woman-kind below,
  With a rope's end round the man, handy and brave—
      He was pitched to his death at a blow,
  For all his dreadnought breast and braids of thew:
  They could tell him for hours, dandled the to and fro
    Through the cobbled form-fleece, what could he do
With the burl of the fountains of air, buck and the flood of the wave?

XVII   They fought with God's cold—
      And they could not and fell to the deck
  (Crushed them) or water (and drowned them) or rolled
      With the sea-romp over the wreck.
  Night roared, with the heart-break hearing a heart-broke rabble,
  The woman's wailing, the crying of child without check—
    Till a lioness arose breasting the babble,
A prophetess towered in the tumult, a virginal tongue told.

XVIII   Ah, touched in your bower of bone
      Are you! turned for an exquisite smart,
  Have you! make words break from me here all alone,
      Do you!—mother of being in me, heart.
  O unteachably after evil, but uttering truth,
  Why, tears! is it? tears; such a melting, a madrigal start!
    Never-eldering revel and river of youth,
What can it be, this glee? the good you have there of your own?

XIX   Sister, a sister calling
      A master, her master and mine!
    And the inboard seas run swirling and hawling;

The rash smart sloggering brine
Blinds her; but she that weather sees one thing, one;
Has one fetch in her: she rears herself to divine
Ears, and the call of the tall nun
To the men in the tops and the tackle rode over the storm's brawling.

XX   She was first of a five and came
      Of a coifèd sisterhood,
   (O Deutschland, double a desparate name!
     O world wide of its good!
 But Gertrude, lily, and Luther, are two of a town,
  Christ's lily and beast of the waste wood:
    From life's dawn it is drawn down,
Abel is Cain's brother and breasts they have sucked the same.)

XXI   Loathed for a love men knew in them,
      Banned by the land of their birth,
   Rhine refused them. Thames would ruin them;
     Surf, snow, river and earth
 Gnashed: but thou art above, thou Orion of light;
  Thy unchancelling poising palms were weighing the worth,
    Thou martyr-master: in thy sight
Storm flakes were scroll-leaved flowers, lily showers—sweet heaven
  was astrew in them.

XXII   Five! the finding and sake
      And cipher of suffering Christ.
   Mark, the mark is of man's make
     And the word of it Sacrificed.
 But he scores it in scarlet himself on his own bespoken,
  Before-time-taken, dearest prizèd and priced—
    Stigma, signal, cinquefoil token
For lettering of the lamb's fleece, ruddying of the rose flake.

XXIII   Joy fall to thee, father Francis,
      Drawn to the Life that died;
   With the gnarls of the nails in thee, niche of the lance, his
     Lovescape crucified
 And seal of his seraph-arrival! and these thy daughters
  And five-livèd and leavèd favour and pride,
    Are sisterly sealed in wild waters,
To bathe in his fall-gold mercies, to breathe in his all-fire glances.

XXIV   Away in the loveable west,
      On a pastoral forehead of Wales,
   I was under a roof here, I was at rest,
     And they the prey of the gales;
  She to the black-about air, to the breaker, the thickly

▶▶▶▶

Falling flakes, to the throng that catches and quails
    Was calling "O Christ, Christ, come quickly":
The cross to her she calls Christ to her, christens her wild-worst Best.

XXV   The majesty! what did she mean?
    Breathe, arch and original Breath.
  Is it love in her of the being as her lover had been?
    Breathe, body of lovely Death.
 They were else-minded then, altogether, the men
Woke thee with a *we are perishing* in the weather of Gennesareth.
    Or is it that she cried for the crown then,
The keener to come at the comfort for feeling the combating keen?

XXVI   For how to the heart's cheering
    The down-dugged ground-hugged grey
  Hovers off, the jay-blue heavens appearing
    Of pied and peeled May!
 Blue-beating and hoary-glow height; or night, still higher,
 With belled fire and the moth-soft Milky Way,
    What by your measure is the heaven of desire,
The treasure never eyesight got, nor was ever guessed what for the
    hearing?

XXVII No, but it was not these.
    The jading and jar of the cart,
  Time's tasking, it is fathers that asking for ease
    Of the sodden-with-its-sorrowing heart,
 Not danger, electrical horror; then further it finds
The appealing of the Passion is tenderer in prayer apart:
    Other, I gather, in measure her mind's
Burden, in wind's burly and beat of endragoned seas.

XXVIII But how shall I . . . make me room there:
    Reach me a . . . Fancy, come faster—
  Strike you the sight of it? look at it loom there,
    Thing that she . . . there then! the Master,
Ipse, the only one, Christ, King, Head:
 He was to cure the extremity where he had cast her;
    Do, deal, lord it with living and dead;
Let him ride, her pride, in his triumph, despatch and have done with
    his doom there.

XXIX   Ah! there was a heart right!
    There was a single eye!
  Read the unshapeable shock night
    And knew the who and the why;
 Wording it how but by him that present and past,
Heaven and earth are word of, worded by?—

The Simon Peter of a soul! to the blast
Tarpeian-fast, but a blown beacon of light.

XXX   Jesu, heart's light,
     Jesu, maid's son,
   What was the feast followed the night
     Thou hadst glory of this nun?—
  Feast of the one woman without stain.
  For so conceivèd, so to conceive thee is done;
   But here was heart-throe, birth of a brain,
Word, that heard and kept thee and uttered thee outright.
XXXI   Well, she has thee for the pain, for the
     Patience; but pity of the rest of them!
   Heart, go and bleed at a bitterer vein for the
     Comfortless unconfessed of them—
  No not uncomforted: lovely-felicitous Providence
  Finger of a tender of, O of a feathery delicacy, the breast of the
   Maiden could obey so, be a bell to, ring of it, and
Startle the poor sheep back! is the shipwreck then a harvest, does
  tempest carry the grain for thee?

XXXII   I admire thee, master of the tides,
     Of the Yore-flood, of the year's fall;
   The recurb and the recovery of the gulf's sides,
     The girth of it and the wharf of it and the wall;
  Stanching, quenching ocean of a motionable mind;
  Ground of being, and granite of it: past all
     Grasp God, throned behind
Death with a sovereignty that heeds but hides, bodes but abides;

XXXIII With a mercy that outrides
     The all of water, an ark
   For the listener; for the lingerer with a love glides
     Lower than death and the dark;
  A vein for the visiting of the past-prayer, pent in prison,
  The-last-breath penitent spirits—the uttermost mark
     Our passion-plunged giant risen,
The Christ of the Father compassionate, fetched in the storm of his
  strides.

XXXIV Now burn, new born to the world,
     Double-natured name,
   The heaven-flung, heart-fleshed, maiden-furled
     Miracle-in-Mary-of-flame,
  Mid-numbered He in three of the thunder-throne!
  Not a dooms-day dazzle in his coming nor dark as he came;
     Kind, but royally reclaiming his own;
A released shower, let flash to the shire, not a lightning of fire
  hard-hurled.

➤➤➤

XXXV Dame, at our door
        Drowned, and among our shoals,
      Remember us in the roads, the heaven-haven of the Reward:
        Our King back, oh, upon English souls!
    Let him easter in us, be a dayspring to the dimness of us, be a
      crimson-cresseted east,
      More brightening her, rare-dear Britain, as his reign rolls,
        Pride, rose, prince, hero of us, high-priest,
  Our hearts' charity's hearth's fire, our thoughts' chivalry's throng's
    Lord.

A Hymn to God the Father

Ben Jonson

Hear me, O God!
  A broken heart
  Is my best part:
Use still Thy rod,
  That I may prove,
  Therein, Thy love.

If Thou hadst not
  Been stern to me,
  But left me free,
I had forgot
  Myself and Thee.

For sin's so sweet,
  As minds ill bent
  Rarely repent
Until they meet
  Their punishment.

Who more can crave
  Than Thou hast done:
  That gav'st a Son
To free a slave?
  First made of nought,
  Withal since bought.

Sin, Death, and Hell
  His glorious Name
  Quite overcame,
Yet I rebel
  And slight the same.

But I'll come in
  Before my loss
  Me farther toss,
As sure to win
  Under His Cross.

A Hymn on the Nativity of My Savior

I sing the birth, was born tonight,
The Author both of life and light;
  The angels so did sound it,
And like the ravished shepherds said,
Who saw the light and were afraid,
  Yet searched, and true they found it.

The Son of God, the Eternal King,
That did us all salvation bring,
  And freed the soul from danger;
He whom the whole world could not take,
The Word, which heaven and earth did make,
  Was now laid in a manger.

The Father's wisdom willed it so,
The Son's obedience knew no No,
  Both wills were in one stature;
And as that wisdom had decreed,
The Word was now made flesh indeed,
  And took on Him our nature.

What comfort by Him do we win?
Who made Himself the Prince of sin
  To make us heirs of glory?
To see this Babe, all innocence;
A Martyr born in our defence;
  Can man forget this story?

George MacDonald

Shall the Dead Praise Thee?

I cannot praise Thee. By his instrument
   The master sits, and moves nor foot nor hand;
For see the organ pipes, this, that way bent,
   Leaning, o'erthrown, like wheat-stalks tempest fanned!

I well could praise Thee for a flower, a dove,
   But not for Life that is not life in me;
Not for a being that is less than Love—
   A barren shoal half lifted from a sea.

Unto a land where no wind bloweth ships
   Thy Wind one day will blow me to my own:
Rather I'd kiss no more their loving lips
   Than carry them a heart so poor and prone.

I bless Thee, Father, Thou art what Thou art,
   That Thou dost know Thyself what Thou dost know—
A perfect, simple, tender, rhythmic heart,
   Beating its blood to all in bounteous flow.

And I can bless Thee too for every smart,
   For every disappointment, ache, and fear;
For every hook Thou fixest in my heart,
   For every burning cord that draws me near.

But prayer these wake, not song. Thyself I crave.
   Come Thou, or all Thy gifts away I fling.
Thou silent, I am but an empty grave:
   Think to me, Father, and I am a king!

My organ pipes will then stand up awake,
   Their life soar, as from smoldering wood the blaze;
And swift contending harmonies shall shake
   Thy windows with a storm of jubilant praise.

Jesus Despised!

Despised! Rejected by the priest-led roar
Of the multitude! The imperial purple flung
About the form the hissing scourge had stung,
Witnessing naked to the truth it bore!
True Son of Father true, I Thee adore.
Even the mocking purple truthful hung
On Thy true shoulders, bleeding its folds among,
For Thou wast King, art King for evermore!
"I know the Father: He knows Me the Truth."
Truth-Witness, therefore, the one essential King,
With Thee I die, with Thee live worshipping!
O human God, O Brother, eldest born,
Never but Thee was there a Man in sooth,
Never a true crown but Thy crown of thorn!

Prayer

We doubt the Word that tells us: Ask,
And ye shall have your prayer:
We turn our thoughts as to a task,
With will constrained and rare.

And yet we have; these scanty prayers
Yield gold without alloy:
O God, but he that trusts and dares
Must have a boundless joy!

Rondel

I do not know Thy final will;
    It is too good for me to know:
    Thou willest that I mercy show,
That I take heed and do no ill,
That I the needy warm and fill,
    Nor stones at any sinner throw;
But I know not Thy final will—
    It is too good for me to know.

I know Thy love unspeakable—
    For love's sake able to send woe!
    To find Thine own Thou lost didst go,
And wouldst for men Thy blood yet spill!—
How should l know Thy final will,
    Godwise too good for me to know!

John Milton

The Hymn

It was the winter wild,
While the heaven-born child
All meanly wrapped in the rude manger lies;
Nature, in awe to him,
Had doffed her gaudy trim,
With her great Master so to sympathize:
It was no season then for her
To wanton with the Sun, her lusty paramour.

Only with speeches fair
She woos the gentle air
To hide her guilty front with innocent snow,
And on her naked shame,
Pollute with sinful blame,
The saintly veil of maiden white to throw;
Confounded, that her Maker's eyes
Should look so near upon her foul deformities.

But he, her fears to cease,
Sent down the meek-eyed Peace:
She, crowned with olive green, came softly sliding
Down through the turning sphere,
His ready harbinger,
With turtle wing the amorous clouds dividing;
And, waving wide her myrtle wand,
She strikes a universal peace through sea and land.

No war or battle's sound
Was heard the world around;
The idle spear and shield were high uphung;
The hookéd chariot stood,
Unstained with hostile blood;
The trumpet spake not to the arméd throng;
And kings sat still with awful eye,
As if they surely knew their sovran Lord was by.

But peaceful was the night
Wherein the Prince of light
His reign of peace upon the earth began.
The winds, with wonder whist,
Smoothly the waters kissed,
Whispering new joys to the mild Ocean,

Who now hath quite forgot to rave,
While birds of calm sit brooding on the charméd wave.

The stars, with deep amaze,
Stand fixed, in steadfast gaze,
Bending one way their precious influence,
And will not take their flight,
For all the morning light,
Or Lucifer that often warned them thence;
But in their glimmering orbs did glow,
Until their Lord himself bespake, and bid them go.

And though the shady gloom
Had given day her room,
The Sun himself withheld his wonted speed,
And hid his head for shame,
As his inferior flame
The new-enlightened world no more should need:
He saw a greater Sun appear
Than his bright throne or burning axletree could bear.

The shepherds on the lawn,
Or ere the point of dawn,
Sat simply chatting in a rustic row;
Full little thought they then
That the mighty Pan
Was kindly come to live with them below:
Perhaps their loves, or else their sheep,
Was all that did their silly thoughts so busy keep.

When such music sweet
Their hearts and ears did greet
As never was by mortal finger struck,
Divinely-warbled voice
Answering the stringéd noise,
As all their souls in blissful rapture took:
The air, such pleasure loth to lose,
With thousand echoes still prolongs each heavenly close.

Nature, that heard such sound
Beneath the hollow round
Of Cynthia's seat the airy region thrilling,
Now was almost won
To think her part was done,
And that her reign had here its last fulfilling:
She knew such harmony alone
Could hold all Heaven and Earth in happier union.

At last surrounds their sight

►►►►

A globe of circular light,
That with long beams the shamefaced Night arrayed;
The helméd cherubim
And sworded seraphim
Are seen in glittering ranks with wings displayed,
Harping loud and solemn choir,
With unexpressive notes, to Heaven's new-born Heir.

Such music (as 'tis said)
Before was never made,
But when of old the sons of morning sung,
While the Creator great
His constellations set,
And the well-balanced world on hinges hung,
And cast the dark foundations deep,
And bid the weltering waves their oozy channel keep.

Ring out, ye crystal spheres,
Once bless our human ears,
If ye have power to touch our senses so;
And let your silver chime
Move in melodious time;
And let the bass of heaven's deep organ blow;
And with your ninefold harmony
Make up full consort to th'angelic symphony.

For, if such holy song
Enwrap our fancy long,
Time will run back and fetch the age of gold;
And speckled vanity
Will sicken soon and die;
And leprous sin will melt from earthly mold;
And Hell itself will pass away,
And leave her dolorous mansions to the peering day.

Yea, Truth and Justice then
Will down return to men,
Orbed in a rainbow; and, like glories wearing,
Mercy will sit between,
Throned in celestial sheen,
With radiant feet the tissued clouds down steering;
And Heaven, as at some festival,
Will open wide the gates of her high palace-hall.

But wisest Fate says no,
This must not yet be so;
The Babe lies yet in smiling infancy
That on the bitter cross
Must redeem our loss,
So both himself and us to glorify:

Yet first, to those enchained in sleep,
The wakeful trump of doom must thunder through the deep

With such a horrid clang
As on Mount Sinai rang,
While the red fire and smoldering clouds outbrake:
The aged Earth, aghast,
With terror of that blast,
Shall from the surface to the center shake,
When, at the world's last session,
The dreadful Judge in middle air shall spread his throne.

And then at last our bliss
Full and perfect is,
But now begins; for from this happy day
The old Dragon under ground,
In straiter limits bound,
Not half so far casts his usurpéd sway,
And, wroth to see his kingdom fail,
Swings the scaly horror of his folded tail.

The Oracles are dumb;
No voice or hideous hum
Runs through the archéd roof in words deceiving.
Apollo from his shrine
Can no more divine,
With hollow shriek the steep of Delphos leaving.
No nightly trance or breathéd spell
Inspires the pale-eyed priest from the prophetic cell.

The lonely mountains o'er,
And the resounding shore,
A voice of weeping heard and loud lament;
From haunted spring, and dale
Edged with poplar pale,
The parting genius is with sighing sent;
With flower-inwoven tresses torn
The Nymphs in twilight shade of tangled thickets mourn.

In consecrated earth,
And on the holy hearth,
The Lars and Lemures moan with midnight plaint;
In urns and altars round,
A drear and dying sound
Affrights the flamens at their service quaint;
And the chill marble seems to sweat,
While each peculiar power forgoes his wonted seat.

Peor and Baalim
Forsake their temples dim,

With that twice-battered God of Palestine;
And moonéd Ashtaroth,
Heaven's queen and mother both,
Now sits not girt with tapers' holy shine:
The Libyc Hammon shrinks his horn;
In vain the Tyrian maids their wounded Thammuz mourn.

And sullen Moloch, fled,
Hath left in shadows dread
His burning idol all of blackest hue;
In vain with cymbals' ring
They call the grisly king,
In dismal dance about the furnace blue;
The brutish gods of Nile as fast,
Isis, Orus, and the dog Anubis, haste.

Nor is Osiris seen
In Memphian grove or green,
Trampling the unshowered grass with lowings loud;
Nor can he be at rest
Within his sacred chest;
Nought but profoundest Hell can be his shroud;
In vain, with timbreled anthems dark,
The sable-stoléd sorcerers bear his worshiped ark.

He feels from Judah's land
The dreaded Infant's hand;
The rays of Bethlehem blind his dusky eyn;
Nor all the gods beside
Longer dare abide,
Not Typhon huge ending in snaky twine:
Our Babe, to show his Godhead true,
Can in his swaddling bands control the damnéd crew.

So when the sun in bed,
Curtained with cloudy red,
Pillows his chin upon an orient wave,
The flocking shadows pale
Troop to th' infernal jail;
Each fettered ghost slips to his several grave,
And the yellow-skirted fays
Fly after the night-steeds, leaving their moon-loved maze.

But see! the Virgin blest
Hath laid her Babe to rest.
Time is our tedious song should here have ending:
Heaven's youngest-teeméd star
Hath fixed her polished car,
Her sleeping Lord with handmaid lamp attending;
And all about the courtly stable
Bright-harnessed angels sit in order serviceable.

When I Consider

When I consider how my light is spent
  Ere half my days in this dark world and wide,
  And that one talent which is death to hide
  Lodged with me useless, though my soul more bent
To serve therewith my Maker, and present
  My true account, lest he returning chide;
  "Doth God exact day-labor, light denied?"
  I fondly ask; but Patience to prevent .
That murmur, soon replies, "God doth not need
  Either man's work or his own gifts; who best
  Bear his mild yoke, they serve him best. His state
Is kingly. Thousands at his bidding speed
  And post o'er land and ocean without rest;
  They also serve who only stand and wait."

At a Solemn Music

Blest pair of sirens, pledges of heaven's joy,
Sphere-born harmonious sisters, voice and verse,
Wed your divine sounds, and mixed power employ,
Dead things with inbreathed sense able to pierce,
And to our high-raised fantasy present
That undisturbed song of pure consent
Ay sung before the sapphire-colored throne
To him that sits thereon,
With saintly shout and solemn jubilee
Where the bright seraphim in burning row
Their loud uplifted angel trumpets blow,
And the cherubic host in thousand choirs
Touch their immortal harps of golden wires
With those just spirits that wear victorious palms,
Hymns devout and holy psalms
Singing everlastingly;
That we on earth with undiscording voice
May rightly answer that melodious noise;
As once we did, till disproportioned sin
Jarred against nature's chime and with harsh din
Broke the fair music that all creatures made
To their great Lord, whose love their motion swayed
In perfect diapason, whilst they stood
In first obedience and their state of good.
O may we soon again renew that song
And keep in tune with heaven, till God ere long
To his celestial consort us unite,
To live with him and sing in endless morn of light.   361

Psalm 136

Let us with a gladsome mind
Praise the Lord for He is kind:
For His mercies aye endure,
Ever faithful, ever sure.

Let us blaze His Name abroad,
For of gods He is the God:
For His mercies aye endure,
Ever faithful, ever sure.

He, with all-commanding might,
Filled the new-made world with light:
For His mercies aye endure,
Ever faithful, ever sure.

He the golden-tresséd sun
Caused all day his course to run;
For His mercies aye endure,
Ever faithful, ever sure.

And the moon to shine by night,
'Mid her spangled sisters bright:
For His mercies aye endure,
Ever faithful, ever sure.

All things living He doth feed;
His full hand supplies their need:
For His mercies aye endure,
Ever faithful, ever sure.

Let us therefore warble forth
His high majesty and worth:
For His mercies aye endure,
Ever faithful, ever sure.

Ode on the Morning
of Christ's Nativity

This is the month, and this the happy morn,
Wherein the Son of Heaven's Eternal King,
Of wedded maid and virgin mother born,
Our great redemption from above did bring;
For so the holy sages once did sing,
   That he our deadly forfeit should release,
And with his Father work us a perpetual peace.

That glorious form, that light unsufferable,
And that far-beaming blaze of majesty,
Wherewith he wont at Heaven's high council-table
To sit the midst of Trinal Unity,
He laid aside, and, here with us to be,
   Forsook the courts of everlasting day,
And chose with us a darksome house of mortal clay.

Say, Heavenly Muse, shall not thy sacred vein
Afford a present to the Infant God?
Hast thou no verse, no hymn, or solemn strain,
To welcome him to this his new abode,
Now while the heaven, by the Sun's team untrod,
   Hath took no print of the approaching light,
And all the spangled host keep watch in squadrons bright?

See how from far upon the eastern road
The star-led wizards haste with odors sweet!
Oh run, prevent them with thy humble ode,
And lay it lowly at his blessed feet;
Have thou the honor first thy Lord to greet,
   And join thy voice unto the angel choir
From out his secret altar touched with hallowed fire.

How Soon Hath Time

How soon hath time, the subtle thief of youth,
   Stolen on his wing my three-and-twentieth year!
   My hasting days fly on with full career,
   But my late spring no bud nor blossom showeth.
Perhaps my semblance might deceive the truth
   That I to manhood am arrived so near;
   And inward ripeness doth much less appear,
   That some more timely-happy spirits endueth.
Yet be it less or more or soon or slow,
   It shall be still in strictest measure even,
   To that same lot, however mean or high,
Toward which Time leads me, and the will of Heaven;
   All is, if I have grace to use it so,
   As ever in my great Taskmaster's eye.

John Newton

How Sweet the Name

How sweet the Name of Jesus sounds
In a believer's ear!
It soothes his sorrows, heals his wounds,
And drives away his fear.

It makes the wounded spirit whole
And calms the troubled breast;
'Tis manna to the hungry soul,
And to the weary rest.

Dear Name! the Rock on which I build,
My Shield and Hiding-place,
My never-failing Treasury filled
With boundless stores of grace.

By Thee my prayers acceptance gain,
Although with sin defiled;
Satan accuses me in vain,
And I am owned a child.

Jesus! my Shepherd, Husband, Friend,
My Prophet, Priest, and King;
My Lord, my Life, my Way, my End,
Accept the praise I bring.

Weak is the effort of my heart
And cold my warmest thought;
But when I see Thee as Thou art,
I'll praise Thee as I ought.

Till then I would Thy love proclaim
With every fleeting breath;
And may the music of Thy Name
Refresh my soul in death.

May the Grace
of Christ Our Savior

May the grace of Christ our Savior
And the Father's boundless love,
With the Holy Spirit's favor,
Rest upon us from above.

Thus may be abide in union
With each other and the Lord,
And possess, in sweet communion,
Joys which earth cannot afford.

Glorious Things
of Thee Are Spoken

Glorious things of thee are spoken,
   Zion, city of our God;
He whose Word cannot be broken
   Formed thee for His own abode.
On the Rock of Ages founded,
   What can shake thy sure repose?
With salvation's walls surrounded
   Thou may'st smile at all thy foes.

See, the streams of living waters,
   Springing from eternal love,
Well supply thy sons and daughters
   And all fear of want remove.
Who can faint while such a river
   Ever flows their thirst t'assuage?
Grace which like the Lord, the Giver,
   Never fails from age to age.

Savior, if of Zion's city
   I, through grace, a member am,
Let the world deride or pity,
   I will glory in Thy Name.
Fading is the worldling's pleasure,
   All his boasted pomp and show;
Solid joys and lasting treasure
   None but Zion's children know.

Amazing Grace!

Amazing grace! how sweet the sound
That saved a wretch like me!
I once was lost, but now am found,
Was blind, but now I see.

'Twas grace that taught my heart to fear,
And grace my fears relieved;
How precious did that grace appear
The hour I first believed!

Through many dangers, toils, and snares
I have already come;
'Tis grace hath brought me safe thus far,
And grace will lead me home.

When we've been there ten thousand years,
Bright shining as the sun,
We've no less days to sing God's praise
Than when we first begun.

Francis Quarles

Why Dost Thou Shade Thy Lovely Face?

JOB 13:24

Why dost Thou shade Thy lovely face? O, why
Does that eclipsing hand so long deny
The sunshine of Thy soul-enlivening eye?

Without that Light, what light remains in me?
Thou art my Life, my Way, my Light; in Thee
I live, I move, and by Thy beams I see.

Thou art my Life; if Thou but turn away,
My life's a thousand deaths. Thou art my Way;
Without Thee, Lord, I travel not but stray.

My Light Thou art; without Thy glorious sight
Mine eyes are darkened with perpetual night.
My God, Thou art my Way, my Life, my Light.

Thou art my Way; I wander if Thou fly:
Thou art my Light; if hid, how blind am I!
Thou art my Life; if Thou withdraw, I die.

Mine eyes are blind and dark; I cannot see.
To whom, or whither, should my darkness flee
But to the Light? And who's that Light but Thee?

My path is lost; my wandering steps do stray;
I cannot safely go, nor safely stay.
Whom should I seek but Thee, my Path, my Way?

O, I am dead: to whom shall I, poor I,
Repair? To whom shall my sad ashes fly
But Life? And where is life but in Thine eye?

And yet Thou turnst Thy face and fly'st me;
And yet I sue for grace and Thou deny'st me;
Speak, art Thou angry, Lord, or only try'st me?

Unscreen those heavenly lamps or tell me why
Thou shad'st Thy face. Perhaps Thou thinkest no eye
Can view those flames, and not drop down and die.

If that be all, shine forth and draw Thee nigher;
Let me behold and die, for my desire
Is phoenix-like to perish in that fire.

Death-conquered Lazarus was redeemed by Thee;
If I am dead, Lord, set death's prisoner free.
Am I more spent, or stink I worse than he?

If my puffed light be out, give leave to tine
My flameless snuff at that bright Lamp of Thine;
O what's Thy Light the less for lighting mine?

If I have lost my path, great Shepherd, say,
Shall I still wander in a doubtful way?
Lord, shall a lamb of Israel's sheepfold stray?

Thou art the pilgrim's Path, the blind man's Eye,
The dead man's Life; on Thee my hopes rely.
If Thou remove, I err, I grope, I die.

Disclose Thy sunbeams; close Thy wings and stay;
See, see, how I am blind, and dead, and stray,
O Thou, that art my Light, my Life, my Way.

Christina Rossetti

If I Could Trust Mine Own Self

If I could trust mine own self with your fate,
  Shall I not rather trust it in God's hand?
  Without Whose Will one lily doth not stand,
Nor sparrow fall at His appointed date;
  Who numbereth the innumerable sand,
Who weighs the wind and water with a weight,
To Whom the world is neither small nor great,
  Whose knowledge foreknew every plan we planned.
Searching my heart for all that touches you,
  I find there only love and love's goodwill
Helpless to help and impotent to do,
Of understanding dull, of sight most dim;
And therefore I commend you back to Him
  Whose love your love's capacity can fill.

Good Friday

Am I a stone, and not a sheep,
  That I can stand, O Christ, beneath Thy cross,
  To number drop by drop Thy Blood's slow loss,
And yet not weep?

Not so those women loved
  Who with exceeding grief lamented Thee;
  Not so fallen Peter weeping bitterly;
Not so the thief was moved;

Not so the Sun and Moon
  Which hid their faces in a starless sky,
A horror of great darkness at broad noon—
  I, only I.

Yet give not o'er,
  But seek Thy sheep, true Shepherd of the flock;
Greater than Moses, turn and look once more
  And smite a rock.

A Christmas Carol

In the bleak mid-winter
  Frosty wind made moan,
Earth stood hard as iron,
  Water like a stone;
Snow had fallen, snow on snow,
  Snow on snow,
In the bleak mid-winter
  Long ago.

Our God, Heaven cannot hold him,
  Nor earth sustain;
Heaven and earth shall flee away
  When he comes to reign:
In the bleak mid-winder
  A stable-place sufficed
The Lord God Almighty
  Jesus Christ.

Enough for him whom cherubim
  Worship night and day,
A breastful of milk
  And a mangerful of hay;
Enough for him whom angels
  Fall down before,
The ox and ass and camel
  Which adore.

Angels and archangels
  May have gathered there,
Cherubim and seraphim
  Thronged the air,
But only his mother
  In her maiden bliss
Worshipped the Beloved
  With a kiss.

What can I give him,
  Poor as I am?
If I were a shepherd
  I would bring a lamb,
If I were a wise man
  I would do my part,—
Yet what I can I give him,
  Give my heart.

Who Shall Deliver Me?

God, strengthen me to bear myself,
That heaviest weight of all to bear,
Inalienable weight of care.

All others are outside myself;
I lock my door and bar them out,
The turmoil, tedium, gad-about.

I lock my door upon myself,
And bar them out; but who shall wall
Self from myself, most loathed of all?

If I could once lay down myself,
And start self-purged upon the race
That all must run! Death runs apace.

If I could set aside myself,
And start with lightened heart upon
The road by all men overgone!

God, harden me against myself,
This coward with pathetic voice
Who craves for ease, and rest, and joys:

Myself, arch-traitor to myself;
My hollowest friend, my deadliest foe,
My clog whatever road I go.

Yet One there is can curb myself,
Can roll the strangling load from me,
Break off the yoke and set me free.

A Better Resurrection

I have no wit, no words, no tears;
    My heart within me like a stone
Is numbed too much for hopes or fears.
    Look right, look left, I dwell alone;
I lift mine eyes, but dimmed with grief
    No everlasting hills I see;
My life is in the falling leaf:
    O Jesus, quicken me.

My life is like a faded leaf,
    My harvest dwindled to a husk:
Truly my life is void and brief
    And tedious in the barren dusk;
My life is like a frozen thing,
    No bud nor greenness can I see;
Yet rise it shall—the sap of Spring;
    O Jesus, rise in me.

My life is like a broken bowl,
    A broken bowl that cannot hold
One drop of water for my soul
    Or cordial in the searching cold;
Cast in the fire the perished thing;
    Melt and remould it, till it be
A royal cup for Him, my King:
    O Jesus, drink of me.

Heaven Overarches

Heaven overarches earth and sea,
    Earth-sadness and sea-bitterness.
Heaven overarches you and me:
A little while and we shall be—
Please God—where there is no more sea
    Nor barren wilderness.

Heaven overarches you and me,
    And all earth's gardens and her graves.
Look up with me, until we see
The day break and the shadows flee:
What though tonight wrecks you and me
    If so tomorrow saves?

Before the Beginning

Before the beginning Thou hast foreknown the end,
  Before the birthday the death bed was seen of Thee:
Cleanse what I cannot cleanse, mend what I cannot mend,
  O Lord All Merciful, be merciful to me.

While the end is drawing near I know not mine end;
  Birth I recall not, my death I cannot foresee:
O God, arise to defend, arise to befriend,
  O Lord All Merciful, be merciful to me.

None Other Lamb

None other Lamb, none other Name,
  None other Hope in heaven or earth or sea,
None other Hiding-place from guilt and shame,
  None besides Thee.

My faith burns low, my hope burns low—
  Only my heart's desire cries out in me,
By the deep thunder of its want and woe,
  Cries out to Thee.

Lord, Thou art Life though I be dead,
  Love's Fire Thou art, however cold I be:
Nor heaven have I, nor place to lay my head,
  Nor home, but Thee.

From *Gifts and Graces*

If thou be dead, forgive and thou shalt live;
  If thou hast sinned, forgive and be forgiven;
God waiteth to be gracious and forgive
  And open heaven.

Set not thy will to die and not to live;
  Set not thy face as flint refusing heaven;
Thou fool, set not thy heart on hell: forgive
  And be forgiven.

The Three Enemies

"Sweet, thou art pale."
     "More pale to see
Christ hung upon the cruel tree
And bore His Father's wrath for me."

"Sweet, thou art sad."
     "Beneath a rod
More heavy, Christ for my sake trod
The winepress of the wrath of God."

"Sweet, thou art weary."
     "Not so Christ,
Whose mighty love of me sufficed
For Strength, Salvation, Eucharist."

"Sweet, thou art footsore."
     "If I bleed,
His feet have fled; yea in my need
His heart once bled for mine indeed."

THE WORLD

"Sweet, thou art young."
     "So He was young
Who for my sake in silence hung
Upon the Cross with passion wrung."

"Look, thou art fair."
     "He was more fair
Than men, Who deigned for me to wear
A visage marred beyond compare."

"And thou hast riches."
     "Daily bread:
All else is His: Who, living, dead,
For me lacked where to lay His head."

"And life is sweet."
     "It was not so
To Him, Whose cup did overflow
With mine unutterable woe."

"Thou drinkest deep."
      "When Christ would sup,
He drained the dregs from out my cup:
So how should I be lifted up?"

"Thou shalt win Glory."
      "In the skies,
Lord Jesus, cover up mine eyes
Lest they should look on vanities."

"Thou shalt have Knowledge."
      "Helpless dust!
In Thee, O Lord, I put my trust:
Answer Thou for me, Wise and Just."

"And Might."—
      "Get thee behind me. Lord,
Who has redeemed and not abhorred
My soul, oh keep it by Thy Word."

from *The World. Self-destruction*

LORD, SAVE US, WE PERISH

O Lord, seek us, O Lord, find us
  In Thy patient care;
Be Thy Love before, behind us,
  Round us, everywhere:
Lest the god of this world blind us,
  Lest he speak us fair,
Lest he forge a chain to bind us,
  Lest he bait a snare.
Turn not from us, call to mind us,
  Find, embrace us, bear;
Be Thy Love before, behind us,
  Round us, everywhere.

Trust Me, I Have Not Earned

Trust me, I have not earned your dear rebuke—
   I love, as you would have me, God the most;
   Would lose not Him, but you, must one be lost,
Nor with Lot's wife cast back a faithless look,
Unready to forego what I forsook;
   This say I, having counted up the cost,
   This, though I be the feeblest of God's host,
The sorriest sheep Christ shepherds with His crook.
Yet while I love my God the most, I deem
   That I can never love you over-much;
   I love Him more, so let me love you too;
   Yea, as I apprehend it, love is such
I cannot love you if I love not Him,
I cannot love Him if I love not you.

If Only

If I might only love my God and die!
But now He bids me love Him and live on,
Now when the bloom of all my life is gone,
The pleasant half of life has quite gone by.
My tree of hope is lopped that spread so high;
And I forget how summer glowed and shone,
While autumn grips me with its fingers wan,
And frets me with its fitful windy sigh.
When autumn passes, then must winter numb,
And winter may not pass a weary while,
But when it passes, spring shall flower again:
And in that spring who weepeth now shall smile;
Yea, they shall wax who now are on the wane—
Yea, they shall sing for love when Christ shall come.

Christopher Smart

Learning

Come, come with emulative strife,
To learn the Way, the Truth, and Life,
　　Which Jesus is in One;
In all sound doctrines He proceeds
From Alpha to Omega leads,
　　E'en Spirit, Sire, and Son.

Sure of the exceeding great reward,
Midst all your learning, learn the Lord—
　　This was thy doctrine, Paul;
And this thy lecture should persuade,
Though thou hadst more of human aid
　　Than thy blest brethren all.

Humanity's a charming thing,
And every science of the ring;
　　Good is the classic lore.
For these are helps along the road
That leads to Zion's blest abode
　　And Heavenly Muse's store.

But greater still in each respect,
He that communicates direct,
　　The Tutor of the soul,
Who without pain, degrees, or parts,
While He illuminates our hearts,
　　Can teach at once the whole.

For Sunday

Arise, arise, the Lord arose
On this triumphant day:
Your souls to piety dispose;
Arise to bless and pray.

Ev'n rustics do adorn them now,
Themselves in roses dress;
And to the clergyman they bow
When he begins to bless.

Their best apparel now arrays
The little girls and boys,
And better than the preacher, prays
For heaven's eternal joys.

Beauty

Christ, keep me from the self-survey
  Of beauties all Thine own;
If there is beauty, let me pray,
  And praise the Lord alone.

Pray—that I may the fiend withstand,
  Where'er his serpents be;
Praise—that the Lord's almighty hand
  Is manifest in me.

It is not so—my features are
  Much meaner than the rest;
A glow-worm cannot be a star,
  And I am plain at best.

Then come, my Love, Thy grace impart,
  Great Savior of mankind;
O come and purify my heart
  And beautify my mind.

Then will I Thy carnations nurse
  And cherish every rose,
And empty to the poor my Purse
  Till grace to glory grows.

Good-Nature to Animals

The man of mercy (says the Seer)
   Shows mercy to his beast;
Learn not of churls to be severe,
   But house and feed at least.

Shall I melodious prisoners take
   From out the linnet's nest,
And not keep busy care awake
   To cherish every guest?

What, shall I whip in cruel wrath
   The steed that bears me safe;
Or 'gainst the dog, who plights his troth,
   For faithful service chafe?

In the deep waters throw thy bread,
   Which thou shalt find again,
With God's good interest on thy head,
   And pleasure for thy pain.

Let thine industrious silk-worms reap
   Their wages to the full,
Nor let neglected dormice sleep
   To death within thy wool.

Know when the frosty weather comes,
   'Tis charity to deal
To wren and redbreast all thy crumbs,
   The remnant of thy meal.

Though these some spirits think but light
   And deem indifferent things,
Yet they are serious in the sight
   Of Christ, the King of Kings.

The Nativity of Our Lord and Savior Jesus Christ

Where is this stupendous Stranger?
　Swains of Solyma, advise;
Lead me to my Master's manger,
　Show me where my Savior lies.

O Most Mighty! O Most Holy!
　Far beyond the seraph's thought,
Art Thou then so mean and lowly
　As unheeded prophets taught?

O the magnitude of meekness!
　Worth from worth immortal sprung;
O the strength of infant weakness,
　If eternal is so young!

If so young and thus eternal,
　Michael tune the shepherd's reed,
Where the scenes are ever vernal,
　And the loves be love indeed!

See *the* God blasphemed and doubted
　In the schools of Greece and Rome;
See the powers of darkness routed,
　Taken at their utmost gloom.

Nature's decorations glisten
　Far above their usual trim;
Birds on box and laurels listen,
　As so near the cherubs hymn.

Boreas no longer winters
　On the desolated coast;
Oaks no more are riven in splinters
　By the whirlwind and his host.

Spinks and ouzles sing sublimely,
　"We too have a Savior born";
Whiter blossoms burst untimely
　On the blest Mosaic thorn.

God all-bounteous, all-creative,
　Whom no ills from good dissuade,
Is incarnate and a Native
　Of the very world He made.

Robert Southwell

The Burning Babe

As I in hoary winter's night stood shivering in the snow,
Surprised I was with sudden heat which made my heart to glow;
And lifting up a fearful eye to view what fire was near,
A pretty babe all burning bright did in the air appear;
Who, scorchéd with excessive heat, such floods of tears did shed
As though his floods should quench his flames which with his tears
   were fed.
"Alas," quoth he, "but newly born in fiery heats I fry,
Yet none approach to warm their hearts or feel my fire but I!
My faultless breast the furnace is, the fuel wounding thorns,
Love is the fire, and sighs the smoke, the ashes shame and scorns;
The fuel justice layeth on, and mercy blows the coals,
The metal in this furnace wrought are men's defiléd souls,
For which, as now on fire I am to work them to their good,
So will I melt into a bath to wash them in my blood."
With this he vanished out of sight and swiftly shrunk away,
And straight I calléd unto mind that it was Christmas day.

The Flight into Egypt

Alas! our Day is forced to fly by night!
   Light without light, and sun by silent shade.
O Nature, blush, that sufferest such a wight,
   Who in Thy sun this dark eclipse hath made;
Day to his eyes, light to his steps deny,
Who hates the Light which graceth every eye.

Sun being fled, the stars do loose their light,
   And shining beams in bloody streams they drench;
A cruel storm of Herod's mortal spite
   Their lives and lights with bloody showers doth quench:
The tyrant, to be sure of murdering One,
For fear of sparing Him doth pardon none.

O blessed babes! first flowers of Christian Spring,
   Who though untimely cropped, fair garlands frame;
With open throats and silent mouths you sing
   His praise, Whom age permits you not to name;
Your tunes are tears, your instruments are swords,
Your ditty death, and blood in lieu of words!

The Nativity of Christ

Behold the Father is His daughter's Son,
    The bird that built the nest is hatched therein;
The old of years an hour hath not outrun,
    Eternal life to live doth now begin,
The Word is dumb, the mirth of heaven doth weep,
Might feeble is, and force doth faintly creep.

O dying souls! behold your Living Spring!
    O dazzled eyes! behold your Sun of Grace!
Dull ears, attend what word this Word doth bring!
    Up, heavy hearts, with joy your Joy embrace!
From death, from dark, from deafness, from despairs,
This Life, this Light, this Word, this Joy repairs.

Gift better than Himself God doth not know—
    Gift better than his God no man can see;
This Gift doth here the Giver given bestow,
    Gift to this Gift let each receiver be:
God is my Gift, Himself He freely gave me;
God's gift am I, and none but God shall have me.

Man altered was by sin from man to beast;
    Beast's food is hay, hay is all mortal flesh;
Now God is flesh and lies in manger pressed
    As hay, the brutest sinner to refresh:
O happy field wherein this fodder grew,
Whose taste doth us from beasts to men renew!

Edmund Spenser

Most Glorious Lord of Life

Most glorious Lord of Life, that on this day
Didst make Thy triumph over death and sin:
And having harrowed hell, didst bring away
Captivity, thence captive, us to win:
This joyous day, dear Lord, with joy begin,
And grant that we for whom Thou diddest die,
Being with Thy dear blood clean washed from sin,
May live forever in felicity.
And that Thy love we weighing worthily,
May likewise love Thee for the same again:
And for Thy sake that all like dear didst buy,
With love may one another entertain.
So let us love, dear love, like as we ought;
Love is the lesson which the Lord us taught.

Edward Taylor

Meditation I

What love is this of Thine that cannot be
    In Thine infinity, O Lord, confined,
Unless it in Thy very Person see
    Infinity and finity conjoined?
    What hath Thy Godhead, as not satisfied,
    Married our manhood, making it its bride?

Oh, matchless Love! filling heaven to the brim!
    O'er-running it—all running o'er beside
This world! Nay, overflowing hell, wherein
    For Thine elect there rose a mighty tide!
    That there our veins might through Thy Person bleed
    To quench those flames that else would on us feed.

Oh! that Thy love might overflow my heart!
    To fire the same with love, for love I would.
But oh! my straitened breast! my lifeless spark!
    My fireless flame! What chilly love and cold?
    In measure small! In manner chilly! See.
    Lord, blow the coal: Thy love enflame in me.

Huswifery

Make me, O Lord, Thy spinning wheel complete.
　　Thy Holy Word my distaff make for me.
Make mine affections Thy swift flyers neat
　　And make my soul Thy holy spool to be.
　　My conversation make to be Thy reel
　　And reel the yarn thereon spun of Thy wheel.

Make me Thy loom then; knit therein this twine;
　　And make Thy Holy Spirit, Lord, wind quills;
Then weave the web Thyself. The yarn is fine.
　　Thine ordinances make my fulling mills.
　　Then dye the same in heavenly colors choice,
　　All pinked with varnished flowers of Paradise.

Then clothe therewith mine understanding, will,
　　Affections, judgment, conscience, memory,
My words and actions, that their shine may fill
　　My ways with glory and Thee glorify.
　　Then mine apparel shall display before ye
　　That I am clothed in holy robes for glory.

Am I Thy Gold?

Am I Thy gold? Or purse, Lord, for Thy wealth,
　　Whether in mine or mint refined for Thee?
I'm counted so, but count me o'er Thyself,
　　Lest gold-washed face and brass in heart I be.
　　I fear my Touchstone touches when I try
　　Me and my counted gold too overly.

Am I new minted by Thy stamp indeed?
　　Mine eyes are dim; I cannot clearly see.
Be Thou my spectacles that I may read
　　Thine image and inscription stamped on me.
　　If Thy bright image do upon me stand,
　　I am a golden angel in Thy hand.

Lord, make my soul Thy plate; Thine image bright
　　Within the circle of the same enfoil.
And on its brims in golden letters write
　　Thy superscription in an holy style.
　　Then I shall be Thy money, Thou my hoard;
　　Let me Thy angel be, be Thou my Lord.

Francis Thompson

"In No Strange Land"

O world invisible, we view thee,
O world intangible, we touch thee,
O world unknowable, we know thee,
Inapprehensible, we clutch thee!

Does the fish soar to find the ocean,
The eagle plunge to find the air—
That we ask of the stars in motion
If they have rumor of thee there?

Not where the wheeling systems darken
And our benumbed conceiving soars!
The drift of pinions, would we hearken,
Beats at our own clay-shuttered doors.

The angels keep their ancient places;
Turn but a stone, and start a wing!
'Tis ye, 'tis your estranged faces,
That miss the many-splendored thing.

But, when so sad thou canst not sadder,
Cry—and upon thy so sore loss
Shall shine the traffic of Jacob's ladder
Pitched betwixt Heaven and Charing Cross.

Yea, in the night, my Soul, my daughter,
Cry, clinging Heaven by the hems;
And lo, Christ walking on the water
Not of Gennesareth, but Thames!

The Hound of Heaven

I fled Him, down the nights and down the days:
I fled Him, down the arches of the years;
I fled Him, down the labyrinthine ways
Of my own mind; and in the mist of tears
I hid from Him, and under running laughter.
       Up vistaed hopes I sped;
       And shot, precipitated,
Adown Titanic glooms of chasmed fears,
  From those strong Feet that followed, followed after.
      But with unhurrying chase,
      And unperturbèd pace,
    Deliberate speed, majestic instancy,
      They beat—and a Voice beat
      More instant than the Feet—
"All things betray thee, who betrayest Me."

       I pleaded, outlaw-wise,
By many a hearted casement, curtained red,
Trellised with intertwining charities;
(For, though I knew His love Who followèd,
      Yet was I sore adread
Lest, having Him, I must have naught beside).
But, if one little casement parted wide,
  The gust of His approach would clash it to.
  Fear wist not to evade, as Love wist to pursue.
Across the margent of the world I fled,
   And troubled the gold gateways of the stars,
   Smiting for shelter on their clangèd bars;
     Fretted to dulcet jars
And silvern chatter the pale ports o' the moon.
I said to Dawn: Be sudden—to Eve: Be soon;
  With thy young skiey blossoms heap me over
    From this tremendous Lover—

➤➤➤➤

387

Float thy vague veil about me, lest He see!
    I tempted all His servitors, but to find
My own betrayal in their constancy,
In faith to Him their fickleness to me,
    Their traitorous trueness, and their loyal deceit.
To all swift things for swiftness did I sue;
    Clung to the whistling mane of every wind.

        But whether they swept, smoothly fleet,
        The long savannahs of the blue;
            Or whether, Thunder-driven,
            They clanged his chariot 'thwart a heaven,
Plashy with flying lightnings round the spurn o' their feet:
    Fear wist not to evade as Love wist to pursue.
            Still with unhurrying chase,
            And unperturbèd pace,
        Deliberate speed, majestic instancy,
            Came on the following Feet,
            And a Voice above their beat—
        "Naught shelters thee, who wilt not shelter Me."

I sought no more that after which I strayed
        In face of man or maid;
But still within the little children's eyes
        Seems something, something that replies,
They at least are for me, surely for me!
I turned to them very wistfully;
But just as their young eyes grew sudden fair
        With dawning answers there,
Their angel plucked them from me by the hair.
"Come then, ye other children, Nature's—share
With me" (said I) "your delicate fellowship;
        Let me greet you lip to lip,
        Let me twine with you caresses,
            Wantoning
        With our Lady-Mother's vagrant tresses,
            Banqueting
        With her in her wind-walled palace,
        Underneath her azured dais,
        Quaffing, as your taintless way is,
            From a chalice
Lucent-weeping out of the dayspring."
        So it was done:
I in their delicate fellowship was one—
Drew the bolt of Nature's secrecies.

I knew all the swift importings
On the wilful face of skies;
I knew how the clouds arise
Spumèd of the wild sea-snortings;
   All that's born or dies
Rose and drooped with; made them shapers
Of mine own moods, or wailful or divine;
   With them joyed and was bereaven.
   I was heavy with the even,
   When she lit her glimmering tapers
   Round the day's dead sanctities.
   I laughed in the morning's eyes.
I triumphed and I saddened with all weather,
   Heaven and I wept together,
And its sweet tears were salt with mortal mine;
Against the red throb of its sunset-heart
   I laid my own to beat,
   And share commingling heat;
But not by that, by that, was eased my human smart.
In vain my tears were wet on Heaven's grey cheek.
For ah! we know not what each other says,
   These things and I; in sound *I* speak—
Their sound is but their stir, they speak by silences.
Nature, poor stepdame, cannot slake my drouth;
   Let her, if she would owe me,
Drop yon blue bosom-veil of sky, and show me
   The breasts o' her tenderness:
Never did any milk of hers once bless
     My thirsting mouth.
     Nigh and nigh draws the chase,
     With unperturbèd pace,
   Deliberate speed, majestic instancy;
    And past those noisèd Feet
    A voice comes yet more fleet—
   "Lo! naught contents thee, who content'st
   not Me."

Naked I wait Thy love's uplifted stroke!
My harness piece by piece Thou hast hewn from me,
   And smitten me to my knee;
   I am defenceless utterly.
   I slept, methinks, and woke,
And, slowly gazing, find me stripped in sleep.
In the rash lustihead of my young powers,
   I shook the pillaring hours

➤➤➤➤

And pulled my life upon me; grimed with smears,
I stand amid the dust o' the moulded years—
My mangled youth lies dead beneath the heap.
My days have crackled and gone up in smoke,
Have puffed and burst as sun-starts on a stream.
          Yea, faileth now even dream
The dreamer, and the lute the lutanist;
Even the linked fantasies, in whose blossomy twist
I swung the earth a trinket at my wrist,
Are yielding; cords of all too weak account
For earth with heavy griefs so overplussed.
          Ah! is Thy love indeed
A weed, albeit an amaranthine weed,
Suffering no flowers except its own to mount?
          Ah! must—
          Designer infinite!—
Ah! must Thou char the wood ere Thou canst limn with it?
My freshness spent its wavering shower i' the dust;
And now my heart is as a broken fount,
Wherein tear-drippings stagnate, spilt down ever
          From the dank thoughts that shiver
Upon the sighful branches of my mind.
          Such is; what is to be?
The pulp so bitter, how shall taste the rind?
I dimly guess what Time in mists confounds;
Yet ever and anon a trumpet sounds
From the hid battlements of Eternity;
Those shaken mists a space unsettle, then
Round the half-glimpsed turrets slowly wash again.
          But not ere him who summoneth
          I first have seen, enwound
With glooming robes purpureal, cypress-crowned;
His name I know, and what his trumpet saith.
Whether man's heart or life it be which yields
          Thee harvest, must Thy harvest-fields
          Be dunged with rotten death?

          Now of that long pursuit
          Comes on at hand the bruit;
        That Voice is round me like a bursting sea:
          "And is thy earth so marred,
          Shattered in shard on shard?
        Lo, all things fly thee, for thou fliest Me!
        Strange, piteous, futile thing!
Wherefore should any set thee love apart?
Seeing none but I makes much of naught" (He said),

"And human love needs human meriting:
How hast thou merited—
Of all man's clotted clay the dingiest clot?
Alack, thou knowest not
How little worthy of any love thou art!
Whom wilt thou find to love ignoble thee,
Save Me, save only Me?
All which I took from thee I did but take,
Not for thy harms,
But just that thou might'st seek it in My arms.
All which thy child's mistake
Fancies as lost, I have stored for thee at home:
Rise, clasp My hand, and come!"

Halts by me that footfall:
Is my gloom, after all,
Shade of His hand, outstretched caressingly?
"Ah, fondest, blindest, weakest,
I am He Whom thou seekest!
Thou dravest love from thee, who dravest Me."

To a Snowflake

What heart could have thought you?—
Past our devisal
(O filigree petal!)
Fashioned so purely,
Fragilely, surely,
From what Paradisal
Imagineless metal,
Too costly for cost?
Who hammered you, wrought you,
From argentine vapor?—

"God was my Shaper.
Passing surmisal,
He hammered, He wrought me,
From curled silver vapor,
To lust of His mind:—
Thou couldst not have thought me!
So purely, so palely,
Tinily, surely,
Mightily, frailly,
Insculped and embossed,
With His hammer of wind,
And His graver of frost."

Thomas Traherne

Poverty

As in the house I sat
Alone and desolate,
No creature but the fire and I
The chimney and the stool, I lift mine eye
Up to the wall,
And in the silent hall
Saw nothing mine
But some few cups and dishes shine,
The table and the wooden stools
Where people used to dine;
A painted cloth there was,
Wherein some ancient story wrought
A little entertained my thought
Which light discovered through the glass.

I wondered much to see
That all my wealth should be
Confined in such a little room,
Yet hope for more I scarcely durst presume.
It grieved me sore
That such a scanty store
Should be my all;
For I forgot my ease and health,
Nor did I think of hands or eyes,
Nor soul nor body prize;
I neither thought the sun,
Nor moon, nor stars, nor people, mine,
Though they did round about me shine;
And therefore was I quite undone.

Some greater things, I thought,
Must needs for me be wrought,
Which till my pleased mind could see,
I ever should lament my poverty.
I fain would have
Whatever Bounty gave,
Nor could there be
Without, or love or Deity.
For, should not He be infinite
Whose hand created me?
Ten thousand absent things
Did vex my poor and absent mind,

Which, till I be no longer blind,
Let me not see the King of Kings.

His love must surely be
Rich, infinite, and free;
Nor can He be thought a God
Of grace and power, that fills not His abode,
His holy court,
In kind and liberal sort;
Joys and pleasures,
Plenty of jewels, goods, and treasures
(To enrich the poor, cheer the forlorn)
His palace must adorn,
And given all to me.
For till *His* works *my* wealth became,
No love or peace did me enflame;
But now I have a Deity.

First Day

Hail, sacred Light, which highly dost excel
And dost our sorrows and our fears dispel!
When first appearing, thou didst strike the sight
With darting beams, all glorious, fair, and bright,
And wondrous charming. Oh! how great and full
Of sparkling glory! Oh! how beautiful!
How sweet thy shine! How ravishing thy rays!
Proclaiming loud thy great Creator's praise
When marvelously He had now decreed
That day should night, and night should day succeed,
That this His works and wonders might display
And shadow forth His own eternal day,
Whilst that should temper the day's increasing drought,
Moisten the air, and make the earth to sprout.
He gave the Word, and day did straight appear,
Till day at length declined, and night drew near.
Night, which hovering with her sable wing,
Doth ease and rest to wearied mortals bring.
Thus nights and days, and days and nights do fly,
Returning in their course successively—
Each with its comforts, though of different kinds,
Both for our active and our drooping minds.
Since then both day and night such blessings bring,
By day and night let's bless our Lord and King,
The King of all the World, in whom we move
And live and are, the mighty God above.

On Christmas Day

Shall dumpish melancholy spoil my joys
      While angels sing
      And mortals ring
   My Lord and Savior's praise?
Awake from sloth, for that alone destroys;
'Tis sin defiles; 'tis sloth puts out thy joys.
  See how they run from place to place,
  And seek for ornaments of grace;
  Their houses decked with sprightly green
  In winter makes a summer seen;
      They bays and holly bring
        As if 'twere spring!

Shake off thy sloth, my drowsy soul, awake;
      With angels sing
      Unto thy King,
   And pleasant music make.
Thy lute, thy harp, or else thy heart-strings take,
And with thy music let thy sense awake.
  See how each one the other calls
  To fix his ivy on the walls;
  Transplanted there it seems to grow
  As if it rooted were below.
      Thus He, who is thy King,
        Makes winter, spring.

Shall houses clad in summer liveries
      His praises sing
      And laud thy King,
   And wilt not thou arise?
Forsake thy bed and grow, my soul, more wise;
Attire thyself in cheerful liveries:
  Let pleasant branches still be seen
  Adorning thee, both quick and green,
  And, which with glory better suits,
  Be laden all the year with fruits—
      Inserted into Him,
        For ever spring.

'Tis He that Life and Spirit doth infuse;
      Let everything
      The praises sing
   Of Christ the King of Jews,
Who makes things green, and with a spring infuse
A season which to see it doth not use.
  Old winter's frost and hoary hair

With garlands crowned, bays doth wear;
The nipping frost of wrath being gone,
To Him the manger made a throne.
    Due praises let us sing,
      Winter and spring.

See how, their bodies clad with finer clothes,
      They now begin
      His praise to sing
    Who purchased their repose,
Whereby their inward joy they do disclose;
Their dress alludes to better works than those.
  His gayer weeds and finer band,
  New suit and hat into his hand
  The plowman takes; his neatest shoes
  And warmer gloves he means to use;
    And shall not I, my King,
      Thy praises sing?

See how their breath doth smoke and how they haste
      His praise to sing
      With cherubim;
    They scarce a breakfast taste,
But through the streets, lest precious time should waste,
When service doth begin, to church they haste.
  And shall not I, Lord, come to Thee,
  The beauty of thy Temple see?
  Thy Name with joy I will confess,
  Clad in my Savior's righteousness;
    'Mong all Thy servants sing
      To Thee, my King.

'Twas Thou that gavest us cause for fine attires;
      Even Thou, O King,
      As in the spring,
    Dost warm us with Thy fires
Of love: Thy blood hath bought us new desires;
Thy righteousness doth clothe with new attires.
  Made fresh and fine, let me appear
  This day divine, to close the year;
  Among the rest let me be seen
  A living branch and always green,
    Think it a pleasant thing
      Thy praise to sing.

At break of day, O how the bells did ring!
      To Thee, my King,
      The bells did ring;
    To Thee the angels sing.

►►►►

Thy goodness did produce this other spring,
For this it is they make the bells to ring:
  The sounding bells do through the air
  Proclaim Thy welcome far and near,
  While I alone with Thee inherit
  All these joys beyond my merit.
      Who would not always sing
        To such a King?

I all these joys, above my merit, see
      By Thee, my King,
      To whom I sing,
      Entire conveyed to me.
My treasure, Lord, Thou makest Thy people be
That I with pleasure might Thy servants see.
  Even in their rude external ways
  They do set forth my Savior's praise
  And minister a Light to me,
  While I by them do hear to Thee
      Praises, my Lord and King,
        Whole churches ring.

Hark, how remoter parishes do sound!
      Far off they ring
      For Thee, my King,
      Even round about the town.
The churches scattered over all the ground
Serve for Thy praise, who art with glory crowned.
  This city is an engine great
  That makes my pleasure more complete;
  The Sword, the Mace, the Magistrate,
  To honor Thee attend in state.
      The whole assembly sings;
        The minster rings.

Henry Vaughan

Peace

My soul, there is a country
 Far beyond the stars,
Where stands a winged sentry
 All skillful in the wars;
There above noise and danger
 Sweet peace sits crowned with smiles,
And One born in a manger
 Commands the beauteous files;
He is thy gracious Friend,
 And (O my soul, awake!)
Did in pure love descend
 To die here for thy sake;
If thou canst get but thither,
 There grows the flower of peace,
The Rose that cannot wither,
 Thy Fortress and thy Ease.
Leave then thy foolish ranges;
 For none can thee secure,
But One Who never changes,
 Thy God, thy Life, thy Cure.

Easter Hymn

Death and darkness, get you packing,
Nothing now to man is lacking;
All your triumphs now are ended,
And what Adam marred is mended;
Graves are beds now for the weary,
Death a nap to make more merry;
Youth now, full of pious duty,
Seeks in thee for perfect beauty;
The weak and aged, tired with length
Of days, from thee look for new strength;
And infants with thy pangs contest
As pleasant, as if with the breast.
 Then, unto Him Who thus hath thrown
Even to contempt thy kingdom down,
And by His blood did us advance
Unto His own inheritance,
To Him be glory, power, praise,
From this, unto the last of days.

The Dwelling Place

JOHN 1:38–39

What happy, secret fountain,
  Fair shade, or mountain,
Whose undiscovered virgin glory
Boasts it this day, though not in story,
Was then Thy dwelling? Did some cloud,
Fixed to a tent, descend and shroud
My distressed Lord? Or did a star
Beckoned by Thee, though high and far,
In sparkling smiles haste gladly down
To lodge Light, and increase her own?
My dear, dear God! I do not know
What lodged Thee then, nor where, nor how;
But I am sure, Thou dost now come
Oft to a narrow, homely room,
Where Thou too hast but the least part;
My God, I mean my sinful heart.

The World

I saw Eternity the other night,
Like a great ring of pure and endless light,
      All calm as it was bright;
And round beneath it, time in hours, days, years,
      Driven by the spheres
Like a vast shadow moved, in which the world
      And all her train were hurled.
The doting lover in his quaintest strain
      Did there complain;
Near him, his lute, his fancy, and his flights,
      Wit's sour delights,
With gloves and knots, the silly snares of pleasure,
      Yet his dear treasure,
All scattered lay, while he his eyes did pour
      Upon a flower.

The darksome statesman, hung with weights of woe,
Like a thick midnight fog, moved there so slow,
    He did not stay nor go;
Condemning thoughts—like sad eclipses—scowl
    Upon his soul,
And clouds of crying witnesses without
    Pursued him with one shout.
Yet digged the mole, and lest his ways be found,
    Worked underground,
Where he did clutch his prey; but One did see
    That policy.
Churches and altars fed him; perjuries
    Were gnats and flies;
It rained about him blood and tears, but he
    Drank them as free.

The fearful miser on a heap of rust
Sat pining all his life there, did scarce trust
    His own hands with the dust,
Yet would not place one piece above, but lives
    In fear of thieves.
Thousands there were frantic as himself
    And hugged each one his pelf;
The downright epicure placed heaven in sense
    And scorned pretence;
While others, slipped into a wide excess,
    Said little less;
The weaker sort, slight, trivial wares enslave,
    Who think them brave;
And poor, despisèd Truth sat counting by
    Their victory.

Yet some, who all this while did weep and sing,
And sing and weep, soared up into the ring;
    But most would use no wing.
Oh, fools, said I, thus to prefer dark night
    Before true light!
To live in grots and caves and hate the day
    Because it shows the way;
The way which from this dead and dark abode
    Leads up to God—
A way where you might tread the sun, and be
    More bright than he!
But as I did their madness so discuss,
    One whispered thus,
"This ring the Bridegroom did for none provide,
    But for His bride."

Ascension Hymn

Dust and clay
Man's ancient wear!
Here you must stay,
But I elsewhere;
Souls sojourn here, but may not rest;
Who will ascend must be undressed.

And yet some
That know to die
Before death come,
Walk to the sky
Even in this life; but all such can
Leave behind them the old man.

If a star
Should leave the sphere,
She must first mar
Her flaming wear
And after fall, for in her dress
Of glory, she cannot transgress.

Man of old
Within the line
Of Eden could
Like the sun shine,
All naked, innocent, and bright,
And intimate with heaven as light;

But since he
That brightness soiled,
His garments be
All dark and spoiled,
And here are left as nothing worth
Till the Refiner's fire breaks forth.

Then comes He
Whose mighty light
Made His clothes be
Like heaven, all bright:
The Fuller, Whose pure blood did flow
To make stained men more white than
snow.

He alone
And none else can
Bring bone to bone
And rebuild man,
And by His all-subduing might
Make clay ascend more quick than light.

Christ's Nativity

Awake, glad heart! Get up and sing;
It is the birthday of thy King.
 Awake! awake!
 The sun doth shake
Light from his locks, and all the way
Breathing perfumes, doth spice the day.

Awake, awake! Hark, how the wood rings,
Winds whisper, and the busy springs
 A consort make.
 Awake! awake!
Man is their high priest and should rise
To offer up the sacrifice.

I would I were some bird or star
Fluttering in woods or lifted far
 Above this inn
 And road of sin!
Then either star or bird should be
Shining or singing still to Thee.

I would I had in my best part
Fit rooms for Thee! or that my heart
 Were so clean as
 Thy manger was!
But I am all filth, and obscene;
Yet, if Thou wilt, Thou canst make clean.

Sweet Jesu! Will then! Let no more
This leper haunt and soil Thy door;
 Cure him, ease him,
 O release him!
And let once more by mystic birth
The Lord of Life be born in earth.

The Relapse

My God how gracious art Thou! I had slipt
     Almost to hell,
And on the verge of that dark, dreadful pit
     Did hear them yell,
But O Thy love, Thy rich, almighty love
     That saved my soul,
And checked their fury when I saw them move
     And heard them howl!
O my sole Comfort, take no more these ways,
     This hideous path,
And I will mend my own without delays.
     Cease Thou Thy wrath!
I have deserved a thick, Egyptian damp,
     Dark as my deeds,
Should mist within me and put out that lamp
     Thy Spirit feeds;
A darting conscience full of stabs and fears,
     No shade but yew.
Sullen and sad eclipses, cloudy spheres,
     These are my due.
But He that with His blood (a price too dear)
     My scores did pay
Bid me, by virtue from Him, challenge here
     The brightest day.
Sweet, downy thoughts, soft lily-shades, calm streams,
     Joys full and true,
Fresh, spicy mornings and eternal beams—
     These are His due.

Joy to the World

Isaac Watts

Joy to the world! the Lord is come;
Let earth receive her King.
Let every heart prepare Him room
And heaven and nature sing.

Joy to the earth! the Savior reigns;
Let men their songs employ,
While fields and floods, rocks, hills, and plains
Repeat the sounding joy.

No more let sins and sorrows grow,
Nor thorns infest the ground;
He comes to make His blessings flow
Far as the curse is found.

He rules the world with truth and grace
And makes the nations prove
The glories of His righteousness
And wonders of His love.

From All That Dwell Below the Skies

From all the dwell below the skies
Let the Creator's praise arise;
Let the Redeemer's Name be sung
Through every land by every tongue.

Eternal are Thy mercies, Lord;
Eternal truth attends Thy Word:
Thy praise shall sound from shore to shore,
Till suns shall rise and set no more.

In every land begin the song;
To every land the strains belong:
In cheerful sounds all voices raise
And fill the world with loudest praise.

Our God, Our Help in Ages Past

Our God, our Help in ages past,
  Our Hope for years to come,
Our Shelter from the stormy blast,
  And our eternal Home.

Under the shadow of Thy throne
  Thy saints have dwelt secure;
Sufficient is Thine arm alone,
  And our defence is sure.

Before the hills in order stood,
  Or earth received her frame,
From everlasting Thou art God,
  To endless years the same.

Thy Word commands our flesh to dust,
  "Return, ye sons of men":
All nations rose from earth at first,
  And turn to earth again.

A thousand ages in Thy sight
  Are like an evening gone;
Short as the watch that ends the night
  Before the rising sun.

The busy tribes of flesh and blood
  With all their lives and cares
Are carried downwards by Thy flood
  And lost in following years.

Time like an ever-rolling stream
  Bears all its sons away;
They fly forgotten as a dream
  Dies at the opening day.

Like flowery fields the nations stand
  Pleased with the morning light;
The flowers beneath the mower's hand
  Lie withering ere 'tis night.

Our God, our Help in ages past,
  Our Hope for years to come,
Be Thou our Guard while troubles last,
  And our eternal Home.

Jesus Shall Reign
Where'er the Sun

Jesus shall reign where'er the sun
Does his successive journeys run;
His Kingdom stretch from shore to shore,
Till moons shall wax and wane no more.

People and realms of every tongue
Dwell on His love with sweetest song,
And infant voices shall proclaim
Their early blessings on His Name.

Blessings abound where'er He reigns;
The prisoner leaps to lose his chains,
The weary find eternal rest,
And all the sons of want are blest.

Let every creature rise and bring
Peculiar honors to our King,
Angels descend with songs again
And earth repeat the loud Amen!

Alas! and Did My
Savior Bleed

Alas! and did my Savior bleed,
And did my Sovereign die?
Would He devote that sacred head
For such a worm as I?

Was it for crimes that I have done
He groaned upon the tree?
Amazing pity, grace unknown,
And love beyond degree!

Well might the sun in darkness hide,
And shut his glories in,
When Christ, the mighty Maker, died
For man the creature's sin.

Thus might I hide my blushing face
While His dear cross appears;
Dissolve, my heart, in thankfulness!
And melt, mine eyes, to tears!

When I Survey
the Wondrous Cross

When I survey the wondrous cross
On which the Prince of Glory died,
My richest gain I count but loss,
And pour contempt on all my pride.

Forbid it, Lord, that I should boast,
Save in the death of Christ, my God!
All the vain things that charm me most,
I sacrifice them through His blood.

See from His head, His hands, His feet,
Sorrow and love flow mingled down;
Did e'er such love and sorrow meet,
Or thorns compose so rich a crown?

Were the whole realm of nature mine,
That were a present far too small;
Love so amazing, so divine,
Demands my soul, my life, my all.

Am I a Soldier
of the Cross?

Am I a soldier of the cross,
A follower of the Lamb?
And shall I fear to own His cause
Or blush to speak His Name?

Must I be carried to the skies
On flowery beds of ease
While others fought to win the prize
And sailed through bloody seas?

Are there no foes for me to face?
Must I not stem the flood?
Is this vile world a friend to grace
To help me on to God?

Since I might fight if I would reign,
Increase my courage, Lord;
I'll bear the toil, endure the pain,
Supported by Thy Word.

The Day of Judgment

AN ODE IN ENGLISH SAPPHIC

When the fierce north wind with his airy forces
Rears up the Baltic to a foaming fury,
And the red lightning with a storm of hail comes
        Rushing amain down,

How the poor sailors stand amazed and tremble,
While the hoarse thunder, like a bloody trumpet,
Roars a loud onset to the gaping waters,
        Quick to devour them!

Such shall the noise be and the wild disorder,
(If things eternal may be like these earthly)
Such the dire terror, when the great Archangel
        Shakes the creation,

Tears the strong pillars of the vault of heaven,
Breaks up old marble, the repose of princes;
See the graves open, and the bones arising,
        Flames all around them!

Hark, the shrill outcries of the guilty wretches!
Lively bright horror and amazing anguish
Stare through their eyelids, while the living worm lies
        Gnawing within them.

Thoughts like old vultures prey upon their heart-strings,
And the smart twinges, when the eye beholds the
Lofty Judge frowning, and a flood of vengeance
        Rolling afore him.

Hopeless immortals! how they scream and shiver,
While devils push them to the pit wide-yawning
Hideous and gloomy, to receive them headlong
        Down to the center.

Stop here, my fancy: (all away ye horrid
Doleful ideas); come, arise to Jesus;
How He sits God-like! and the saints around Him
        Throned, yet adoring!

Oh may I sit there when He comes triumphant
Dooming the nations! then ascend to glory
While our hosannas all along the passage
        Shout the Redeemer!

Charles Wesley

Free Grace

And can it be, that I should gain
An interest in the Savior's blood?
Died He for me, who caused His pain,
For me, who Him to death pursued?
Amazing Love! How can it be
That Thou, my God, shouldst die for me?

'Tis Mystery all! The Immortal dies!
Who can explore His strange design?
In vain the first-born seraph tries
To sound the depths of Love divine.
'Tis Mercy all! Let earth adore;
Let angel minds inquire no more.

He left His Father's throne above,
(So free, so infinite His Grace!)
Emptied Himself of all but Love,
And bled for Adam's helpless race:
'Tis Mercy all, immense and free!
For, O my God, it found out me!

Long my imprisoned spirit lay,
Fastbound in sin and nature's night:
Thine eye diffused a quickening ray;
I woke; the dungeon flamed with light;
My chains fell off, my heart was free;
I rose, went forth, and followed Thee.

Still the small inward voice I hear
That whispers all my sins forgiven;
Still the atoning blood is near
That quenched the wrath of hostile heaven:
I feel the life His wounds impart;
I feel my Savior in my heart.

No condemnation now I dread;
Jesus, and all in Him, is mine:
Alive in Him, my living Head,
And clothed in Righteousness divine,
Bold I approach the eternal throne,
And claim the crown, through Christ, my own.

O For a Thousand Tongues

O for a thousand tongues to sing
My great Redeemer's praise,
The glories of my God and King,
The triumphs of His grace.

My gracious Master and my God,
O help me to proclaim,
To spread through all the earth abroad
The honors of Thy name.

Jesus! the Name that charms our fears,
That bids our sorrows cease;
Tis music in the sinner's ears,
Tis life and health and peace.

He breaks the power of canceled sin,
He sets the prisoner free;
His blood can make the foulest clean;
His blood availed for me.

Hear Him, ye deaf; His praise, ye dumb,
Your loosened tongues employ;
Ye blind, behold your Savior come,
And leap, ye lame, for joy!

Blest Be
That Sacred Covenant Love

Blest be that sacred covenant love,
    Uniting though we part;
We may be called far off to move,
    We still are one in heart.

Joined in one Spirit to our Head,
    Where He appoints, we go;
And while we in His footsteps tread,
    Show forth His praise below.

O may we ever walk with Him
    And nothing know beside:
Naught else desire, naught else esteem
    But Jesus Crucified.

Hark! the Herald Angels Sing

Hark! the herald angels sing,
"Glory to the newborn King;
Peace on earth and mercy mild,
God and sinners reconciled!"
Joyful, all ye nations, rise,
Join the triumph of the skies;
With the angelic host proclaim,
"Christ is born in Bethlehem!"
  Hark! the herald angels sing,
   "Glory to the newborn King!"

Christ, by highest heaven adored,
Christ, the Everlasting Lord!
Late in time behold Him come,
Offspring of the virgin's womb.
Veiled in flesh the Godhead see;
Hail the Incarnate Deity!
Pleased as man with men to dwell,
Jesus, our Immanuel.
  Hark! the herald angels sing,
   "Glory to the newborn King!"

Hail, the heavenborn Prince of Peace!
Hail, the Sun of Righteousness!
Light and life to all He brings,
Risen with healing in His wings.
Mild He lays His glory by,
Born that man no more may die,
Born to raise the sons of earth,
Born to give them second birth.
  Hark! the herald angels sing,
   "Glory to the newborn King!"

Christ, Whose Glory

Christ, whose glory fills the skies,
  Christ the true and only Light,
Sun of Righteousness, arise,
  Triumph o'er the shades of night!
Day-spring, from on high, be near!
Day-star, in my heart appear!

Dark and cheerless is the morn
  Unaccompanied by Thee;
Joyless is the day's return,
  Till Thy mercy's beams I see;
Till they inward light impart,
Glad my eyes and warm my heart.

Visit then this soul of mine,
  Pierce the gloom of sin and grief!
Fill me, Radiancy Divine,
  Scatter all my unbelief!
More and more Thyself display,
Shining to the perfect day.

Come, Thou Long-expected Jesus

Come, Thou long-expected Jesus,
Born to set Thy people free;
From our fears and sins release us;
Let us find our rest in Thee.
Israel's Strength and Consolation,
Hope of all the earth Thou art;
Dear Desire of every nation,
Joy of every longing heart.

Born Thy people to deliver,
Born a child and yet a King,
Born to reign in us forever,
Now Thy gracious Kingdom bring.

By Thine own eternal spirit
Rule in all our hearts alone;
By Thine all-sufficient merit
Raise us to Thy glorious throne.

Love Divine,
All Loves Excelling

Love Divine, all loves excelling,
Joy of heaven, to earth come down,
Fix in us Thy humble dwelling,
All Thy faithful mercies crown!
Jesus, Thou art all compassion,
Pure unbounded Love Thou art;
Visit us with Thy salvation—
Enter every trembling heart.

Breathe, O breathe Thy loving Spirit
Into every troubled breast!
Let us all in Thee inherit,
Let us find the promised rest.
Take away the love of sinning;
Alpha and Omega be;
End of faith, as its Beginning,
Set our hearts at liberty.

Come, Almighty to deliver,
Let us all Thy life receive;
Suddenly return, and never,
Nevermore Thy temples leave.
Thee we would be always blessing,
Serve Thee as Thy hosts above;
Pray, and praise Thee without ceasing,
Glory in Thy perfect love.

Finish, then, Thy new creation;
Pure and spotless let us be.
Let us see Thy great salvation
Perfectly restored in Thee,
Changed from glory into glory
Till in heaven we take our place,
Till we cast our crowns before Thee,
Lost in wonder, love, and praise.

Henry Wotton

A Hymn to My God in a Night of My Late Sickness

O Thou great Power, in whom I move,
For whom I live, to whom I die,
Behold me through Thy beams of love,
Whilst on this couch of tears I lie,
And cleanse my sordid soul within
By Thy Christ's blood, the bath of sin.

No hallowed oils, no grains I need,
No rags of saints, no purging fire,
One rosy drop from David's Seed
Was worlds of seas to quench Thine ire.
O precious ransom, which once paid
That *Consummatum Est* was said:

And said by Him that said no more,
But sealed it with His sacred breath.
Thou then, that hast dispunged my score,
And dying, was the death of Death,
Be to me now—on Thee I call—
My Life, my Strength, my Joy, my All.

Medieval Poems, Renaissance Madrigals, Spirituals

A Medieval Poem of the Nativity

Let us gather hand in hand
And sing of bliss without an end:
The devil has fled from earthly land,
And Son of God is made our Friend.

A Child is born in man's abode,
And in that Child no blemish showed.
That Child is God, that Child is Man,
And in that Child our life began.

Be blithe and merry, sinful man,
For your marriage peace began
    When Christ was born.
Come to Christ, your peace is due
Because He shed His blood for you,
    Who were forlorn.

Sinful man, be blithe and bold,
For heaven is both bought and sold,
    Through and through.
Come to Christ and peace foretold:
His life He gave a hundredfold
    To succor you.

So let us gather hand in hand
And sing of bliss without an end:
The devil has fled from earthly land,
And Son of God is made our Friend.

Rejoice and Be Merry!

Rejoice and be merry in song and in mirth!
O praise our Redeemer, all mortals of earth!
For this is the birthday of Jesus our King,
Who brought us salvation—His praises we'll sing!

From an old church gallery book discovered in Dorset, England

Two Renaissance Madrigals

Ye People All

Ye people all in one accord
    Clap hands and eke rejoice;
Be glad and sing unto the Lord
    With sweet and pleasant voice.

Sing praises to our God, sing praise,
    Sing praises to our King,
For God is King of all the earth,
    All thankful praises sing.

John Hopkins

O All Ye Nations

O all ye nations of the Lord,
    Praise ye the Lord always;
And all ye people everywhere
    Set forth His noble praise.
For great His kindness is to His,
    His truth endures for aye;
Wherefore praise ye the Lord our God,
    Praise ye the Lord I say.

Thomas Norton

Swing Low, Sweet Chariot

I looked over Jordan, and what did I see?
A band of angels comin' after me.

If you get there before I do,
Tell all my friends I'm comin' too.

The brightest day that ever I saw—
When Jesus washed my sins away.

Swing low, sweet chariot, comin' fo' to carry me home;
Swing low, sweet chariot, comin' fo' to carry me home.

Go Down, Moses

When Israel was in Egypt land,
   Let my people go!
Oppressed so hard they could not stand,
   Let my people go!

"Thus saith the Lord," bold Moses said,
   "Let my people go!
If not, I'll smite your firstborn dead!
   Let my people go!"

Were You There?

Were you there when they crucified my Lord?
Sometimes it causes me to tremble.
Were you there when they crucified my Lord?

Were you there when they nailed Him to the tree?
Sometimes it causes me to tremble.
Were you there when they nailed Him to the tree?

Were you there when they laid Him in the tomb?
Sometimes it causes me to tremble.
Were you there when they laid Him in the tomb?

Were you there when He rose from the dead?
Sometimes it causes me to tremble.
Were you there when He rose from the dead?

Biographies,
Acknowledgments,
Indexes

Biographies of Contemporary Poets

Carol Addink (now Carol Van Klompenburg) is a graduate of Dordt College with an M.A. in drama from the University of Minnesota.

Charlene Anderson was a poetry editor of *Decision* and a graduate of North Central Bible College.

W. H. Auden, English poet and critic, became an American citizen in 1939. Two of his notable works are *For the Time Being* and *Age of Anxiety.*

Margaret Avison is a Canadian poet and the author of *The Dumbfounding.* Her poetry has been published in many periodicals and anthologies.

Josiah Bancroft is a 1975 graduate of Calvin College, now teaching English at Brianwood Christian High School in Birmingham, Alabama.

Cor Barendrecht is the literary editor of *Calvinist-Contact* and the editor of *For the Time Being* for several years. Cor observes that "the poem should be an artistic statement or comment relating to the faith and to the life of the Christian in this world now."

Joseph Bayly is on the editorial staff of the David C. Cook Publishing Co. and *Eternity.* He is also the writer of many books, among them *I Saw Gooley Fly, The Gospel Blimp, Psalms of My Life* (poetry), and *View from a Hearse.*

Daniel Berrigan is a teacher, priest, apologist, and poet. He has taught theology at Fordham University and Le Moyne College. Besides books in various genres, his shorter writings and poetry have appeared in *Saturday Review, The Atlantic Monthly, Poetry, Thought,* and *Commonweal.*

Paul Borgman is Chairman of the English Department at Northwestern College in Orange City, Iowa. He has a Ph.D. from the University of Chicago. Principal subjects of his writings and speeches are Flannery O'Connor, John Updike, and Willa Cather. Paul says, "I have been on my Christian pilgrimage for as long as I can remember."

Brother Antonius (William Everson) was born in 1912 in Sacramento, California. Moving from Christian Science through pantheism and agnosticism to Catholicism, be became a Dominican in 1951. Among his books are *The Crooked Lines of God* and *The Hazards of Holiness.*

Matthew R. Brown is a graduate of Saginaw Valley State College with a B.A. in English. He is completing a volume of poetry to be entitled *The Iron Crucifix.* His aesthetic, in the tradition of Herbert and Hopkins, is the following: "My poems are aimed first at the praise of God and His works. I see the contemporary poetic scene as full of despair and evil—poetry will always reflect society—and would like to show my fellow poets, not another cult or system of belief, but Jesus Himself."

Sietze Buning was born to Reformed parents in Middleburg, Iowa, in 1930. Sietze teaches in the English department of Calvin College under the pseudonym Stanley Wiersma and publishes in various genres and voices.

Joseph Campbell (1881–1944) was an Irish poet and author of six books of poetry, including *The Mountainy Singer*. For a time he was also an instructor at Fordham University.

Thomas John Carlisle is the pastor the Stone Street Presbyterian Church of New York. He has written four books of poetry: *You! Jonah!*, *Celebration!*, *Mistaken Identity*, and *Journey With Job*.

Albert Howard Carter, III, teaches comparative literature at Eckerd College. He is also a photograhpic artist.

E. Margaret Clarkson, a Toronto school teacher, is the author of *Rivers Among the Rocks* and *Clear Shining After Rain*.

Jack Clemo is a blind poet who lives with his wife and mother in Cornwall, England. Jack has written *The Map of Clay*, *Cactus on Carmel*, *The Echoing Tip*, *Broad Autumn*, *Wilding Graft* (a novel), and *The Invading Gospel* (autobiography).

Edmund Clowney is the President of Westminster Seminary.

David Cochrane is attending Hope College as an English major. He has also written a number of short stories.

Hugh Cook is a graduate of Calvin College with an M.A. from Simon Fraser University. Hugh teaches American literature and creative writing at Dordt College. His hope regarding Christian poetry is this: "May our poems be psalms of praise in God's ear, and may they serve to the coming of His glorious Kingdom."

E. Neil Culbertson was a chaplain's assistant during the Vietnam War; he is now attending Dordt College and writing for *Canon*.

Countee Cullen was reared by foster parents in a Methodist parsonage, earned an M.A. at Harvard, and published several volumes of poetry and prose. Among them are *Copper Sun*, *The Black Christ*, and *On These I Stand*.

Joann Deems is a 1973 graduate of the University of Nebraska, past president of the Omaha Writers' Club, and a member of the Nebraska Poetry Association.

Dave DeGroot is a graduate of Dordt College with an M.A. in journalism from the University of Missouri.

Sandra Duguid is a graduate of Houghton College, with an M.A. in creative writing from Johns Hopkins. She is now teaching at The King's College.

Colin Duriez lived for two years in Istanbul and now lives in Coleraine, Northern Ireland. He has edited an anthology of Christian poetry entitled *Making Eden Grow*. Colin affirms that "Christian poetry tries, however imperfectly, to be centered upon the God who made both the poet and his world. It thus reflects the very nature of reality, which is meant to be directed towards Christ: it exists in and through and for Him."

T. S. Eliot is the poet of "The Waste Land"; after his conversion to

Christianity, he wrote such notable works as "Ash Wednesday," "Choruses from The Rock," and *Murder in the Cathedral.* In "Choruses from The Rock," Eliot alludes to the poet when he writes: "Lord, shall we not bring these gifts to Your service? / . . . The Lord who created must wish to create, / And employ our creation again in His service."

Gracia Fay Ellwood is a poet, essayist, and pastor's wife. She has also written a book on fantasy entitled *Good News from Tolkien's Middle Earth.* A graduate of Calvin College, Gracia has an M.A. in Theology from the University of Chicago Divinity School. Many of her poems have been published by *The Reformed Journal.*

Robert Emshoff was born in 1946 and reborn at Trinity Christian College. He has a B.A. in philosophy from Calvin College, and he did graduate work in English at the University of Wisconsin. Working as an investigator and photographer, he claims as his profession Christ, and as his aesthetic: "The heavens declare the glory of God and the little hills sing His praise."

Mia Fagerstrom is a graduate of Hope College and is now attending the University of Chicago. She became a Christian in 1975. Mia has won the Sandrine Award for Proficiency in Literature.

Dan Hawkins has published poetry in *Eternity* and *Christianity and Literature.* Dan affirms that each poem is a gift from the Father, a gift of words that comes down through the poet to shed new light on His world and His truth.

Helen Hoffman is a graduate of Calvin College living in Grand Rapids. She writes, "My poems are an offering of thanks to God."

Hester Hogan is the wife of Orlin Hogan, who teaches in the Mexican Seminary of the Christian Reformed Church in Chula Vista.

Ralph Huizenga is a Christian school teacher in Abbotsford, British Columbia. Ralph also writes short stories.

Roderick Jellema grew up in Holland, Michigan. He presently teaches English at the University of Maryland and is co-director of the Washington National Poetry Center.

James Weldon Johnson was Executive Secretary of the NAACP and a professor of creative writing at Fisk University. His works include *Fifty Years and Other Poems* and *Along This Way.*

Carolyn Keefe teaches in the speech department and is Director of Forensics at West Chester State College.

Ron Klug has been a book editor at Augsburg Publishing House and president of the Minnesota Christian Writers Guild. Ron is also the author of *The Strange Young Man in the Desert.* With an A.B. from Dr. Martin Luther College and graduate work at the University of Wisconsin, Ron is now teaching English at The American School, Ft. Dauphin, Madagascar.

Bonnie Kuipers is a student at Dordt College and on the staff of KDCR, a Christian FM station. She is an English major from Platte, South Dakota and writes for *Canon*.

Howard Laing has an M.A. in English from North Texas State University, a Th.M. from Dallas Theological Seminary, and he is presently completing his Ph.D. in English at Baylor University. Howard has also taught freshman English for seven years and has been the pastor of two congregations.

John Leax teaches English at Houghton College. Harold Shaw recently published a volume of John's poems entitled *Reaching Into Silence*. "My poems are written to be enjoyed," writes John, "and to be a witness to what the Lord has done."

Madeleine L'Engle is the author of twenty-three books: poetry, plays, novels, fantasy, science fiction, and autobiography. She has been an actress and is the wife of the actor Hugh Franklin. Madeleine comments that poetry is for her a form of prayer.

C. S. Lewis is the writer of *The Screwtape Letters, Perelandra, The Great Divorce, The Narnia Chronicles, Christian Reflections*, and a few score other books, including his spiritual autobiography *Surprised by Joy*.

Heather Marsman is a Barrie, Ontario, wife and mother. She attended the University of Toronto and the University of Waterloo. Heather writes that "poetry is one of man's expressed responses to God's created reality. The mature Christian poet will potentially produce the truest reflection, for he sees that reality derives its meaning from God the Creator."

Elva McAllaster is chairman of languages, literature, and fine arts at Greenville College. She has also written many essays and articles, as well as *Strettam*, a novel.

Susan McCaslin has an M.A. in English from Simon Fraser University. She is now teaching English and creative writing at Trinity Western College in British Columbia.

Gladys McKee is a member of the Poetry Society of America and has published poems in various periodicals.

Diana Mee was born and raised in White Plains, New York. She graduated from Houghton College, where she studied under John Leax. Diana is now an editor with Baker Book House.

John Meeter is a retired minister of the Christian Reformed Church and editor of two volumes of B. B. Warfield's shorter writings.

Merle Meeter is a teacher of English at Dordt College and author of *Literature and the Gospel, Canticles to the Lion-Lamb*, and *Prince of God*.

Beth Merizon is the former associate editor of *Christian Home and School*. She has written many poems, reviews, and essays (notably on Milton and Bradstreet) in several publications.

Thomas Merton was an American Trappist monk and the author of many books of prose as well as poetry. Among them are *Emblems of a Season of Fury, Thoughts in Solitude,* and *The Seven Storey Mountain* (autobiography).

Calvin Miller is the pastor of the Westside Baptist Church in Omaha. He has a Ph.D. from Midwestern Baptist Seminary and is the author of *Once Upon a Tree, Burning Bushes and Moon Walks,* and *The Singer,* a poetic narrative on the Christ. *The Song,* a sequel, has just been published.

Vassar Miller has written three volumes of poetry: *Wage War on Silence, My Bones Being Wiser,* and *Onions and Roses.*

William R. Mitchell is the Dean of Arts and Sciences at Oklahoma Baptist University. He has a Ph.D. in English from the University of Oklahoma, and has published poetry in *The Christian Century, Laurel Review,* and *The Living Church.* Dr. Mitchell thinks of his poetry and its purpose as follows: "I must cast my poems on their own resources, since they are no longer mine to give or take back, but belong to God. So let them thrive or perish, as He wills."

Stephen Mosley attended Western Illinois University and is a graduate of Wheaton College. Steve is currently working in Christian journalism and film production.

Karl Neerhof is a teacher of English at Valley Christian High School in Bellflower, California.

E. William Oldenburg taught English literature at Grand Valley State College until God took him to Himself through an automobile collision in 1974.

Evangeline Paterson is the wife of John Paterson, a geographer in Leicester, England, and the mother of three children. She has organized several poetry workshops. A volume of her poetry is entitled *The Sky Is Deep Enough.*

Johanna Patterson works in the circulation department of *Christianity Today.* Widowed six years ago, she is now active in singles work.

Ken Peeders was born and reared in Brooklyn. He is now Instructor in English at Fergus Falls State Community College.

Eugene Peterson is a pastor in the United Presbyterian Church U.S.A. After attending Seattle Pacific College, New York Theological Seminary, and Johns Hopkins, he is now the minister of Christ Our King Church in Bel Air, Maryland.

Marie Post is a Grand Rapids poet, wife, and mother. A book of her poetry is entitled *I Had Never Visited an Artist Before.* She is the syndicated poet of the *Grand Rapids Press,* and she has published in many periodicals, as well as *For the Time Being.* Marie says that "poetry should express one's Christian faith without sounding pedantic."

Eugene Rubingh is the Secretary of Foreign Missions of the Christian Reformed Church and author of *Sons of Tiv.*

Mary Ruch lives in Dumont, New Jersey, and has written a book of poetry entitled *Stained Glass Windows*.

Luci Shaw was born in England, graduated from Wheaton College, and is the author of *Listen to the Green* and *The Secret Trees*, as well as the editor of *Sightseers Into Pilgrims* and *The Risk of Birth*. On the core of Christian Poetry, Luci affirms that "unifying the works of Christian poets is their common belief in a potent, pervasive, actively self-revealing, redeeming God."

Phil Silva was born in Michigan and educated in elementary school as a Roman Catholic. He has a B.A. in English from Michigan State University. For some three years he worked at various artistic activities in San Diego. On Independence Day, 1975, he testifies, he was truly set free from materialism, impersonal sex, and libertarian movements by an encounter with Jesus Christ, who is now the Lord of his life.

John W. Simons is one of the modern poets in the supplemented edition of *Joyce Kilmer's Anthology of Catholic Poets*.

Edith Sitwell, an English poet and literary critic, is the author of many books of poetry, essay, and biography—among them, *The Canticle of the Rose, Aspects of Modern Poetry*, and *Alexander Pope*.

Lenora Speyer is the author of *Slow Wall: Poems–Together With Nor Without Music and Further Poems* (Random House).

Kathleen Speyers was born in Utrecht and reared in London, Ontario. She is now a student at Calvin College. "If Jesus Christ were not in some way the center of my poetry," Kathleen professes, "it would all be meaningless and void."

Ruthe Spinnanger was born in Norway and educated in the United States. Her poetry has been published in *Christianity Today, Eternity*, and *Moody Monthly*.

T. A. Straayer, a Grand Rapids native, is a senior at Calvin College.

Elmer F. Suderman has a Ph.D. from the University of Kansas and is Chairman of the English Department at Gustavus Adolphus College. His background is Mennonite, but he belongs to the Methodist Church and also serves as a lay preacher.

Robert D. Swets is a former literary editor of the Calvin College *Chimes* and the present editor of *For the Time Being*.

Fred Tamminga has poems in *Six Days*, and has published several other works of fiction, drama, and poetry (for example, *Believe It Or...* and *Bunk Among Dragons*).

Henrietta Ten Harmsel is a professor of English at Calvin College, and author of several books, including a translation of poems entitled *Jacob Revius: Dutch Metaphysical Poet*.

Nancy Thomas is a Quaker missionary serving with her husband Hal and their two children among the Aymara Indians of Bolivia.

John H. Timmerman teaches English at Calvin College. His poetry has appeared in several publications, especially *The Reformed Journal* and *The Banner*.

Nancy Todd is a graduate of Covenant College with an A.B. in English. She grew up in Columbia, Illinois, in a rural community.

Cornelius Van Bruggen is a member of the Christian Reformed Church who has had many of his poems published in *The Banner*.

Sandy Van Den Berg is employed at Handicap Village in Sheldon, Iowa. She is a graduate of Dordt College.

Debbie Vandenburg, from Thornton, Colorado, is an English major at Dordt College.

Randall Vander Mey is a graduate of Calvin College, presently working on his Ph.D. in English at the University of Pennsylvania. He has also taken courses at the University of Iowa's Writers' Workshop.

Charles Van Gorkom teaches English in the Terrace, British Columbia, Christian School.

Joe Veltman was born in Friesland. He is a graduate of Calvin College and Calvin Seminary.

Clarence Walhout is a professor of English at Calvin College and the author of many essays on literary criticism.

Jeanne Murray Walker is a professor of literature and creative writing at Haverford College. Jeanne is a graduate of Wheaton College with a Ph.D. from the University of Pennsylvania.

Debbie Wallis graduated from Covenant College in 1973. Now a student at Missouri Baptist Hospital of Nursing, she also works as an aide in a local nursing home.

Chad Walsh is Professor of English and writer in residence at Beloit College. He has written five books of poetry, including *The Psalm of Christ*.

David Waltner-Toews was reared in a Mennonite Brethren community in Winnipeg. After a working world tour, Dave went back to school and graduated from Goshen College. He has published poetry in several principal Canadian periodicals.

Eugene Warren grew up on a Kansas farm and now teaches English at the University of Missouri, Rolla. His books of poetry are *Christographia: Poems* and *The Fifth Season*.

James E. Warren, Jr. is a member of the United Methodist Church and was head of the English department at Lovett School in Atlanta, where he is now Poet-in-Residence. Jim has published nine books of poetry and numerous essays.

Charles Waugaman is pastor of the West Harpswell Baptist Church. His publications include *Patterns of Passing* and *A Harvest of Willows*.

Laura Weller was raised in northern Michigan, graduated from Ferris State College, and is now an editor with Baker Book House.

Nancy G. Westerfield teaches English at Kearney State College. She has published poems in *Christianity Today, Christian Advocate, Christian Century,* and *Arizona Quaterly.* She observes, "Sometimes I tell myself ruefully that I should find someBody more important than God to write my poetry about—but I know of none."

Dorann Williams is a Dordt College student from Sheboygan, Wisconsin, who write for the Dordt *Diamond* and *Canon.*

Sherwood Wirt, the former editor of *Decision,* has also written *The Social Conscience of the Evangelical, Passport to Life City, Love Song* (Augustine's *Confessions*), and *Afterglow.*

Norberto Wolf is a minister of the Reformed Church in Mar del Plata, Argentina.

Mildred Zylstra is a professor of English at Calvin College and a frequent contributor of poems and short stories to *The Banner* and *The Reformed Journal.*

Biographies of Historic Poets

Anne Bradstreet (1612–1672) was an American Puritan poet who wrote the first significant English poetry in the United States. Her poems range in subject from the historical to the domestic and personal.

Elizabeth Barrett Browning (1806–1861) was the wife of Robert Browning, and is better known for her romantic love poetry than for her few Christian sonnets.

John Bunyan (1628–1688) was a dissenting Baptist minister who endured sustained persecution for preaching the Gospel of the Lord Jesus Christ. His main works are *The Pilgrim's Progress* and *Grace Abounding to the Chief of Sinners* (autobiography).

John Byrom (1692–1763) was a Cambridge Fellow and later a teacher of shorthand as well as a poet.

Thomas Campion (1567–1620) was a poet, musician, and medical doctor who wrote both Christian and secular poetry to be set to music.

G. K. Chesterton (1874–1936) was a brilliant Catholic Christian apologist, novelist, essayist, poet, and public speaker. Chesterton also wrote *Orthodoxy*, *Heretics*, and the Father Brown detective stories.

William Cowper (1731–1800) was a major English pre-romantic poet of everyday life. He also wrote the *Olney Hymns* with his friend John Newton.

Richard Crashaw (1613–1649) was a mystical Catholic poet who praised the majesty and grace of God in *Carmen Deo Nostra, Steps to the Temple,* and *Sacred Epigrams.*

John Donne (1572–1633) changed the direction of his poetry after he became a Christian. As well as writing his hymns and holy sonnets, Donne composed many sermons and meditations.

John Dryden (1631–1700) was a playwright, Poet Laureate, and Historiographer Royal. His most famous poems are odes and political satires.

Giles Fletcher (1586–1623) was a Fellow at Trinity College until he took a country parish in 1618. His elder brother Phineas was also a poet and pastor.

Felicia Hemans (1794–1835), an English poet also, wrote many essays on foreign literatures, as well as much romantic poetry in traditional forms.

George Herbert (1593–1633) dedicated his rhetorical and poetic talents to God when he was a student at Cambridge. He became an Anglican pastor and wrote a single volume of poetry entitled *The Temple*. Herbert said that his poetry was "a picture of the many spiritual conflicts that have passed betwixt God and my soul, before I could subject mine to the will of Jesus my Master, in whose service I have now found perfect freedom."

Gerard Manley Hopkins (1844–1889) was a Jesuit Christian who sought out the inscape, the God-created individuality, of a person or thing and then expressed it in sprung verse rhythms and richly variegated diction.

Ben Jonson (1572–1637) was an Elizabethan playwright, poet, and critic, a contemporary of Shakespeare.

George MacDonald (1824–1905) was a Scottish novelist, poet, and Congregational minister. He wrote much fiction and several moral fantasies with occasional biblical resonances.

John Milton (1608–1674) wrote his épics *Paradise Lost* and *Paradise Regained*, the tragic drama *Samson Agonistes*, "Lycidas," the "Nativity Ode," and many shorter poems, as well as several major polemical essays, such as *Areopagitica*.

John Newton (1725–1807) was a pastor and friend of William Cowper. Before his conversion, Newton was a ship's captain in the slave trade. He wrote the *Olney Hymns* with Cowper.

Francis Quarles (1592–1644) was a Royalist and a member of the Church of England. His very popular book of poems, *Emblems,* was published in 1635.

Christina Rossetti (1830–1894) was an English Episcopalian poet who suffered prolonged illness, but whose poems are hymns of joy and adoration to God.

Christopher Smart (1722–1771) was an English poet who enjoyed wandering and observing in the fields as well as working in his study.

Robert Southwell (1561–1595) was a Jesuit priest and poet who was persecuted and eventually martyred for his Christian faith.

Edmund Spenser (1552–1599) was a Protestant Christian poet of the English renaissance and author of *The Faerie Queene*.

Edward Taylor (1645–1729), an English-born American colonist, became a Puritan pastor and poet, the author of two series of *Sacramental Meditations,* love poems to God in Christ.

Francis Thompson (1859–1907) wrote *The Hound of Heaven,* one of the finest odes in the language. Thompson said, "To be the poet of the return to nature is somewhat, but I would be the poet of the return to God."

Thomas Traherne (1637–1674) was a metaphysical poet and the author of *Christian Ethics* and other meditations.

Henry Vaughan (1622–1695) was a metaphysical Christian poet, notably influenced by his contemporaries Herbert and Donne.

Isaac Watts (1674–1748) was a theologian, pastor, and hymnist. He published *Hymns, The Psalms of David,* and *Divine and Moral Songs for Children.*

Charles Wesley (1707–1788) was the poet of the evangelical revival, a gifted preacher and writer of about 6,500 hymns.

Henry Wotton (1568–1639) was English ambassador to Venice and a friend of John Donne.

Acknowledgments

My thanks to all the poets who permitted me to include poems of theirs in this volume. My gratitude also to the publishing houses, periodicals, and boards listed below.

A.D. Publications, Inc. for the Jonah poems by Thomas John Carlisle, For "Five Days Before Friday," "Supper With Jesus Christ," and "that gust" (these poems are also printed in *Celebration!*, Eerdmans); "Under the Sun" (this is reprinted in *Mistaken Identity*, Eerdmans). Also for "Perhaps the Socrates He Had Never Read" by Chad Walsh. Copyright *A.D.* Used by permission.

Ball State University Forum for "Adam in the Garden" by Elmer F. Suderman.

The Banner for poems by Cor Barendrecht, Sietze Buning, Helen Hoffman, Hester Hogan, John Meeter, Merle Meeter, William Oldenburg, Marie Post, Eugene Rubingh, Luci Shaw, Robert Swets, Fred Tamminga, John H. Timmerman, Cornelius Van Bruggen, Clarence Walhout, Norberto Wolf, and Mildred Zylstra.

Colorado Quarterly for "The Sureness of This Hour" by John Leax.

Cor Barendrecht for "Swimmers at Leelanau Schools" (used by permission.)

Bulletin Board for "Christ Writing on the Sand" by Nancy G. Westerfield.

Calvin Seminary Corps for permission to reprint "Eve 2" and "Love Looks" by Joe Veltman.

The Canadian Forum for "Wald Heim" by David Waltner-Toews.

The Christian Century Foundation for "Benediction for Danny" (July 24, 1968 *Christian Century*) by William R. Mitchell, and for "Sister Bertha" by Jeanne Murray Walker (January 29, 1969 *Century*). Copyright 1968 and 1969, Christian Century Foundation. Reprinted by permission.

Christianity Today for "The Singing Christ" by Edmund Clowney; "After the Stroke," "The Dove," and "Grandmother; Dying" by John Leax; "Book Review," "From Jaffa," "The Next Morning: Twenty Songs for Twenty Voices," "Rehearsal," and "Treasures of Darkness" by Elva McAllaster; "Sing the Lord, Wisely" by Gladys McKee; "The Crystal Hexagon" by Beth Merizon; "The Pawn" and "Primordial Pattern" by Johanna Patterson; "John the Baptist" and "Mourning Prayers" by Eugene Peterson; "Parable" and "The Poet—Silent After Pentecost" by Luci Shaw; "In the Year That King Uzziah Died" by Ruthe Spinnanger; "The Leader" and "Three Prophets" by Nancy Thomas; "Two Hymns Waiting for Music" by Chad Walsh; "A Conversion (1741)," "All These Breads," "Christographia XXIII," "Dancing the Rainbow," "Darkness," "Idols in a Museum," "A Reason for Hammers," and "The Stones of the City" by Eugene Warren; "The Lowly Eternal" by Charles Waugaman;

by Countee Cullen. Copyright 1947. Used by permission.

His for "The Word," ". . . Person, or a Hymn on and to the Holy Ghost" (March, 1968) by Margaret Avison; for "The Trading Post" (February, 1975) and "Love Seeking" (May, 1976) by Carolyn Keefe; for "To Ask, To Seek, To Knock" (April, 1968) by Elva McAllaster; for "The Story of the Turkish Bath" (May, 1971) by Stephen Mosley; for "Hard God" (June, 1972) by Nancy Thomas; and for "A City to Come" (April, 1975) by Eugene Warren. Reprinted by permission of *His*, student magazine of Intervarsity Christian Fellowship, copyright 1968, 1971, 1972, 1974, 1975, 1976.

Insight for "The Few" by Bonnie Kuipers, copyright 1976, the Young Calvinist Federation, Grand Rapids, Michigan. Reprinted by permission.

Interest for the poems of Luci Shaw that were later published in *Listen to the Green* (Harold Shaw Publishers, 1971). Reprinted by permission. "Royalty" and "Tithes" appear also in Virginia Mollenkott's *Adam Among the Television Trees*.

Jawbone for "A Bestiary for the Birth of Christ" by Jeanne Murray Walker. (From *Jawbone*, Volume II, Number 1, 1976. Used by permission.)

Ktaadn Poetry Press for "The Current" by John Leax. Copyright 1971 by John Leax. Used by permission.

John Leax for "Geography of Love" (used by permission).

The Liveright Company for the poems of John W. Simons.

The Living Church for "Compound Metaphors for Sunday Morning" by John Leax, for "Before or After" by James E. Warren, Jr.

Lyric for "Heed Not the Withered Gods" by James E. Warren, Jr.

The Macmillan Company for poems by Christina Rossetti, from *Selected Poems by Christina Rossetti*, Marya Zaturenska, ed. Reprinted by permission.

The Mennonite for "Shake My Eye" by Matthew Brown and for "Crucify Him" by Elmer F. Suderman.

Mennonite Life for "Thy Kingdom Come" by Elmer F. Suderman.

The Mennonite Reporter for "If He Were Born Today" by David Waltner-Toews.

Methuen and Co. Ltd. for "Broad Autumn" and "Josephine Butler" from *Broad Autumn*, copyright 1975; "Harpoon," and "Wedding Eve" from *The Echoing Tip*, copyright 1971; and for "Priest Out of Bondage" and "The Winds" from *The Map of Clay*, copyright 1961. All poems by Jack Clemo. Reprinted by permission.

Moody Press for "Prayer from a Stryker Frame" by Margaret Clarkson. Copyright 1972. Moody Press, Moody Bible Institute of Chicago. Used by permission.

Press.

Wisconsin Poetry Magazine for "Came Slowly Forth" by James E. Warren, Jr.

Word Books for "If Christ Had Lept from the Cross" by Sandra Duguid, from *Adam Among the Television Trees.* Copyright 1971. Reprinted by permission.

The World Publishing Co. for "Lazarus" and "Thirst" from *Encounters* by Daniel Berrigan. Copyright 1960. Used by permission.

World Vision for "Ezekiel Saw His Wheel" by Nancy Thomas, from the November, 1974 issue of *World Vision.* Reprinted by permission.

Yale University Press for "Meditation #1" by Edward Taylor. Copyright 1960, Yale University Press. Reprinted by permission.

Index of Poets

Addink, Carol, 3
Anderson, Charlene M., 4
Auden, W. H., 5
Avison, Margaret, 7

Bancroft, Josiah, 16
Barendrecht, Cor W., 18
Bayly, Joseph, 22
Berrigan, Daniel, 24
Borgman, Paul, 25
Bradstreet, Anne, 295
Brother Antoninus, 28
Brown, Matthew, 29
Browning, Elizabeth Barrett, 300
Buning, Sietze, 32
Bunyan, John, 301
Byrom, John, 302

Campbell, Joseph, 37
Campion, Thomas, 304
Carlisle, Thomas John, 38
Carter, Albert Howard, III, 4
Chesterton, G. K., 305
Clarkson, E. Margaret, 42
Clemo, Jack, 44
Clowney, Edmund P., 50
Cochrane, David, 52
Cook, Hugh, 54
Cowper, William, 306
Crashaw, Richard, 312
Culbertson, E. Neil, 55
Cullen, Countee, 59

Deems, Joann, 61
DeGroot, Dave, 64
Donne, John, 314
Dryden, John, 320
Duguid, Sandra, 65
Duriez, Colin, 70

Eliot, T. S., 73
Ellwood, Gracia Fay, 74
Emshoff, Robert, 78

Fagerstrom, Mia, 81
Fletcher, Giles, 321

Hawkins, Dan, 82
Hemans, Felicia, 322
Herbert, George, 323

Hogan, Hester, 83
Hopkins, Gerard Manley, 335
Hopkins, John, 418
Huizenga, Ralph, 84

Jellema, Roderick, 86
Johnson, James Weldon, 86
Jonson, Ben, 353

Keefe, Carolyn, 88
Klug, Ron, 95
Kuipers, Bonnie, 96

Laing, Howard, 98
Leax, John, 101
L'Engle, Madeleine, 110
Lewis, C. S., 113

MacDonald, George, 354
Marsman, Heather, 114
McAllaster, Elva, 116
McCaslin, Susan, 125
McKee, Gladys, 128
Mee, Diana, 129
Meeter, John, 130
Meeter, Merle, 133
Merizon, Beth, 140
Merton, Thomas, 141
Miller, Calvin, 144
Miller, Vassar, 148
Milton, John, 356
Mitchell, William R., 150
Mosley, Stephen, 156

Neerhof, Karl, 157
Newton, John, 365
Norton, Thomas, 418

Oldenburg, E. W., 158

Paterson, Evangeline, 162
Patterson, Johanna, 165
Peeders, Ken, 166
Peterson, Eugene H., 167
Post, Marie J., 169

Quarles, Francis, 368

Rossetti, Christina, 370
Rubingh, Eugene, 176

Ruch, Mary, 180

Shaw, Luci, 181
Silva, Phil, 194
Simons, John W., 196
Sitwell, Edith, 198
Smart, Christopher, 377
Southwell, Robert, 381
Spenser, Edmund, 383
Speyer, Leonora, 199
Speyers, Kathleen, 201
Spinnanger, Ruthe T., 202
Straayer, T. A., 203
Suderman, Elmer F., 204
Swets, Robert D., 207

Tamminga, Fred W., 214
Taylor, Edward, 384
Ten Harmsel, Henrietta, 219
Thomas, Nancy, 222
Thompson, Francis, 386
Timmerman, John H., 228
Todd, Nancy, 230
Traherne, Thomas, 392

Van Bruggen, Cornelius, 232
Van Den Berg, Sandy, 233
Vandenburg, Debbie, 234
VanderMey, Randall, 235
Van Gorkom, Charles, 237
Vaughan, Henry, 397
Veltman, Joe, 238

Walhout, Clarence, 240
Walker, Jeanne Murray, 243
Wallis, Debbie, 248
Walsh, Chad, 249
Waltner-Toews, David, 254
Warren, Eugene, 260
Warren, James E., Jr., 272
Watts, Isaac, 403
Waugaman, Charles A., 277
Weller, Laura, 279
Wesley, Charles, 408
Westerfield, Nancy, 281
Williams, Dorann, 286
Wirt, Sherwood E., 287
Wolf, Norberto, 290
Wotton, Henry, 413

Zylstra, Mildred, 291

Index of Titles

Aaron, 331
about death and life, 217
about God with us, 217
Adam in the Garden, 206
Adam's Uncle, 267
After His Kind, 157
After the Stroke, 104
Agon, 125
Agony in the Garden, The, 322
Aim of Art, The, 134
Alas! and Did my Savior Bleed, 405
All Out or Oblation, 7
All These Breads, 263
Alston Chapel, 273
Altar, The, 330
Am I a Soldier of the Cross? 406
Am I Thy Gold? 385
Amazing Grace! 367
And Then God Spoke, 278
Angel Vision, 182
Anniversary, 171
Annunciation (Buning), 35
Annunciation (Carter), 42
Annunciation (Donne), 319
Apologist's Evening Prayer, The, 113
As an Orchard, Sing, 267
As Kingfishers Catch Fire, 337
As Spring the Winter, 299
As Weary Pilgrim, 295
Ascension, 170
Ascension Hymn, 400
Ashes, 162
Assurance, 173
At a Solemn Music, 361
At Communion, 111
At Galilee, 175
At the Round Earth's, 318

Babel: A Warning, 96
Ballad of the Dragon, 218
Baptism of Jesus, The, 167
Bareback in Kansas, 268
Barnfloor and Winepress, 336
Barnyard Miracle, 36
Bass, 103
Batter My Heart, 315
Be Still and Know That I Am God, 237
Beauty, 378
Beauty of the Law, The, 127
Before or After, 275

Before the Beginning, 373
Benediction, 154
Benediction for Danny, 154
Bestiary for the Birth of Christ, A, 243
Bethlehem Outcast, 148
Better Resurrection, A, 372
Blest Be That Sacred Covenant Love, 409
Blood Thaw, 83
Bloody Sweat, 220
Book Review, 123
Brain, The, 144
Branch, The, 31
Brass Salvation, The, 101
Brazen Serpent, 219
Breaking Trinity, 212
Broad Autumn, 45
Brothers and Sisters, 115
Burning Babe, The, 381

Caged Skylark, The, 343
Came Slowly Forth, 276
Carol for Christmas Morning, 34
Carrion Comfort, 335
Catch, 174
Cereal Boxes, 249
Chaff, 55
Christ Came Juggling, 263
Christ Risen Was Rarely Recognized, 183
Christ, Whose Glory, 411
Christ Writing in the Sand, 285
Christmas Carol, A, 371
Christmas Couplets With Bells On, 214
Christmas Mourning, 149
Christographia XXIII, 265
Christ's Nativity, 401
Circuit, 11
City to Come, A, 262
Cleansing, The, 81
Collar, The, 325
Come, Thou Long-Expected Jesus, 411
Coming and Going, 38
Communion for the Aged, 205
Complaint, God's Patience, 67
Compound Metaphors for Sunday
   Morning, 103
Confidence, 175
Conversion (1741), A, 266
Coronation, 77
Counselor to the Almighty, 38
Covenant Celebration, 230

Crazy Man Myself Sometimes, A, 56
Creation (Kuipers), 97
Creation (Revius), 219
Creature Praise, 97
Crucifixion, 54
Crucifixion: Communion Service, 65
Crucifixion Hymn, 312
Crucify Him! 204
Crystal Hexagon, The, 140
Current, The, 107

Dancing the Rainbow, 264
Darkness, 265
David, 201
Day of Judgment, The, 407
Dear God, 82
Death, 334
Death Drowned, 55
Deathbed, 162
Deepest Apologetic, The, 131
Defunct, 226
De Profundis, 304
Discovery, 179
Dissension, 133
Dove, The, 103
Dream Combat at Claibourne Church, 91
Dumbfounding, The, 13
Dwelling Place, The, 398

Easter (Herbert), 326
Easter (Keefe), 89
Easter (VanderMey), 235
Easter Day, 312
Easter Hymn, 397
Easter Morning: Romans 13:12, 151
Easter Morning: 10:00 A.M., 233
Easter Wings, 327
Elijah, 125
Elohimmyyahweh, 78
Endtime, 126
Enoch, 186
Epiphany on a Plot of Moonlight, 150
Et Incarnatus Est, 75
Eutychus, 158
Eve 2, 238
Everyone Begins, 57
Exile, 164
Experience in April, 174
Ezekiel Saw His Wheel, 226

Fatherhood Is a School of Humility, 252
Faucet, The, 122
Feed My Sheep, 180
Few, The, 97

Fields Are Already White for Harvest, The, 29
Filling Out the Forms, 133
Finding the Word, 101
Fire on the Berkshires, October 1974, 187
First Day, 393
Five Days Before Friday, 40
Flat Person, 162
Flesh, World, Devil, 26
Flight into Egypt, The, 381
Fly, The, 166
Fool, The, 76
For a Friend Dying, 164
For Everything There Is a Season, 71
For Fifty Years of Music: For Seymour Swets, 210
For Sunday, 378
For Tinkers Who Travel on Foot, 8
Four-Square Gospel, 86
Free Grace, 408
From All That Dwell Below the Skies, 403
From Behind Closed Doors, 171
From "For the Time Being," 5
From Gifts and Graces, 373
From Jaffa, 119
From The Equation of Mystery, 98
From "The World. Self-destruction," 375
Furrow, The, 84

Game of Backsliding, The, 134
Gardener, The, 127
Geography of Love, The, 108
Getting Inside the Miracle, 185
Glorious Things of Thee Are Spoken, 366
Go Down, Moses, 419
God in the Cave, 139
God's Grandeur, 339
Golden Echo, The, 340
Good Friday, 370
Good Friday, 1613, Riding Westward, 314
Good-Nature to Animals, 379
Grackle, Grackle, Grackle, 132
Grandfather (Culbertson), 58
Grandfather (Swets), 208
Grandmother: Dying, 102
Gratefulness, 333
Grave Grows Firm with Grasses, The, 273
Great Intruder, The, 41
Groundhog, The, 186

Haman, 160
Hard God, 222
Hark, the Herald Angels Sing, 410

Harpoon, 48
He Bore Our Griefs, 221
"He Is Not Here," 168
he who would be great among you, 184
Hearing, A, 10
Heaven Harvester, 287
Heaven Overarches, 372
Heed Not the Withered Gods, 274
Heritage, 59
Higher Vision, 54
His Workmanship, 57
Holy Night, 246
Hound of Heaven, The, 387
House of Calvin, 199
How Soon Hath Time, 364
How Sweet the Name, 365
Hurrahing in Harvest, 344
Huswifery, 385
Hymn, The, 356
Hymn for Christmas Day, A, 302
Hymn for the Church Militant, A, 305
Hymn on and to the Holy Ghost, 12
Hymn on the Nativity of My Savior, A, 353
Hymn to God My God in My Sickness, 316
Hymn to God the Father, A (Donne), 318
Hymn to God the Father, A (Jonson), 353
Hymn to God the Holy Ghost, A, 211
Hymn to My God in a Night of My Late Sickness, A, 413

I Am the Mountainy Singer, 37
I Came Upon a Man, 145
I Waste Dead, 4
I Will Sing a New Song, 250
Idols in a Museum, 262
If Christ Had Lept, 65
If He Were Born Today, 254
If I Could Trust Mine Own Self, 370
If Only, 376
If Poisonous Minerals, 317
I'm Tired, 248
In Canterbury Cathedral, 158
in deserto vox clamantis, 178
In His Sameness of Grace: Our Church, Burning, 282
In Memoriam, 177
In Memory of E. William Oldenburg, 207
In Memory of My Dear Grandchild, 296
"In No Strange Land," 386
In Thankful Remembrance, 297
In the Beginning, 170
In the Hospital, 114

"In the Year That King Uzziah Died," 202
Incarnation, 90
Individuation, 224
Invader, The, 144
Ironies of Love, The, 264
Isaiah, 228
It Still Sings, 63

Jacob, 241
Jesus Despised! 355
Jesus, Flesh Torn, 195
Jesus Our Hope, 35
Jesus Shall Reign Where'er the Sun, 405
Jews, The, 324
John in Gethsemane, 287
John the Baptist, 168
John 3, 29
Joining, The, 193
Jordan (I), 323
Joseph, 25
Josephine Butler, 46
Joseph's Lullaby, 95
Journey of the Magi, 73
Joy to the World, 403
Just a Housecat, 62
Just Before Dawn on a Winter Morning, 130

Lament, 240
Lamp, The, 122
Lantern Out of Doors, The, 337
Last Birth, The, 96
last Word, the, 69
Later, 126
Lazarus (Berrigan), 24
Lazarus (Hawkins), 82
Leaden Echo, The, 340
Leader, The, 224
Learning, 377
Let All the World in Every Corner Sing, 330
Let Light Ride In, 260
Light, Everything Is Light, 246
Light Giver, 155
Light Shining Out of Darkness, 307
Like Ilium, 141
Literalist of the Gospel, 135
Living Crèche, 281
Longing to Be With Christ, 306
Look, The, 300
Lord, Let Me Recall the Fall, 195
Lord, Open Our Eyes, 279
Love Divine All Loves Excelling, 412
Love Looks, 238

Love Seeking, 89
Love Story, 145
Love (III), 332
Lowly Eternal, The, 278

Malnutrition, 234
Man Overboard, 170
Manna, 125
Maranatha, 223
March Message, 232
Master, 127
Matthew 22, 313
May the Grace of Christ Our Savior, 366
May 20: Very Early Morning, 191
Meaning of the Look, The, 300
Medieval Poem of the Nativity, A, 417
Meditation on I Peter 1:3–4, 227
Meditation on Psalm 139:7–12, 154
Meditation on Psalm 142, 260
Meditation I, 384
Messenger, The, 215
Messias, 142
Miss Pettigrew and Tree, 163
Miss Weld, 68
Morning Prayers, 167
Most Glorious Lord of Life, 383
Mustard Field, 189
My Desire Is, 17
My Father's Acres, 102
My Soul Thirsts for God, 311
My Spirit Longs for Thee, 303

Name, 21
Nativity, The, 113
Nativity of Christ, The, 382
Nativity of Our Lord and Savior Jesus
   Christ, The, 380
Negotiation With a Higher Power, 41
New Moon, 242
Next Morning, The: Twenty Songs for
   Twenty Voices, 120
9 A.M. Sunday, 169
No Matter What, 15
No Silent Night, 248
Node, 79
None Other Lamb, 373
Northern Lights, 201
November 22, 1963, 74

O All Ye Nations, 418
O Black and Unknown Bards, 86
O For a Thousand Tongues, 409
O Sapientia, 111
O Simplicitas, 110

Oasis, 169
Oblation, 149
Obedience, 32
Occasional Meditations, 296
October Comes to Glen Lake, 132
Ode on the Morning of Christ's Nativity,
   363
Of Birds and Bards, 138
Oh My Black Soul, 317
Old-Testament Gospel, 308
On Bellini's "St. Francis in Ecstasy," 261
On Christmas Day, 394
On Fragrant Hay, 124
On Our Crucified Lord Naked and
   Bloody, 313
On Prayer, 72
On That Eighth Day, 16
On the Day of His Deliverance, 29
On the Eve of Snow White, 238
On the Resurrection, 289
Orchard View, 172
Our Father on Earth in Transit, 136
Our God, Our Help in Ages Past, 404
Out of the Ruined Nursery, 137
Over the Fields of Summer, 277

Palm Sunday, 172
Palm Sunday: Good Friday, 321
Parable (Shaw), 185
Parable, (Warren), 272
Paradise, 328
Paradox, 148
Passion Week, 28
Pawn, The, 165
Peace, 397
Perfect Wresting, 30
Perhaps the Socrates, 251
Perspective on St. Joseph's Day, 61
Pied Beauty, 339
Placed by the Gideons, 283
Pneuma, 190
Poem for a Girl Who Limps, 105
Poem for Melissa, 101
Poem Written on Request, 105
Poet—Silent After Pentecost, The, 186
Poverty, 392
Power Failure, 186
Praise for the Fountain Opened, 310
Prayer, 355
Prayer (I), 332
Prayer from a Stryker Frame, 42
Priest Out of Bondage, 47
Primordial Pattern, 165
Prisoner, The, 283

Prophet, 88
Psalm, 173
Psalm at Children's Hospital, A, 22
Psalm for Maundy Thursday, A, 23
Psalm for Today, A, 290
Psalm 136, 362
Psalms of Nihilism Revisited, The, 146

Quatrains for a Christmas Card, 216

Reading the Rites, 281
Reason for Hammers, A, 260
Reception, 140
Reckoning, 179
Red Jordan, 74
Redemption, 328
Rehearsal, 119
Rejoice and Be Merry! 417
Relapse, The, 402
Reminder, 157
Reprisal, The, 323
Requiem for Innocence, A, 152
Restaurant Conversation, 129
Resurrection, 247
Resurrection Rondeau, 135
Rib Cage, 192
Risk of Birth, The, 112
Roman Lock, The, 288
Rondel, 355
Royalty, 185

Sand Castles, 54
Seascape: Recalling the Wind, 79
Second Lazarus, 112
Seek the Lord! 304
Sestina for Professor William Blisset, 14
Shake My Eye, 30
Shall the Dead Praise Thee? 354
She Did, 245
Simeon's Light Remembered, 196
Sing the Lord, Wisely, 128
Singing Christ, The, 50
Singularity of Shells, The, 186
Sin's Round, 329
Sister Bertha, 247
Smiling Eyes Approach All Pain, 231
Snake, The, 102
Snowstorm, 255
Some Thought That It Was Merely Joy, 176
Somewhere, 274
Song of the Lambs, 126
Spring, 343
Spring and Fall, 342

Spring Song, 180
Spring Stanzas, 65
Star in the East, 213
Starlight Night, The, 335
Still Falls the Rain, 198
Stone Has Rolled Away, The, 249
Stones of the City, The, 270
Storm, The, 329
Story of the Turkish Bath, The, 156
Suffering of Christ, 221
Summer, 291
Sunday Morning, 106
Sunlight Splintered, 194
Sunset Crucifixion: Camera Shot, 233
Supper With Jesus Christ, 39
Sureness of this Hour, The, 107
Swaddling the Word, 20
Swimmers at LeeLanau Schools, 21
Swing Low, Sweet Chariot, 419

Tables and Stars, 52
Te Deum Laudamus, 173
Tearing Veil, The, 66
Tested, 49
Thanksgiving in a Supermarket Line, 277
that gust, 38
That Nature Is a Heraclitean Fire, 338
Theometry, 150
They Were Going Somewhere, 62
Thirst, 34
This Easter, 118
Thou Art Indeed Just, Lord, 344
Thou Hast Made Me, 315
Though Still in Filth I Run, 64
Three Enemies, The, 374
Three Prophets, 225
Thy Kingdom Come, 205
Time, 333
Tithes, 181
To a Christmas Two-Year-Old, 184
To a Snowflake, 391
To Ask, To Seek, To Knock, 116
To Dr. Clyde S. Kilby, 188
To Jesus on Easter, 149
To See How He Dwells Heartward, 194
Today's Special, 134
Today's Too Daft a Day, 275
Tracking Fields, 229
Trading Post, The, 88
Travail Hymn, 136
Treasures of Darkness: After Catastrophe, 123
Tree Thoughts, 130
Trinity Sunday, 331

Truly This Was the Son of God, 31
Trust Me, I Have Not Earned, 376
Turnabout, 288
Twin, The, 125
Two Hymns Waiting for Music, 253
Two Inscapes, 31

Unacceptables, 284
Under the Sun, 40
Upon the Burning of Our House, 298
Upon Viewing, 239
Urban Churchyard, 284

Veni Creator Spiritus, 320
Very Little Cross, A, 147

Wald Heim, 256
Walk in Fog, 80
Walking With God, 309
Way of All Flesh, The, 3
Were You There? 420
Whale and the Tiger, The, 197
When I Consider, 361
When I Survey the Wondrous Cross, 406

When Will We Dance Again? 204
"Whence? What? Whither?" 72
Whiteheat, 286
Whitewash, 203
Who Shall Deliver Me? 371
Who Would True Valor See, 301
Why Are We by All Creatures? 319
Why Dost Thou Shade Thy Lovely Face?
   368
Windhover, The, 342
Windows, The, 324
Winds, The, 44
Wings, 240
Word, The, 9
Word to World, 18
Words Are a Dying Sun, 70
World, The, 398
Worm, The, 105
Wreck of the *Deutschland*, The, 345

Ye People All, 418

Zone of Death, 28